BERSERK IN THE ANTARCTIC

David Mercy

summersdale

BERSERK IN THE ANTARCTIC

First published by Lyons Press Ltd in 2004 as *Berserk: My Voyage to the Antarctic in a Twenty-Seven-Foot Sailboat*

This edition published in 2006 by Summersdale Publishers Ltd.

Summersdale Publishers Ltd
46 West Street
Chichester
West Sussex
PO19 1RP
UK

www.summersdale.com

Printed and bound in Great Britain.

ISBN 1 84024 479 8

for my father

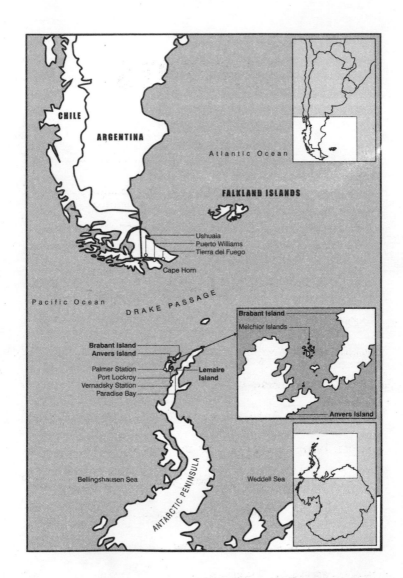

CONTENTS

Prologue...7

Chapter One – How I Came to the *Berserk*........................11

Chapter Two – A Little Training Cruise............................42

Chapter Three – Leaving for Antarctica...........................66

Chapter Four – The First Storm.......................................81

Chapter Five – We Go On: The Crossing.........................100

Chapter Six – Arrival...112

Chapter Seven – Antarctica..120

Chapter Eight – Antarctica II: Sniffing Out the Wind.....160

Chapter Nine – Mad Russians and Uncle Sam................191

Chapter Ten – The Last Anchorage.................................218

Chapter Eleven – The Second Storm...............................227

Chapter Twelve – The Ride Home...................................239

Chapter Thirteen – Civilisation......................................267

PROLOGUE

'This is suicide!' Manuel screamed frantically. 'We've got to go back before it's too late!'

He grabs me by the collar with both hands balled into fists like a madman and shakes wildly. Though he is shouting right in my face, the wind blows so fiercely, so loudly, I can barely hear him. We are in the middle of a hurricane, riding it out on the swamped decks of a tiny sailing boat, a speck in a sea of madness. A week earlier, none of us had ever met before – and now we are reliant upon each other, and upon this fragile, dilapidated boat, for our lives.

Maybe he is right. Maybe we are going to die. We are being smacked flush in the face by a major hurricane-strength storm just south of Cape Horn, like we have walked into the ring against the heavyweight champion of the world and are getting punched right in the nose before having a chance to lift a glove. We are on our way to Antarctica in a 27-foot fibreglass sailing boat our 21-year-old Norwegian captain named *Berserk*. It's our first day out at sea, the first time Manuel and I have really sailed, and the seas are enormous. The waves tower high over the mast and break down upon us constantly, tossing the boat over on its side. We're always one wave away from capsizing.

We've reached a point beyond fear. No longer do I fight Death – I have accepted it. I just don't want to die with Manuel screaming in my ear, that's all. I met him ten minutes before we got on board – ten minutes before we met Jarle. We're three strangers out here at sea doing battle with the worst possible conditions in the world, but for some odd reason, I'm still happy. The question is: why?

Manuel gets right up in my face and shouts again. 'We're going to fucking die!' His eyes look like overweight Marine recruit Private Pyle's in the Stanley Kubrick film *Full Metal Jacket* right before he blows his drill sergeant to oblivion.

He loosens his grip but his eyes remain the same. 'Jarle, we've got to go back!' he shouts up to the captain. He frantically bounces around the inside of the cabin like a cockroach, grabbing onto anything he can hold in the storm.

He tries to reason with me. 'David, he's just a boy. He's only a boy,' he explains quietly and calmly. 'He's only twenty-one. Remember all the mistakes you made at that age?' He speaks with reason and assuredness that are not called for during such a harrowing scene, in such a difficult moment. It is almost eerie, a moment of quiet in the middle of raging, deafening violence – as unnatural and disconcerting as the panicked shouting.

Manuel doesn't let up. 'He didn't listen to the report,' he shrieks. 'He knew we were heading out into a storm.' Manuel thinks he's crazy. Is that true? No way. As Jarle likes to say: 'Crazy, but not stupid.' He would never intentionally head out into this. No right-thinking human would.

But Manuel would argue that Jarle – the 'crazy Viking' I had heard about – is indeed not a right-thinking human. That is his point. Jarle's original statement – that once we left for Antarctica, there would be no turning back, no matter what, that our next port of call would be South Africa – should be abrogated immediately.

'He's making all the wrong decisions!' he screams again, almost irrational. 'We've got to turn back before it's too late!! While we still have a chance!! Jarle – we've got to go back!!' His face turns plum red.

'Jarle, you're not Shackleton!' he shrieks. It is a slap in the face, aimed directly at the young captain's beloved idol. Jarle's goal in leaving Antarctica would be to retrace the famed explorer's life-saving sail to South Georgia, and he has mentioned this often with pride.

I undress, stripping myself of my wet clothes, listening and thinking about what Manuel said. Maybe he is right. Maybe we should turn back now, while we still have a chance. After all, we are only 12 hours or so from the safety of shore. Another wave crashes into our side, tossing the *Berserk* like a wet napkin. I say nothing. There is nothing to say.

'Jarle, you fucking asshole! I want to go back!' Manuel wails. It is becoming like one of his oft-performed yoga mantras.

Up on deck, the captain breaks his long silence. 'This is a democracy. There are three of us. If two of us vote to go back, we'll let the majority decide.'

He is putting the onus squarely on me.

Manuel runs up to me, again grabbing me by the collar of my sweater. 'David, tell him! Before it's too late!'

I think for a moment. Earlier on deck I had seen my death arriving quickly. Now I silently weigh the state of affairs, sitting on the edge of a bunk. We are still within striking distance of getting back. Manuel is already at the end of his frayed nerves, on the first day of the voyage. It is still uncertain whether the boat can handle the pounding of both the storm and the waters of the fierce Drake Passage. Hell, we aren't really even into the heart of the Drake yet! What more could possibly be waiting for us further out there?! We have already lost a wind pilot, a sea anchor and 20 litres of gas in winds so strong they had blown my colourful Peruvian llama wool cap right off my head in a blink.

And then, in the distance, I hear it on the wind. Like a lone oboe slowly rising to a crescendo. My dear father's voice, echoing. 'David,' it calls to me, 'don't be a hero... hero... hero...'

'Jarle!' I yell up. 'I think we should go back.'

'What?' the disbelieving captain yells down.

'I think we should go back and regroup.'

There is a long moment of silence as Manuel smugly nods his head up and down, close-mouthed in I-told-you-so satisfaction.

'Skull,' Jarle shouts back down, calling me by my chosen pirate name. 'Get dressed and come back up here.'

There was no way I could know it at the time, but the next decision I made would be the turning point in my life. With each monstrous wave, a door was opening wider and wider... and like it or not, I was about to step through.

CHAPTER ONE
HOW I CAME TO
THE *BERSERK*

When I stepped onto the *Berserk* to set sail for Antarctica on 1 January 1999, I had no idea that it would be a life-altering – and ultimately life-affirming – experience. I just thought it would be a good way to see Antarctica.

I had already travelled to the other six continents of the world: fought my way through the heart of the African jungle via canoe on the Congo; driven into a raging river during a flash flood in the Australian outback; beheld with wonder the mysteries of ancient Tibetan sky burials while trekking across China to India; carved salmon on a floating fish processor in the Bering Sea; and sojourned in tarantula-infested teak forest ruins with the Mayans of the Yucatan.

But I had my heart dead-set on seeing all seven continents – and now there was only one left. The hard one. Antarctica. Many people joked that I would swim to Antarctica if that's what it took, and they weren't far off.

The bus pulled into Ushuaia, the southernmost city in the world, on New Year's Eve shortly after 9.30 p.m. local time.

Ushuaia, a beautiful coastal city nestled gently beneath the verdant mountains of Tierra del Fuego, lies at the southernmost tip of Argentina and South America.

I had been on the road since September, on 'the hippy trail' of wayward backpackers from around the world, slowly making my way south amongst the other lost souls banding together in search of fun, frolic, the meaning of life, and of course a good time. To understand the road, you must first understand the nature of the hippy trail. Like formations in a lava lamp, travellers meet, mix, join, separate, and move along – only to reconfigure somewhere else down the road. You never know where you will run into someone that you have seen earlier on the trail; ordinarily it is unexpected in both time and place, but generally always welcome.

It is difficult in this day and age to make one's escape from Modern Life, and my escape was no exception. The older you get, the harder it is. With all the contraptions and gizmos to pay for in one's monthly nut – from mobile phones to access lines to car payments to rent – to simply walk away for a month or two, to disappear, to drop right out of the middle of one's life without a care or worry and leave no trace, requires some planning.

Except in a case like mine: no job, no wife, no kids, no pets, no car – only a garage, where I had lived for 12 years beneath a splendid, sprawling avocado tree whose twisted, gnarled branches sheltered me from reality ever since my days as a film student at UCLA. For me it was easy: simply lock the door to the garage, toss a few things in a backpack, and head south to write my novel, with no itinerary, heading wherever the wind would take me for as long as the cash would last, collecting experiences like butterflies along the way. When I hit the road, I figured the cash I had painstakingly stowed away would last about three months in South America before the well dried up and I was forced to return home and deal with reality.

My first stop was Lima, Peru. After a bleary all-night flight, I took a cab at 5 a.m. to a crowded backpacker's hostel and collapsed immediately in a dorm room filled with snoozing students – only to wake up a few hours later to the sounds of a major morning protest taking place in front of the nearby Peruvian government building, complete with tanks, armoured personnel carriers, riot police, soldiers, and screaming, marching peasant masses. I stepped out onto the veranda, smelling the hot, sticky city, and smiled. I had arrived in South America.

In the span of a few short weeks I had made my way to Machu Picchu and hiked enough of the Inca Trail to watch the magical kingdom appear out of the mists in the early morning dawn, understanding instantly the mystique of the place and how it had remained undiscovered for centuries. I worked my way slowly south, moving along to Lake Titicaca, to the Isle of the Sun, the birthplace of the Incan religion, which unexpectedly turned out be so exceptionally beautiful and peaceful I did not want to leave. Finally, after about a week, I managed to rip myself away from this paradise and move on into Bolivia proper and La Paz, a bustling neon bowl of a city etched right out of the sandy earth near the foothills of the Andes.

Rumour had it that the guards at Santa Cruz prison in La Paz accepted small donations to allow travellers to 'visit' the prison for a time during the day on 'humanitarian missions' to save souls. I went down to the prison with a fellow American woman named Erin and Stuart, a British student whom I had met on the Isle of the Sun and who was now stuck in La Paz for a couple of weeks enduring a series of free rabies shots because he had been bitten by a stray dog a few days after we had split up.

We were met outside the entrance to the prison by the shouts and screams of the inmates within, who were hawking their 'wares' at the tourists outside, namely, us. Finally, the three of us handed over our passports to the guard at the front desk and went inside, led by one of the prisoners, who stood out because he had a long pink scar running across his cheek and a fresh blue-black eye.

This prisoner, who called himself Joe, explained that he had been wrongly sentenced to prison time because he had been set-up by corrupt cops who had brazenly tossed two kilos of pure coke onto his hotel room floor while his hands were unceremoniously cuffed behind his back. The indignity of it all! Now, he was leading these tours because the only way out for him was to purchase a new two-thousand-dollar oak desk for the judge who sentenced him. Luckily, he had almost saved enough to buy his way out.

As he led us to his spacious cell in the wealthiest part of the prison complex, a cell block affectionately known as Beverly Hills, he explained that this was 'easy time' compared to the stint he had done for dealing drugs in Sing-Sing in upstate New York. He had spent a great deal of time in the States (wasn't that wonderful to know); he was half-American and therefore, due to his fluent English, was considered the best of the prison tour guides, which were rotated every three months.

The cell was a two-storey pad bigger than my garage and was attended by a short, squat, young prisoner who acted as Joe's 'butler'. We crawled up a ladder through the hole in the ceiling to his spacious, luxurious bedroom, complete with colour television and stereo, and sat down on his plush couch. Outside, the prison itself was more like a debtors' prison in Victorian England than a penitentiary found in the States. The inmates are given free rein during the day; at night, they are locked into their cells and cell blocks. Joe explained that for a complete tour of the facilities, it would cost us 40 Bolivianos (the equivalent of eight US dollars and quite an exorbitant sum). Erin, wearing shorts, felt immediately uncomfortable, being a woman in a prison filled with miscreants, reprobates, and common criminals, even though Joe reassured her that he was king of the prison and no harm would come to her as long as she was in his company. She couldn't get out of there soon enough. Stuart, too, balked at the rather pricey cost of the tour (we had entered having heard that the grand tour cost only 14 Bolivianos, not 40). I wanted very much to participate – but was uncertain enough of the prospect of taking the tour alone that I joined them in declining Joe's offer. Joe explained that the high price was needed so that the guards would get their share, but the others weren't biting. We were escorted back out through the gates with the admonition: once you leave for the day, you won't be let back in.

We quickly exited the prison and gathered for a huddle in the park across the street. I still very much wanted to go back inside, but was wary of doing so alone. Just as we were ready to call it a day and head out for a beer, we were approached by two other tourists, a tall, blond-haired Brit and his tattooed girlfriend. There is only one reason a tourist comes to that part of town; quickly I asked if anyone wanted to go inside for the tour with me. The Brit was easily convinced, and in we went.

Once again we were led to the cell by Joe, who had been eagerly waiting by the entrance. He sat us down in his cell once again and this time collected our money, which by now we had bargained down to 35 Bolivianos. (I had left the bulk of my cash with Erin, who waited across the street in the park with Stuart.) The Brit looked around at all the fancy equipment and remarked, 'This stuff must've cost a lot – where did you get all the money?' Joe replied, 'Well, I run a little side business here inside the prison – a pharmacy.' He smiled. I thought the whole thing was a joke. Then Joe asked, 'So, are you guys here for the tour, or are you shopping?' I chuckled. 'The tour,' I mumbled.

'Shopping,' the Brit added, after a brief pause. I turned my head in super slow motion and stared at my fellow tourist in disbelief. You have got to be kidding me, I thought to myself. Joe stepped forward and explained that he had pure Bolivian cocaine for four US dollars a gram and bounteous amounts of marijuana at seven Bolivianos a gram. The Brit said that he was interested in buying two grams of the herbs and handed over 14 Bolivianos to Joe. We walked downstairs and Joe called over his little butler. He handed over the cash to his young flunky and the youngster scampered off, disappearing into the prison population. 'OK, let's start the tour,' Joe said.

I was utterly horrified. I wasn't sure about anything that was going on, and certainly wasn't happy about being an American in a Bolivian prison where a drug deal was going down. The guards were corrupt and the prisoners were killers, my passport had been secreted away by the slimy guard at the front door, and American policy in Bolivia had been viewed with mixed results by the indigenous population, who had been growing and using the coca plant for years but were now under attack by the American DEA and all the monetary and political pressure they could apply. I had visions of the guards swooping down on us at any moment and applying their own strong-arm tactics, squeezing out of me every cent they could before tossing me to the wolves, either inside the prison or outside in the political arena.

I began to sweat as Joe led us through the first courtyard to another wing of the prison, explaining the intricacies of the place as he went along. He explained that where he lived, in Beverly Hills, they were able to bolt the doors at either end of the cell block at night to protect themselves from the other prisoners, the toothless ones in 'A Block' on the ground floor, who got wild on *aguardiente* or *pisco* (the local moonshine) and tried to break down those doors, pounding and howling each and every night to get to the massive amounts of pure cocaine stored inside.

He then led us up to a second-tier balcony, from where we could look down on the courtyard. 'This is where we play soccer during the day,' he told us, 'and at night, this is where the beatings and the stabbings take place.' He smiled and led us around the prison via the upper tier; at every intersection to a new area, he mumbled in local dialect to another flunky, who then scampered off. 'This is where the elders play cards during the day,' he pointed out, 'and at night, this is where the beatings and the stabbings take place.' He bragged to us how he had won his five-thousand-dollar cell in a card game when one of the elders put it up as collateral in a bet; cells in Beverly Hills were hard to come by.

We walked on. 'This is where we eat lunch during the day, and at night, where the beatings and the stabbings take place.' I began to sense a pattern. Sweat began to roll down my face even more, the palpable aura of paranoia intense. 'Ah, you don't have to worry about it during the day,' he boasted. 'They wouldn't dare try anything against me. I run the prison.' I asked him how he got his black eye. 'We had a cultural dancing competition between the cell blocks, and things got a little out of hand.' He smiled.

We walked back downstairs and headed for the exit. Along the way, Joe's little butler showed up and they slapped hands. Joe pointed out five tin drums of rubbish, buzzing with flies and waiting for collection. 'There's this week's rubbish,' he said. 'A guy's been missing over on Cell Block C. He's probably chopped up in there somewhere.'

He led us to the front gate, within earshot of the guards. Time to say goodbye. He stuck out his hand to shake the Brit's, and slapped the two grams of dope into his palm. I nervously retrieved my passport from the grinning, clean-cut guard and walked out into the fresh air and sunshine, safely outside the prison walls.

I didn't look back but could still hear the shouting and the hoopla as I rejoined the others in the park across the street. The Brit and his tattooed woman headed off happily to smoke their dope, while I told my companions the tale of intrigue over a beer in a dingy joint across the square. They were equally horrified at my predicament. What a crazy place, where a person goes inside a prison to score the best drugs and the guards themselves run the trade in cahoots with the prisoners. Then, suddenly, it dawned on me, and I smiled at my own foolishness: Joe had been pulling my leg. There really hadn't been a cultural dancing competition at all.

I made my way through the glorious Andes and down into the high reaches of the Amazon basin before hitching a ride out of the jungle on a Bolivian cattle barge. I had hiked out into the bush underneath a blazing sun to a small village on the shore of some nameless river, told to go there by the Bolivian Navy (yes, there really is such a thing) and wait for a cattle barge that would pass by the following morning at the crack of dawn. As I strung up my brand new, market-purchased hammock in an abandoned shack now doubling as a chicken coop, a local villager came running up, panting, to tell me that the barge had arrived early. I quickly packed up my things and ran with the villager down the muddy banks to the water's edge, where we were met by a boatsman in a canoe with a small outboard engine. We whizzed across to the other side of the river, where the barge was tying up against the far shore. Excitedly I asked the eager, young captain if he would take me with them. He smiled and assured me they would – but first they were going to go back to the village to grab a bite to eat. They left me there alone for over two hours with nothing to do but watch another beautiful orange-red Amazonian sunset and listen to the cattle shuffle across the wood planks and moo before finally the delighted crew returned, and upriver we went into the jungle darkness, guided only by a spotlight on a swivel that illuminated the inky water every time the captain yanked on its joystick.

HOW I CAME TO THE *BERSERK*

Travelling on board the barge along with me through the jungle were the smiling Bolivian captain, his precocious young family, three crewmembers oddly reminiscent of the characters who accompanied Dorothy through the Land of Oz, and 156 head of stinking, shuffling longhorn steer. Each night the friendly Scarecrow and I gazed out and up in awe at miraculous meteor showers while reclining on a series of wood planks strategically placed two feet above the shuffling cattle's horns. They stank to high heaven, a mixture of all that a beast entails, uncured hide and acrid urine. Five days later the cattle were driven off the barge with extreme and shocking brutality by the crewmember who reminded me of the Cowardly Lion, who then proudly butchered before my eyes one of the poor sick beasts to provide a month's worth of food for the crew.

I meandered my way down through the Andean silver mines of Potosi and through the salt flats toward the mountains of Chile. Though I had no itinerary planned, I knew in my heart that I wanted to get to Antarctica. Now that I was slowly making my way through South America, Antarctica was the only continent left that I had not visited. As a writer and a filmmaker it was my obligation, duty and desire to see all corners of the world. Antarctica marked the last step in that journey – and I knew it would be the most difficult step to achieve.

But along the way I was certainly enjoying Life. Every day brought a new adventure. Proud to have escaped from the vicious cycle of modern living, though one of the oldest people backpacking along the hippy trail, I felt oddly successful. Before leaving LA, I had been seated before the highest-paid screenwriter in cinema history, who advised me that an opportunity was presenting itself at that time, that I should stay and take advantage of the opportunity to write another screenplay, that the jungle and South America would be waiting for me next year, wouldn't it? I didn't take the advice lightly, respecting this writer as both a friend and an artist.

But I felt something drawing me inexorably down there and could not properly explain it. It seemed that Destiny was calling out to me. One night before the finals of the soccer World Cup, I had a dream that I was lying on the couch and watching the game between France and Brazil. In my dream France scored a goal with less than two minutes to go in the first half and went into the locker room leading the heavily-favoured Brazilians by a score of 2–0. I told a close friend and he mocked me mercilessly.

We watched the game together. The French shockingly scored the first goal but as the half wound down it looked like that would be all they would score. My friend began to rub it in my face. The clock ticked down to zero, but two minutes of extra injury time were added. Suddenly, the French scored again – and my friend finally shut up. The vague dream had proven eerily prescient.

Following in the wake of that dream I mysteriously had another. This one was even more nebulous and vague, communicating more of a feeling than a specific thought. The dream conveyed to me that I would find some answers on this voyage regarding my Destiny. It beckoned me to go, strong as an undertow; there I would find my Fate. I felt it more than I was able to elucidate.

Was I being led inexorably by Fate toward my death? Or was I about to embark on a voyage of discovery that would somehow change my life? I wasn't sure. But whatever it was, the answer was down there – in South America.

The streets of Chile were erupting in chaos as piles of burning rubbish were met by squadrons of riot police when I entered the country across the arid mountainous border with several Brits, who were nervous at the political climate.

Former Chilean dictator Pinochet had been arrested in Spain and was being held by the British to be put on trial. Things calmed quickly, however, further south in the beautiful Chilean Lake District where I sat on a log for days next to a raging river at the conflux of five volcanoes, working on my precious novel.

I then hopped on a ferryboat leaving Puerto Montt for a four-day cruise southward through the Patagonian fjords. It was one big, wild party from start to finish. I met some fellow travellers on the boat, including a long-haired German martial artist named Elmar and his cute girlfriend Frohicke. When we reconvened on the roof of the ship for more drink and merriment, we met a few other people, a couple of Aussies, a Brit, and another German teenager, with whom we eventually backpacked into Torres del Paine National Park in southern Patagonia as a group.

The week-long hike through the wet rugged terrain of Torres del Paine was hard on me; my feet blistered badly. By the time we landed in Punta Arenas, on the Beagle Channel, they were in such lousy shape I could barely walk.

It was in Punta Arenas, holed up on the back bunk bed in a cheap, packed hostel called Backpacker's Paradise for Christmas week to heal my wounds, that I would make my first attempts to find a ride to Antarctica.

Because of the political situation, one avenue that had been available in the past was closed off: the Chilean Navy, which made several supply runs to its Antarctic bases each year and allowed the occasional backpacker to trip along with them, was not allowing any travellers on its vessels this season. The situation for the Chileans was dicey; they felt it was within the realm of possibility that war could break out at any time between them and the British. Still, my first foray took me to the offices of the Chilean Navy, where the young officer at the front desk told me flatly that the Navy would not be taking any travellers with them this year. I was willing to try to bribe them, but he was not the officer to be bribed. He suggested I look for passage on the nearby docks. At the gate to the docks, the guard informed me that an American scientific vessel was due to arrive in several days, scheduled for a run down to Antarctica. Here at last was a legitimate opportunity! The guard told me that the vessel was run by the National Science Foundation, who had offices in the complex. I immediately went to those offices. They were locked. When someone finally arrived, they told me I would have to wait for the vessel.

So wait I did. My friends all headed down south to Ushuaia after a day or two in Punta Arenas. I stayed off my feet, watching HBO on cable with fellow backpackers from around the world and drinking Jack Daniels with the hostel's owner, a friendly, chatty young Chilean named Armando. He ran a fun place and after more than three months on the road, it was good to settle in for some much-needed holiday rest.

Ironically, some of the other travellers had Antarctic dreams or tales of their own. One fellow, a middle-aged Filipino living in Canada, had just returned from a six-day cruise down to Antarctica. We sat over coffee at the picnic table in the hostel's spacious kitchen. My eyes lit up hearing his talc. Another elderly woman also staying at the hostel had been on the same cruise ship. He told me how passage on the cruise ships was expensive – a berth normally started at US$4,500–5,000. He had gone into the cruise ship's office a few hours before the ship was due to leave and had slammed $2,500 cash down on the counter. They'd let him on – even though he was backpacking rabble.

After a three-day crossing of very difficult water, during which time many people became violently seasick, they had arrived in the 'safe' harbours of Antarctica. Once a day the passengers were ferried to shore for a short length of time on rubber rafts with outboard motors. They were issued knee-high rubber boots and wet suits, and they were still chilled to the bone by the fierce Antarctic winds and icy waters. Still, they clambered onto shore – even the elderly woman staying with us at the hostel – and had a bit of a look around.

This certainly wasn't the way I wanted to do things, but it was an option nonetheless. I told him of my desire to get down there another way – any other way – but he scoffed at me and just laughed. 'You'll never do it,' he said, as I continued to pepper him for information, the excitement all too evident in my eyes. 'It's very difficult to get down there,' he told me. 'I got lucky that they were feeling generous that day. They gave me a break.'

I was horrified; I didn't have that kind of money. Even if I did convince them to take me along for a cruise, it would cost me all I had left. I would be left with nothing; my return plane ticket had already expired. I would be forced to hitchhike to Buenos Aires and phone home. It would be the end of my trip.

Plus there was the matter of the short forays onto land with a bunch of other tourists with whom I certainly would not fit in: tourists dressed in formalwear for dinner and waltzing to string quartets by moonlight. I didn't want to eat and I didn't want to dance: I wanted to see Antarctica, and not as it passed by me through the portal window of a formal dining room. I wanted to feel it, touch it, be a part of it.

Still, my fellow traveller told me that Antarctica indeed was as beautiful as I had heard. If I exhausted my options in Punta Arenas, I would head next to Ushuaia. I would try and negotiate a berth on one of the large sailing boats I had been told about, but I didn't have much hope for that, since they catered to wealthy tourists (the travellers who had given me their names were four French doctors on holiday from Martinique whom I had met in the Chilean salt desert known as the Salar de Uyuni, a magical wonderland of blood red lakes, duststorms blowing over flat, dried lakebeds à la Death Valley, geysers, and salt pans that extended as far as the eye could see).

But as a last resort, the cruise ships would have to do. I would make it to Antarctica, I told my companion. Still, things didn't look good; this was the area where many a traveller would turn around. I had seen it before.

My fellow traveller told me one thing that sticks with me to this day. 'You know,' he said, 'it's always more exciting when you're standing at the bottom of the mountain.' Maybe from the bottom of his mountain. He was jaded. He began to ride me about never getting to Antarctica – and not in a very good-natured way, either. We were cordial after that, but from then on something was very different between us.

Then one day, as I sat watching TV in the lobby of the hostel, a young, long-haired American wearing a dirty red-and-white baseball cap waltzed in carrying three six-packs of beer under his arm in a brown paper bag. He sat at the picnic table in the kitchen and began to swig down can after can while waiting for one of the basement Internet computers to free up. His name was John – and he was third mate on the *Lawrence M. Gould*, a scientific vessel which had just arrived in port on its way to Antarctica. The very ship I had been waiting for.

We immediately struck up a friendship. He had the true spirit of a sailor on shore leave coursing through his veins and handed out beers like business cards at a convention to the weary, ragged backpackers gathered round. I began to interrogate him about Antarctica and learned he had made many trips down there through the ice and snow on the *Lawrence M. Gould*. Being a heavy metal fan, I brought up Iron Maiden's 'Rime of the Ancient Mariner' and discovered he played it often while cruising through the treacherous Drake Passage over the loudspeakers in the mammoth ship's bridge. I desperately wanted to go with them on their next trip south.

John was soon unceremoniously tossed from the hostel for drinking his own beer – one of the auberge's rules was that you had to buy beer from them. But before he left, he invited me and another traveller, a blonde British woman, to take a tour of the *Gould* with him the next afternoon.

Excitedly we walked the dock and got our first glimpse of the *Gould*: a large, unwieldy, oblong, almost egg-shaped vessel over 300 feet long and painted day-glo neon orange. The penguins could definitely see it coming through the ice, that's for sure.

John met us at the bottom of the gangplank and led us aboard his majestic ship, outfitted and rigged for scientific work relating to the American bases on the seventh continent. He introduced us to some of his fellow crewmembers, including the noble captain and the ship's chief engineer, a short, jovial North Carolinian who had worked himself up to a position of prominence after a misspent youth and little formal education. The ship was squeaky new – only three years old – and in good shape, though rumour had it that it had to be returned to dry dock after its initial launching because its unusual shape caused it to list to the side. It had all the amenities a crew could possibly want including a full modern gym and a spacious well-stocked kitchen, where we stopped for some dessert and saw a familiar Chilean face from the hostel, a friend of the owner's who had hit the jackpot and contracted on for the voyage as a cook.

But it also soon became apparent that without permission from NOAA (the National Oceanic and Atmospheric Administration) or the NSF (the National Science Foundation), there was no way in hell we were getting on that ship when it finally left port to ferry a new batch of scientists, workers and supplies to the great southern bases.

That night, John invited me out for a farewell dinner and drinks with the crew at the Country Pub, a legendary Punta Arenas American expats hang-out. We all drank like sailors that night. John bought me a jar of Country Pub world-famous smoked salmon prepared by the bar's burly owner, who had arms as thick as tree trunks and a pure American smile (even though he was Chilean) that made everyone feel instantly at home in his presence. John slapped me on the shoulder and wished me luck, leaving me overwhelmed by his kindness and generosity as he walked back to the ship to do his late shift. I stayed at the pub and drank until the wee hours with the friendly engineer, who regaled me with horror stories of his youth in which his mean father would toss him into a dirt pit for bare-knuckle fights with other backwood locals in the hopes of making a man out of him. But he had made a man out of himself, I told him: he had yanked himself up out of that pit through sheer force of will and had made of himself a stunning success with a prominent berth on the *Lawrence M. Gould*, a ship full of friends and countrymen that set sail for Antarctica the next day without me.

A few days after Christmas, my German friends Elmar and Frohicke returned from Ushuaia. They were only in town for the day and were leaving the next morning to fly home and begin their studies. They left a note for me at Backpacker's Paradise and I tracked them down at their hotel.

Later that night at a farewell dinner I told them of the futility of my attempts to find a ship heading to Antarctica. 'Well,' Elmar stammered, looking over at Frohicke uncertainly, 'there is a small sailing boat in Ushuaia. The captain is a Norwegian – a crazy Viking – and he is going to sail down there by himself.'

My eyes lit up. 'I want to go with him!' I exclaimed gleefully.

Elmar frowned. 'Mark said we shouldn't tell you,' he said. 'He knew you would want to go with him – and Mark says he's going to die.'

Mark was a fellow ferry backpacker, a shaggy Generation-X Brit with whom I had hiked and shared a tent in Torres del Paine. Mark had sailed for six months from Australia to Peru via Easter Island on a large yacht, and had related over the campfire how difficult it was at times. I was enthralled by the tale, of course, though at the time had no idea I myself would be heading south in this manner.

Elmar continued relating Mark's assessment of the situation. The 'crazy Viking' and Mark had met on the docks; Mark thought him arrogant. His sailing experience in the Pacific led him to believe that the boat was too small to successfully weather the treacherous seas it would be facing, not to mention the dangers it would face in Antarctica itself.

'When is he leaving?' I prompted.

'Any day now,' Elmar answered.

'I'm going to head down there and try to get on board.'

'Mark knew you would say that – that's why he didn't want us to tell you.'

It was too late – they already had.

The next day I arranged a bus ticket, and on the following morning – 31 December 1998 – I boarded a bus for the 12-hour journey to Ushuaia across the flat tundra of Tierra del Fuego. I watched the Tierra pass by through the window and smiled: I had dreamed of visiting Tierra del Fuego ever since receiving a small blue globe as a present on my seventh birthday. In the years since, I had often thought of Tierra del Fuego: what is there? What is it like? Are my impressions of it going to be anything like I have imagined all this time? As a child I spent hours staring at Tierra del Fuego, the ends of the earth, on that little globe (which still sits in front of me to this day). I was so intrigued by Tierra del Fuego as a youth that I had even done a lengthy book report on Argentina simply because it was there. Before travelling, an impression is much like a black-and-white film; after visiting a locale, it turns to blazing colour. My imagination ran rampant. Now, finally actually passing through it, outside there were only flat barren rocky plains and a few goats. But it made me smile just seeing it nonetheless. Tierra del Fuego. Land of Fire. Tierra del Fuego. The land of my dreams, and there it was.

The bus lumbered and wheezed into Ushuaia's main street station around 9.30 p.m. on New Year's Eve and waiting to greet us was a van sent by the campground on the edge of town that had been recommended by Elmar. In backpacking circles, word gets around quickly regarding the best places to stay; Argentina was 'expensive' compared to Chile, and the most reasonable digs were the campground – provided you had a tent. I didn't and the hostel beds in the campground dorm were full up – but was lucky enough to have met a friendly Swiss traveller on the bus who offered to let me crash in his tent for the night. We threw our packs into the back of the van and headed up to the campground, which was located on the side of a mountain a few miles outside of town.

As we swung off of Main Street for the ride out, we passed by the shore. The driver introduced himself as Boris. Boris, of Russian descent via Spain, pointed out a small sailing boat barely visible in the twilight darkness. 'You see that boat?' he announced to all the passengers. I strained to see, but we were moving quickly past the docks. I could barely make out the tip of a mast. 'That belongs to a crazy Viking who's planning to sail to Antarctica by himself.'

I smiled. 'I know, I want to go with him.'

He turned around and looked at me.

'You're crazy,' he said. 'He's going to die.'

He then explained why: 'The boat is only twenty-seven feet long, and it's made out of fibreglass. As soon as it hits ice it will crack. When you go into the water, you have only four minutes to live before you freeze to death. The Norwegian doesn't even have a lifeboat.'

Boris had been a sailor and let me know it. 'A fibreglass boat that size won't survive the Drake Passage, the roughest seas in the world, where the waves are over forty feet – but even if it does, it can't handle the ice. Take it from me, I've sailed before.'

Well, I hadn't – but I wasn't about to be deterred by the cynical Spaniard. I asked him when the ship was leaving, but he didn't know. 'Any day now,' he said. He continued by telling me that he himself was waiting to go to Antarctica – that was why he was there – but via cruise ship. He was now working and living at the campground until he could afford a ride down there. Upon initially hearing of the Norwegian, however, he had gone down to the docks to assess the situation himself and had spoken to the young captain. They hadn't gotten along, hadn't seen eye to eye. Boris came away from the conversation feeling that the ship and her captain wouldn't make it.

'The name of the boat is *Berserk*,' he stated flatly. 'And so is her captain.'

As we arrived at the campground, I was gleeful: the ship was still there. First thing tomorrow morning I would make my way down to the docks and see if I could join the expedition before it left.

My new Swiss friend and I put up the tent, settled in and joined an incredible New Year's Eve celebration, Argentinian style, complete with a long banquet table, a feast of barbecued meat, dancing, booze and merriment amongst fellow travellers, orchestrated by the campground's owner, a balding hippy who had tied his remaining hair in a long ponytail.

The next morning, we hitched a ride into town – it was quite a walk, and my feet were still wounded – with the campground van. It dropped us off on Main Street and we walked first a few blocks down to the tourist office, which was open on New Year's Day, during the height of tourist season. I went inside and inquired about the cruise ships heading to Antarctica and was handed a detailed photocopied list of all the ships and companies located in Ushuaia. Compared to the one company whose office I had visited during my sojourn in Punta Arenas, this was a bounty. I looked over the list with mixed emotions: it seemed likely a last-minute berth could be secured on one of these vessels, provided they were still operating, but I wasn't sure I would do it. A heavy decision would have to be weighed: was it worth it to blow the rest of my cash on a quick jaunt to Antarctica, which would pass by outside a window in a whizz or dull blur, thus necessitating a return home only a week later after a brief 'been-there done-that' tour of the ice? Or would I be better off turning around from Ushuaia and heading back into the Amazon, which I really wanted to get a better look at? I had lasted for over three months in South America already and had spent far less than expected; at this rate, I could last another three. I was having an amazing time, every day better than the last. Enjoying Life to the utmost. Was it really worth it to end my trip now just so I could say I'd been to Antarctica? It was something I would really need to think about, but luckily I felt I had some time.

I walked back outside into the sunlight and looked around. On a nearby bench a fellow traveller sat comfortably, legs crossed and smoking a cigarette, backpack at his side. He smiled. '*Buenos dias*,' he said, greeting me with a smile. '*Feliz Año Nuevo* – Happy New Year.'

I smiled back. 'Happy New Year to you,' I answered.

'How are you today?' he asked.

'Fine, thank you,' I answered. It was pleasant conversation on a beautiful, sunny day.

'Where are you from?' he asked in Spanish, a normal first question amongst travellers.

'Los Angeles,' I answered. 'And you?'

'I'm Argentinian – but I lived in Los Angeles for seven years!'

He introduced himself as Manuel. He was very jovial, smiling the entire time. As we got to talking about LA, we were joined by a pudgy Brit who asked if we knew of anywhere to get something to eat.

'No, but I could use a cup of coffee,' I answered.

Manuel sprang to his feet. 'Me too.'

My Swiss friend joined us and told us of a café around the corner that the tourist office told him was open. The four of us started off in a group. It was shortly before noon.

As we walked down the street, I realised we were very close to the docks. I stopped. 'There's a boat I want to check out on the docks,' I announced. 'A sailing boat heading for Antarctica. It's right here. I'm gonna go down to the dock and check it out, and I'll meet you guys in five minutes at the café.'

Manuel smiled. 'I'll go with you.'

'OK, see you in a few minutes.' The Swiss and the Brit walked off up the street to the café, while Manuel and I crossed the street and headed for the nearby dock.

We walked into the marina and up the wooden plankway. At the end of the dock, on our left, was the small sailing boat Boris had pointed out the night before. It was tied to another larger sailing boat, which itself was tied up to a third. That one was lashed onto the dock. The small sailing boat on the outside was tiny by comparison; a golf ball in relation to a soccer ball.

A middle-aged man, with a worn sailor's face creased from sun and wind, was down on his hands and knees scrubbing the deck of the middle boat. It was a warm day for Ushuaia, just shy of 20 degrees, sunny, with a steady breeze; the man was dressed in jeans and a striped, longsleeved sailor's shirt. He did not seem to notice our presence on the dock, or if he did, he didn't care to acknowledge it.

'Excuse me,' I mumbled, looking to Manuel for support, 'do you know where I can find the captain of that boat?'

The weathered man looked at me for a moment, turned and looked at the small boat, then looked back again. He pointed toward the end of the dock that we had just come from.

Walking up the dock, carrying six enormous, packed grocery bags, ambled a short, stocky boy with shoulder-length, wavy, dark hair. Following him, like rats after the Pied Piper, struggled four typical backpackers overloaded with camping gear. 'Hallo hallo!' he bellowed, beaming widely.

'I hear you're going to Antarctica,' I answered. 'I want to go with you.'

'When are you leaving?' I added.

He smiled. 'Right now.'

I wasn't expecting that. Still, I answered quickly. 'I need two hours to get my things in order.'

He put his bags down on the dock while the backpackers caught up and unharnessed their loads like prospectors unloading mules. He turned to the others. 'Can you wait here for a few minutes? These two may want to go with me.'

What choice did they have? They were backpackers; they were used to waiting.

'Let's talk on the boat.'

The captain introduced himself: Jarle Andhoey, from Larvik, Norway.

HOW I CAME TO THE *BERSERK*

We followed Jarle (pronounced Yar-la, it was the Norwegian version of Charlie) onto the first big sailing boat next to the dock and followed him across the surface of its bow to the second boat, where the weathered sailor still knelt, scrubbing. Without missing a beat, Jarle greeted him with a warm hallo and asked him 'How's it going?' as he continued across the freshly-cleaned boat to his own. I stepped gingerly, leaving footprints on the surface as the sailor on hands and knees looked on silently and sternly.

For the first time, I got a real look at the *Berserk* up close: it was certainly tiny compared to the two boats we had just crossed. The outdoor cockpit was so small it was barely large enough for the three of us to sit in.

Jarle unlocked a small padlock and lifted three small wooden boards to reveal the dark inside of the tiny boat. He placed the grocery bags down below while Manuel and I sat down in the cockpit excitedly.

'So, you want to go with me,' Jarle said as he returned, smiling. 'Do you have any sailing experience?'

I shook my head. I'd stepped onto a sailing boat only twice in my life, both times as a passenger on day trips.

But I was used to the water. I told Jarle that I had grown up fishing regularly with my father on the Chesapeake Bay, and that I had worked for several months on a floating fish processor in Ugashik Bay, off Pilot Point in the Bering Sea near Alaska's Aleutian Islands. He was especially pleased with my experience in Alaska and instantly began calling me an Alaskan fisherman.

My father's passion in life had always been fishing. He had struggled early in his career as an attorney, but still dragged me with him as he fished for hours, surfcasting from a lonely bay shore or renting a small rowboat with a single outboard engine and cruising the choppy waters to drop a line underneath the busy Bay Bridge. One of our often-told family stories concerns the time when I managed to catch a fish, much to his dismay, when we were cruising full-speed hell bent for leather back to shore in a futile attempt to beat dusk. I had spent many a hot sweltering summer day in the humid sticky stillness of the bay as the small open boat bobbed up and down and raw ground stinking fish guts were tossed overboard as bait chum to attract schools of bluefish – yet I had never been seasick. I was proud of that.

And I let Jarle know it. I really, really wanted to go with him.

'I don't need food and I don't need sleep,' I added. 'And I've never been seasick.'

Manuel and Jarle both laughed.

'What about you?' Jarle said to Manuel.

Manuel then told his tale. He had been living with his sister and working as some sort of tour guide off Peninsula Valdes, about halfway up the Argentinian eastern shore. He had no boating experience whatsoever, but had been going out on small boats that took tourists out to see whales. About a week ago, shortly before Christmas, he had become fed up with his life and had decided to hitchhike down to Ushuaia on a whim, simply because he had never been there before. He had just arrived in town and was smoking his first cigarette on that bench when I met him less than half an hour ago. He wanted to go with us.

Jarle then told us a little bit about himself. He had sailed down to Ushuaia by himself, all the way from home: Larvik, Norway. It had taken him more than a year. He left home at the age of 19, first sailing from Norway down to West Africa; then he had crossed the Atlantic to Brazil. He made his way down the east coast of South America and had fought for three days alone against furious currents and fierce winds spilling out of the Beagle Channel before he was finally able to round Cape Horn for the first time.

There it was: Cape Horn. The stuff of legends. Every young boy who hears a sailor's story can only imagine it.

The name alone invokes the salty spray of the sea, pirate ships flying Jolly Rogers under full sail, monstrous storms – and disastrous shipwrecks.

I looked around the small wood-panelled cabin. A poster taped above the starboard bunk, a map ripped from the pages of an old *National Geographic*, showed a history of explorers, the years of their voyages, and their routes across the Seven Seas. Above the port bunk, along with pictures of Jarle's beloved family, was an animated drawing of a Berserker – a legendary Norse warrior renowned for his intemperate disposition and fierce fighting prowess. I knew right then and there that this kid was the real deal; even Manuel later confided to me that Jarle quite possibly was the modern-day embodiment of that lineage.

I asked Jarle who his favourite explorer was. 'Shackleton,' he answered. 'I am going to retrace his route.'

I had never heard of him. By the end of the trip, I would understand him well.

Now he was heading down to Antarctica. He had been preparing his ship for months now, in the small Chilean Naval port of Puerto Williams, four hours due south on the Beagle Channel by sail. He had returned to Ushuaia for a week simply to pick up some last-minute supplies and provisions that he couldn't get in the small naval town, in particular a steel wind pilot he was planning to fasten to the stern. Unable to find anyone to go with him, he was now prepared to sail down to Antarctica all by himself. The four backpackers were heading to Puerto Williams on Isla Navarino, for a weeklong trek through the island's sawtooth mountains. Jarle was charging them $25 a head for the trip and needed the cash; they were on their way to leaving when they found us waiting on the dock.

Jarle then announced that the trip would cost us US$1,000 each. Manuel's jaw dropped – but I had heard from Mark that this was a common practice. He had paid $3,000 for his berth on the six-month trip across the Pacific. The money would be used to pay for our share of supplies, such as petrol and food staples, and for the necessary upkeep of the boat. Jarle had provisioned for himself for six months, but if we came along it would be necessary to buy more of everything. He knew what to buy, and he knew how much, but he would need the money, in cash, right away.

I agreed instantly, without batting an eyelash. I wouldn't blow my entire wad on the trip, which would take an estimated three to four months, and I would have cash left over when we hit land.

'We're not coming back here,' Jarle added. 'It's too difficult to sail against the prevailing westerly winds. The *Bounty* tried it and made only twenty knots in six months. We're going to go with the winds. After Antarctica, we're going to retrace Shackleton's route to South Georgia Island – and then we're going to cross over the Atlantic to Capetown.'

South Africa. We would be at sea for a month, by my reckoning, once we left South Georgia alone. I gave it some thought. I had always wanted to visit Buenos Aires, and had hoped to get another shot at the Amazon. Still, Antarctica would not come without some sort of sacrifice, and what the heck, I'd never been to South Africa. With my leftover cash I could head to Namibia and Botswana for a safari. I agreed.

Manuel wanted to go too – but he didn't have the cash. He had only $70 and pocket change to his name. Jarle looked at me, then back over at him. I really wanted Manuel to go; I had no idea what kind of workload to expect.

'If we let you go, David and I will be paying for your trip,' Jarle told him. I was willing to do it. 'How will you get back from South Africa?'

'I'll phone my mother or my sister, and they'll wire me the money for a ticket home,' Manuel answered, a smile still etched on his face.

'OK, OK,' said the captain, and like that the crew was born.

We stuck our hands into the middle in an all-for-one, one-for-all gesture of brotherhood and reaffirmation, all smiles and glee, then stood and walked back out of the cabin, where the backpackers still waited on the dock.

Jarle told the backpackers that we wouldn't be leaving for a couple of hours. We were going with them. On the docks, to my surprise, we were suddenly joined by my old friend Gudula, a backpacker from Austria with whom I had toured Machu Picchu. She too was looking for a lift to the island; Jarle quickly agreed to take her along as well (even though we would then be pushing the capacity of the small boat). The backpackers shrugged and headed back to town to spend a couple of hours at a bar while we got our act together.

I told Jarle that I needed to go back to the campground to get my things, and then needed to make a quick phone call. He and Manuel were going to try to find an open store – it was New Year's Day, after all, and choices were limited – and buy whatever extra staples and dry goods they could find. Whatever they couldn't get, we could still potentially get at the small grocery store in Puerto Williams.

It was shortly after noon. We agreed to meet back at the boat at 2 p.m.

We walked to the edge of the docks and split up. My heart was pounding.

I was going to Antarctica.

I flagged down a cab and asked the driver to take me to the campground. When we got there, I told him to wait. The hippy owner and Boris were standing there on the front porch when we arrived.

'I won't be staying tonight – we need to settle up,' I told him hurriedly. 'I'm going to Antarctica.'

'You're what?' the owner asked, a look of consternation on his face.

'I'm going to Antarctica and we're leaving now.'

'With the Norwegian?'

'Yes.'

He shook his head in horror. 'Ai yai yai,' he mumbled loudly, looking over at Boris. 'You're going to die.'

Yeah, whatever. I ran back to the tent and unlocked it, quickly rolling up my sleeping bag and grabbing my pack. I found a piece of scrap paper amongst my things and quickly scribbled a note to my Swiss benefactor. 'Going to Antarctica,' I wrote. 'Thanks for everything. Have a nice life. Dave.' I tossed the spare key inside and locked the tent.

'Seeya,' I said to the owner and Boris as I jumped back into the cab. They simply looked on in dismay, shaking their heads and mumbling to each other as we pulled away.

The cab dropped me down at an ATM near the dock. Jarle wanted me to get him as much cash as I could – but I was unable to withdraw anything. I wasn't sure why; there should be money in the account. But it was New Year's Day and all the banks were closed; the machine was the best I could do. I was completely unsuccessful.

I went to a nearby pay phone and used a prepaid card given to me as a gift by a good friend to call home. I was lucky; my father was home, in suburban DC. I had last spoken to him five weeks ago, on Thanksgiving Day. I hurriedly told him that the conversation had to be quick: I was going to be sailing to Antarctica, and we would be leaving in less than an hour. How big is the boat? he wanted to know. 'Oh, it's big enough. It's small, but not that small,' I told him. There was no way I was going to tell him the exact size. An experienced waterman like him would know exactly what it meant. I was deliberately skirting the issue.

'Does the captain have charts?' he asked.

'Yeah, I think so,' I answered. He seemed competent enough in the ten minutes we had spent together. I told him that we would get a chance to know each other in Puerto Williams, where we would be spending a few days training and getting used to each other.

'Well, if you see that he doesn't know what he's doing, get off the boat,' my father advised sternly. 'Don't be a hero.'

I told him not to worry, because he wouldn't be hearing from me for at least three months, until we reached South Africa.

'Do you have any warm clothes?'

'Some,' I lied.

'Get yourself some warm clothes.'

My father had had his own harrowing experience at sea, accompanied by my cousin Jeff. They had agreed to accompany a captain who was taking his boat from Cabo San Lucas on the southern tip of the Baja Peninsula back up the Pacific to San Diego. They had planned to stop and do some marlin fishing in some of the inlets along the way. But one day out of Cabo the boat's engine quit in high seas, and they had sent out a mayday call that had been intercepted by the Mexican Navy, who was unable to contact them. The Mexican Navy had called American authorities, who in turn called my stepmother, telling her that my father was missing at sea.

My stepmother called me and through the tears of the grieving gave me the bad news. I simply shrugged; no use worrying about it. There was nothing anybody could do to help them. I was certain they were all right. That's just how things are with fishermen.

Of course, they returned safely to regale us with their tale. The delirious captain – ill-prepared and without charts – had locked himself in his cabin while the drifting boat was pounded by furious seas. My father and cousin feared for their lives; it was my cousin who had sent out the distress call. A third passenger, a friend of the captain's and an engineer, had been able to repair the engine well enough to take them into shore, where my father and cousin bolted at first chance and took a local bus, loaded to the gills with goats and chickens, back to the States.

'Being cold and wet and getting pounded in a small boat for three months doesn't sound like fun to me, but if that's what you want to do…' He was being a father; he was morally and ethically obligated to say stuff like that.

But I heeded his advice. I would see if this young captain had his act together in Puerto Williams, and if indeed he didn't know what he was doing, Antarctica or not, I would swallow my pride and get off the boat.

I was the first to arrive back at the dock. The salty sailor was still working on the middle boat.

I thought long and hard if there was anything else I needed. Most of the stores were closed, so clothes were out of the question. Jarle told us he had wet suits we could borrow, and some extra old sweaters. Wool – pure wool – is the only thing that keeps you warm when it gets wet. When we had mentioned our other warm clothes, he simply shook his head and reiterated: 'Wool.'

But no stores were open, and there was no time to look around. What I had with me would be making the trip, nothing more. That's just the way it was. Sure, it would have been nice to have more time to prepare, could've used another day, a normal working day, not New Year's Day, to buy some supplies, some gloves, a sweater, boots, whatever. But that wasn't going to happen.

The sailor looked up at me.

'Do you think this boat can make it through the Drake Passage without falling apart?' I asked. Here was a legitimate sailor. I had heard the tales of the Drake, the portents of doom from all who spoke reverentially of it.

He shrugged. '*Es aventura*,' he said flatly, without emotion. His eyes had a dull glazed thousand-mile stare, like he had seen many, many days at sea.

Aventura – an adventure.

Never would a wise man's words prove more prophetic.

CHAPTER TWO
A LITTLE TRAINING CRUISE

A broad smile hijacked my face as my hand took firm hold of the tiller for the first time. I was draped in a well-worn, faded, mildewed Norwegian sailing jacket that Jarle had tossed to me nonchalantly. We were cruising between the snow-capped peaks that lined the Beagle Channel – named for Darwin's ship that sailed these very same waters before he epiphanised evolution – and Jarle had just moved to the bow to raise the forward sail. The boat bobbed as it spirited through the choppy channel to the delight of the five backpackers who had joined us for the first leg to Puerto Williams, the tiny Chilean port town on the south end of Isla Navarino where we would spend the next few days learning how to be sailors.

Jarle popped a cassette into the tape deck and the mellifluous crooning of Metallica's James Hetfield blared out the first words to their classic *Master of Puppets* cut 'Sanitarium', making me feel instantly at home. We stowed the extra potatoes, onions and pasta in the storage compartments inside the bottom of the boat as we bobbed our heads and rocked out to another Metallica track 'Unforgiven' – and I knew, win or lose, this was going to be fun. At least this kid had some good tunes on board. Now we were cruising through the channel, listening to heavy metal and checking out the sights. Not a bad way to start.

Manuel was buoyant and expectant as well, jovially sharing a cigarette, a smile and conversation with the young backpackers. Gudula snapped a few photographs of us, three happy comrades, as we bounced our way through the golden evening. When I told her I didn't want them, she promised to send them to my father as a gift; she thought he might like them – as a keepsake.

The wind hit hard at one point and the boat lurched over to the side. Squeals of delight mixed with terror escaped from the crowd as they held on tightly to whatever they could get a hold of. One of the backpackers got seasick and threw up. At the tiller I smiled, accepting the tilt of the boat as being part of the nature of sailing, which I knew absolutely nothing about. But I also hoped that this gust would be an anomaly, that the boat listed so far only because the wind kicked unexpectedly, and found myself relieved when Jarle loosened a rope and the boat straightened up again.

A few hours later we reached Puerto Williams and tied our boat on the outside of another sailing boat. Since it was after midnight, we would deal with the authorities in the morning – we had made the leap from Argentinian to Chilean territory. In the meantime, the backpackers bade us farewell and set off into the small town to find accommodation for the evening, wishing us luck.

Because I had a bit more boating experience than Manuel – I at least knew how to read a compass, for example – I naturally assumed the position of first mate. And because I was actually paying for my ride, I was given my choice of bunks.

BERSERK IN THE ANTARCTIC

The inside cabin of the *Berserk* was basically separated into two sections – a rectangular common area in the stern, with two bunks on either side and the 'kitchen' galley area to the port rear; and on the other side of a small open doorway, a triangular bow area used primarily for storage. Jarle pointed to the port stern bunk, where pictures of his family hung, and explained that when we were anchored, that was his bed. Once we were under sail, it would be too difficult for anyone to sleep in the bow, which feels the pounding of the seas to a higher degree. The two stern bunks had canvas harness rigs which could be tied up when the boat was underway; the three of us would rotate on these bunks on a first-come, first-served basis, depending on who was working the shift outside in the cockpit. However, when anchored, we would each have our assigned bunks.

He turned to me and gave me next choice of bunk. I did not need to think about it long. I have always felt very comfortable in confined spaces, so I opted for the starboard bunk on the bow and happily threw my pack into the clutter of supplies to be sorted out later. My own little private room, so to speak, would have its advantages; though the area appeared to be more cramped, it also had access to the front hatch, through which a person would be more easily able to pop up and exit the boat without having to go through the main door. Manuel would sleep across from Jarle in the starboard stern bunk.

I ducked underneath the small hatchway and unfurled my trusty old throwaway sleeping bag on top of the cushions in the tight bow. My 5'6" frame could just barely stretch out. We all chatted a bit, laughing about the absurd adventure of it all, before Jarle announced that we had a long day ahead of us tomorrow and had better get some sleep. When my eyes shut that night, I was giddy with the excitement of it all; what was running through the others' heads I could only imagine.

Getting used to the *Berserk*, living on a boat without a head, constant exposure to the elements, sleeping in close quarters with others, a sky that never darkened completely, living on tight rations – all of this would come with time. We took the first step the next morning.

We slept late – *Berserk* style – before we began our training. Jarle told us he had wet gear for us – yellow rain slickers that made us look like the Gloucester fisherman from a box of frozen fish sticks. But we would definitely need more clothes, specifically more of everything wool – and the supply in town was limited. We would have to barter with other sailors for their leftovers and throw ourselves on their mercy.

We tried on the worn wet gear to determine what fit who. Manuel was worried from the beginning that he was going to be cold, but proudly announced that he was confident the North Face winter jacket he was wearing would be enough. Jarle laughed in his face. He pulled out a couple of old sweaters and tossed them to us; we divied them up. For the rest we were on our own. After taking inventory, we found we needed an extra pair of boots, and as much wool clothing as we could muster, especially socks and underwear.

Meanwhile, Manuel claimed he was completely out of cash. He had given Jarle the last of his reserves and had left himself with nothing to bargain with. He would rely instead on the goodwill of others, myself included. I was only too glad to help out my new shipmate – at this point.

But Manuel easily smoked a pack of cigarettes a day and it was obvious that his supplies eventually would run out. He had a few packs remaining – after that he was out of luck. Lucky for us, Manuel had chosen this trip to give up smoking completely. He boldly announced he was going to stop cold turkey while we crossed the Drake Passage. In the meantime, his few remaining packs would have to last until our departure.

Neither Jarle nor I thought Manuel would realistically be able to pull this off, but he swore up and down it would be no problem. We simply shrugged; without cash to buy cigs, he would have no choice – and there would be no mini market in Antarctica.

The *Berserk* was moored outside a scuttled freighter called the *McElvee*, which had been intentionally grounded in the shallow waters of the harbour and was rusting appropriately in place. The marina office proper was based on the abandoned ship; there was even a cosy little bar that the sailors frequented in the evenings, complete with plush couches and roaring fire. There was also an ice-cold shower on the old boat – though we never used it. Whenever we needed to heed nature's call, we crawled through the pipes of the ol' rust bucket until we found a private spot above the waves and let slip the dogs of war.

Manuel returned from one of these trips to shore proudly holding aloft two pairs of navy-blue woollen knee socks. Manuel, a friendly, affable guy, had struck up a conversation with a jolly, middle-aged Swedish woman from one of the other boats, who had generously donated the socks to the cause. 'I got a pair for you, too,' he smiled as he handed me a pair, which I gratefully accepted.

Now it was my turn to barter. Jarle nudged me toward a nearby boat belonging to a Dutch sailor named Hank. Hank was a stocky bald man of medium build, about 50, who would have been played in the movie version of his life by Austrian actor Klaus Maria Brandauer. He had made numerous trips to the Antarctic in his sizeable schooner and was never shy about letting someone know about it. He also bragged in his inimitable Prussian style that he was part of some self-created, pseudo-bureaucratic European council responsible for administering the Antarctic Treaty, though it came across as a lot of hot air. He was puttering about his boat when I approached from the dock.

'Um, excuse me,' I said by way of introduction, 'um, we're going to Antarctica and I was wondering if you had any extra clothes available?' Hank looked me up and down from his scrubbing bucket, then glanced back over his shoulder at Jarle's boat.

'Do you have any idea what you're doing?' he asked.

Yeah, going to Antarctica, I thought to myself.

'Have you read the Antarctic Treaty?'

I shook my head. One of Jarle's sailing books had it in the appendix in its entirety. 'But I will,' I promised.

Hank stood and explained that he was responsible for ensuring adherence to the Treaty by irresponsible sailors – sailors like Jarle. Manuel arrived just in time to hear that Hank viewed Jarle as reckless – because he felt his boat was ill-prepared for the challenges that lay ahead. There was no proper radio, no lifeboat – and now, two crewmembers without proper clothes. Jarle didn't adhere to rules and wouldn't give a hoot about the Antarctic Treaty, which discussed issues such as dumping of waste – but I assured Hank that we would.

Hank ducked through the hatch of his boat and brought out a handful of old clothes that he undoubtedly kept around to use as wax rags. He sniffed each article before he tossed it over to me, intimating that they had once been worn but not washed since: first, a nice, green Dutch Army sweater made of wool; then, three pairs of thin, green long johns; and then a couple of thin, green, long-sleeved, thermal undershirts. The tags read 'Half-wol' – obviously some sort of hybrid, but better than nothing. He then dragged out a pair of old rubber boots – with holes in the bottom – and a weathered pair of cracked rubber gloves.

Manuel was excited as a lap dog; he was deathly afraid of being cold and wanted all of it, anything he could get his hands on. 'How much for the lot?' I asked.

'Seventy-five dollars,' Hank answered sternly. 'US.'

'Seventy-five dollars?' I asked incredulously. It was a fortune down here. But Hank knew he had me over a barrel.

'Take it or leave it.' He was strong-arming me and I knew it.

'Take it, take it!' Manuel begged, like an exuberant contestant on a game show, maybe *The Price Is Right* or *Let's Make a Deal*.

'I'll throw in the hat.' Hank, acting like he was doing me a great favour, tossed over a warm, blue, Smurf-looking hat that covered the head, leaving only the face exposed like an Arthurian knight. It sealed the deal.

As I reluctantly handed over the cash to a delighted Hank, I knew we had been ripped off – but we had no choice. We simply needed the clothes.

We went back to the boat and divided the clothing. Manuel groused constantly about the cold – so Jarle handed him a pair of thick, hand-knitted, white woollen long johns that were more than worth their weight in gold. An attractive young French mother from yet another nearby boat – the sailing community in these southern waters was tight and knew Jarle well – had personally knitted two pairs for young Jarle, who seemed to charm women everywhere he went. He gave one pair to Manuel and kept the other for himself.

Manuel and I split Hank's clothing. Because he already had the precious white wool long johns, I kept two of the others and gave him one. I also kept the military sweater and the hat, resolving to wear both of them every day like a uniform until the end of the voyage.

We augmented our outfits with anything made of wool we could find in the small town, which catered to a tiny cadre of Chilean naval families stationed there. The Argentinians and the Chileans, fierce rivals, each strove to colonise settlements further and further south throughout the uninhabited islands, leapfrogging each other in the hopes of claiming further territory. Puerto Williams was the last real settlement, and indeed there were a handful of small stores in a small gravel town square with some food, some clothes, and believe it or not, a bank, where I went every day at Jarle's behest to try to extract the promised cash. A bald bureaucrat sporting a tie at the southernmost tip of civilisation gave me a difficult time taking out cash with my bank card. Every day we went through the same routine until eventually I went to the local telephone exchange and called my bank on their free phone number. The entire experience seemed completely absurd. Here I was at the end of the world getting ready to put my life on the line and yet still dealing with the most banal reality. There truly seemed to be no escape.

We managed to have some luck, finding a couple of pairs of invaluable, thick, hand-knitted wool socks, as well as some thick neck socks worn in lieu of scarves. Manuel had zero cash, so I made all the purchases and handed out the items fairly. Later on, he managed to miraculously procure for himself a sturdy, green Chilean Naval bodysuit used by the mechanics on the island; I don't know what he gave in trade.

That afternoon we began our first training exercise. For our first manoeuvre Manuel and I had to learn to lower the dinghy. We listened raptly as Jarle instructed us that whenever we hit shore and needed to anchor, one of us would take ropes in the dinghy and row to shore to tie us up; the other would toss the anchor and assist him on the boat.

The yellow dinghy, the size of a half bathtub, seemed to be constructed of nothing more than pressed corncob. Deceptively heavy for its size, Jarle stored it upside down, lashed to the deck right in front of the mast. Lifting it off was a pain in the ass, but a bit easier for two rather than one; hoisting it back on board was another story.

But Jarle was an animal, a true Viking, reminiscent in his own way of Jack London's *Sea Wolf*, Wolf Larsen, and I watched in awe as he hoisted the dinghy, weighted down with the full weight of water, up and out of the sea and onto the deck, all by himself, barefoot.

It seems necessity truly is the mother of invention. Jarle, who had done a great deal of solo sailing to get down to Tierra del Fuego on his own, including three days against the wind as he tried to turn the Horn east to west alone, driven to tears of exasperation before finally succeeding, had learned the hard way.

Jarle had set off alone from Larvik, Norway at the age of 19 in the *Berserk*. Larvik, we would learn to know, was the home of a great many historic explorers, including the legendary Thor Heyerdahl, best known for fashioning the raft *Kon-Tiki* and floating it from South America to Polynesia. The eldest son of diplomats, Jarle became fascinated with sailing at a young age; he had been given his first small sailing boat by his beloved grandfather and had learned, by trial and error, the nature of wind and water. At 15 he and some friends set sail south to nearby Denmark in another of his small boats. The overnight voyage, replete with drunken debauchery and near-miss encounters with other ships that resulted in some of his comrades literally jumping overboard in fear, confirmed two things to the young rebel: one, he truly had sailing in his blood; and two, that special love was all his own. He would be hard-pressed to find those who shared it. Thus, he bought and prepped the *Berserk*, a small, 27-foot, fibreglass, Swedish-built Albin Vega lake boat first slapped together in the early 1970s before he was born, hand painted the chosen name in red letters on the side, and set off on his own, first crossing from Norway down to Africa, then making the great leap across the Atlantic to Brazil before skirting the coast south to Tierra del Fuego. Along the way he had picked up various crewmembers (and women) to help him out, but by and large he had made the journey on his own.

Finding people to accompany him to Antarctica, however, had been another story. One by one they had marched down the dock to his boat, including the Spanish/Russian bus driver Boris, and one by one they had walked away, baffled. Many, like Boris, had been frustrated by the very nature of the captain; they simply could not relate. Others, including a young boy from New Zealand, had come aboard only to get scared out of his wits before even leaving port, common sense talked into him by a worried mother.

Eventually Jarle had steeled himself to make the voyage to Antarctica solo and was about to cast off when Manuel and I marched down the dock; whether he truly saw something different in our eyes as he claimed or believed in the kismet of the timing only he knows.

But taking us on board was the easy part. Now he had to turn us into sailors.

It felt like the Olympic tryouts when Manuel and I first set foot in the dinghy to try our hand at rowing, but it was soon apparent that it was not much of a contest. I had a bit of experience, mostly from using a rowboat on the pond near my cousin's summer cottage in Vermont. We each tried our hand at paddling around the placid little lagoon near our mooring. Manuel laughed at his own great difficulty and uncertainty at manipulating the movement of the small dinghy, thrashing around like a baby in a bathtub. As soon as I grabbed hold of the oars, it became apparent who would be the dinghyman. Manuel would be relegated to tossing the anchor.

But in order to secure the ropes properly, we would first need to know how to tie a knot. We didn't have a clue between us. Jarle showed us how to tie a basic reef knot: over then under, like tying a shoelace, curl back around, then over and under again the opposite way. Jarle explained that we would use this knot the most, in fact we could use it for everything, but he also showed us how to tie a sheet bend knot that could be used to secure two separate lines together, just in case.

Manuel and I joked around as we practised tying the knot again and again and again. A seemingly simple task, it would be vital to our survival: the knot would serve as the basis for everything we did, whether it be tying up sails or securing the boat to an anchorage. We sat in the makeshift galley in the back of the *Berserk* and practised tying the knot with rope scraps around ketchup bottles for hours as the boat bobbed gently. There was to be no more time for relaxing. No matter what, we could always be practising our knots.

We also practised raising and lowering the front sail, which Jarle told us was called the jib. One by one we would grab hold of the rope near the mast, drag it with us to the tip of the bow, hook the other end to the sail and hoist it up tautly. Certainly it would take some practice. Certainly it would prove more difficult bouncing on the sea.

Manuel joked that we were the Deadheads of the Sea – the *Berserk*, ill-equipped and stripped to its barebones essence, was akin to one of those old ragged VW vans that used to cruise from city to city filled with dope-sucking hippies following around the Grateful Dead from jam to jam. The *Berserk* fulfilled this mandate head to toe, bow to stern, port to starboard. We ate off of old beat-up plastic plates, drank from worn plastic cups, mixed it all up in one single aluminium cooking pot with a single spoon, went to the bathroom in a red plastic bucket. When we were finished with our meal, one of us would simply wash the dishes perfunctorily over the side of the boat, straight in the salt water without using any soap. The remnants drifted away with the tide to be fed upon by the denizens of the deep.

One afternoon a delighted Manuel returned from one of his many visits to the nearby boats with a small bouquet of wildflowers, which he arranged in a makeshift plastic vase and placed on the shelf in the galley. The flowers had been graciously donated to him by a young, blonde American woman planning to sail, along with two French brothers (the older her boyfriend) down to Antarctica in the sailing boat *Voyeu*. The two struck up a conversation on the dock and seemed to hit it off, and she in turn had given the blushing, hopeful sailor a few flowers to liven up the *Berserk* after undoubtedly hearing reiteration upon reiteration of its squalid conditions.

When Jarle returned from town and saw the flowers, he flipped. He grabbed the flowers out of the vase and tossed them overboard.

'What are you doing?!?' Manuel shrieked.

'There will be no fucking flowers on my boat!' Jarle screamed as we watched them float away. 'This is the *Berserk*!'

Manuel became upset. He indeed appeared a gentle soul, with the word 'harmony' tattooed in green gothic letters across his upper back between the shoulder blades. The word 'harmony' held special significance for Manuel, for it was there, in the town of Harmony, California, where he married his wife. The marriage lasted a week. Eventually Manuel took off, abandoning his bride, and headed south, home to Argentina, after seven years in the US, mostly in LA.

'For a guy with the word "harmony" on his back, he is not a very harmonical guy,' Jarle repeated whenever Manuel would throw a tizzy fit.

Here was his first. He became visibly upset. 'You didn't have to kill them,' he muttered. 'They were given to me as a gift.' When prompted repeatedly as to why he did it, Jarle simply let it be known that this was the *Berserk*. No flowers were allowed on board, and they never would be.

Until then, Jarle and Manuel had gotten along famously, like brothers. At night they would joke and giggle like a bunch of teenage girls, slapping each other giddily across their bunks as they curled up for the night. But here the first chink showed in the armour; it was the first time the two did not get along. It would not be the last. Manuel began to bristle at authority with an irritability and shortness of fuse. That Jarle was so young an authority, that they had been like brothers for the few days they had known each other, made no difference.

That night, before a late dinner, Jarle wrote names on each of our plastic cups in black magic marker. On his own cup he scrawled 'Kaptain'. On mine, he wrote my chosen pirate name: 'Skull'. I had announced earlier that I did not want to be referred to by my given name any longer. This was to be a pirate's adventure, and for that a pirate name was needed. After pondering for a while, I spontaneously blurted out the name 'Skull'. The name stuck and from then on that's how Jarle referred to me. On Manuel's cup Jarle simply wrote 'Flower Child'.

Our personalities, defined.

A few days later we set off for a little practice cruise around the Horn. We were waiting for the metal wind pilot to be soldered per Jarle's specifications by the Chilean Navy's machine shop, and in the meantime, Jarle knew a couple of boats that were going to sail Cape Horn. He wanted to get video images of the *Berserk* in front of the Horn, something he was unable to do when he turned it alone.

A LITTLE TRAINING CRUISE

We set off down the Beagle Channel to find out what we knew, to see what we had learned over the last couple of days – which wasn't much. As we cruised easily down the channel, Jarle asked me to swab the deck. I shrugged and grabbed the bucket, then leaned over the starboard side of the boat to fill it with water. The boat moved at a steady clip and the bucket filled quickly, catching me by surprise as it heavily dragged me down. Not wanting to lose it on our first trip out, I held on to it firmly and started to slide over the rail when Jarle jumped up and grabbed hold of me by the waist, saving me from going overboard. I lost the bucket but gained something far more important, confidence in my captain.

For me, age had nothing to do with it. Either the guy knew what he was doing or he didn't. By saving me and shrugging off the bucket – 'We'll get another one, but don't do it again' – it became apparent we were on the same page.

That night we hit our first storm. It caught me by surprise. One minute we were sailing along the Beagle Channel, ten at night in the dull grey-blue gloom of perpetual Southern Hemisphere light; the next, the boat lurched sideways as if God pursed his cheeks and exhaled a quick puff of wind squarely into the heft of our main sail. The boat tilted over like a ship in a bottle.

We were caught off-guard. The strong headwinds and a driving rain, right in our faces, caused the captain to make his first command decision with us on board: we would anchor for the night and wait it out. Spotting a suitable anchorage, Jarle steered the boat close in to shore to a secluded bay beneath the snow-capped island mountains and we tossed the anchor overboard, where it finally caught hold. But someone would need to keep watch to make sure the boat didn't drift in the night – and, setting precedent, I drew first watch.

Manuel and Jarle crawled into their sleeping bags shortly before midnight. Outside in the cockpit, the world provided a marvellous view: the orange-red-blue glow of the sun as it set on one side of me and rose on the other, simultaneously. The rain stopped, the sky opened, and the evening took on a cool metallic-blue calm. Sea birds fluttered about in the night as the sky kept opening like a flower in bloom, revealing rainbow shades never before imagined. The moon, nearly full, made an appearance, as did the stars and even a bright satellite moving steadily across the night before bright dawn broke from south to north.

Suddenly, I heard a noise, a splash near the boat in the haze of night. My senses trained, honing in. I heard it again: something was swimming nearby. My heart pounded with excitement. It must be a seal. It wasn't – it was a dolphin, and it stayed with us for days.

When we all awoke the next day, we set sail with the wind directly in our faces. It was the first time we were on the tack, and the boat listed at a serious angle as we criss-crossed the channel on our way south. Manuel began to get a queasy look on his face; his smile withered, he leaned over the edge, and he fed the fish with his very own breakfast. It was quite generous of him and he made quite a donation to the deep. It was the first time he had been seasick – but it certainly would not be the last.

We set sail for the Horn, giddy with enough excitement to last a lifetime. After all, this was the place of legend and lore! Cape Horn! How often does a boy dream of adventure as a child, dream of a far-off place, whether it be jungle or mountain or sea – and yet how often does that child grow to manhood and actually get the chance to feel the very fibre of his being bristle, his blood flow thick with the thrill of watching black and white become colour before his very own eyes? These are the days to relish, my friend – and relish this one I did.

The dolphins rode the wake of our bow for the first four hours as we made the slow turn out of the anchorage and headed out into the island seas, filling the entire boat with delight. For years I had been perfecting a 'dolphin call', one that had its origins on the Chesapeake Bay in passing calls to the ospreys nesting on top of blinking red buoys; in the Everglades where the first dolphins answered on their way to the mangrove swamps; and in the Pampas of Bolivia where the pink snub-nosed river dolphins leapt out of the water in glee upon hearing it. I stood on the bow of the *Berserk* with a smile from ear to ear and called to my brothers again and again – and they answered. They jumped out of the water, they swam on their backs and they looked me right in the eye, first with one eye, then after a quick roll with the other. I laid down flat on the bow and held my hand close to the speeding water, and the dolphins leapt out of the water, playfully touching me with their fins.

We sailed out into the open sea and, lo and behold, there she stood majestically, just like a rhino's nose: the Horn. The sails fluttered, slapped taut; the hoary 40-knot wind pinched our cheeks and noses; the sun shone bright, smiling with serendipity; not a cloud lolled in the sky. Jarle steered us toward the Horn; I manned the ropes; and poor Manuel leaned over the edge and hurled, seasick yet again.

Balthazar, a lofty schooner captained by a Frenchman named Bertrand, videotaped us that day from afar as we turned the Horn. Meanwhile, on the *Berserk*, Jarle brought out his little videocamera, which he kept in a watertight case, and aimed it at Manuel.

'How are you doing there, Manuel?' he asked with a wry chuckle.

'Great!' Manuel answered sportingly, 'I just like to look at the fish close up.'

He turned the camera toward me.

'How about you, David?'

'I'm having the time of my life,' I answered, beaming – mostly because we were rounding the legendary Horn – but also because Manuel was tossing his salad overboard right behind me. Eventually he recovered enough to steer while Jarle and I played chess on the way back to our anchorage.

Jarle began bringing out his little videocamera on the first day of our training. He told us that he was making a little video chronicling his expedition, perfectly understandable for a boy who left Norway alone at 19 and now, a mere 21, appeared a seasoned, wild-haired sailor. A video would indeed chronicle his journey, not only from Norway to Antarctica but also from boy to man. It would be something he could show his family and friends.

But I had personally sworn off filming for the trip. In all of my voyages to the other six continents I had never once brought with me a camera. I'm a writer, damn it – and as one of my old professors used to say, 'A writer writes.' Having a camera is intrusive and gets in the way of interacting with people, who view the cameraman with suspicion. That's the last thing I wanted.

In the early 1990s I had spent 13 months in Philadelphia shooting a low-budget independent film; it took me another year to edit. The entire time I had no income. By the time the dust settled, I was two years in arrears in rent (God bless my landlady, though by the time she was paid back I felt a bit like Raskolnikov sneaking down the back stairs in *Crime and Punishment*) and reduced to living off of leftover Kentucky Fried Chicken graciously donated each night at the end of a housemate's shift – original recipe for breakfast, spicy bite sandwiches for lunch, extra crispy and collard greens for dinner, and honey barbecue wings for dessert. Finally

I cracked and having reached the ultimate saturation point became for six months a vegetarian.

In the meantime, the film, *Renaissance*, got distribution throughout the world but not in the US. I began my long, slow crawl out of the gutter, taking soul-crushing, humiliating odd jobs in and out of the film industry to pay my way. I was desperate for work and my girlfriend – even though we were in the process of breaking up – used her connections to get me a well-paying gig as a bookkeeper for a children's game show produced by industry giant Merv Griffin and hosted by Ryan Seacrest, before he ascended to the mantle of *American Idol*. Feeling like a complete sell-out, I drank every night for a week, finding refuge in the bottle, going from bar to bar, until one night I hit a parked car on the way home and kept going. I didn't drink for a while after that.

But the entire time I stayed focused and squirreled away my meagre savings, stuffing cash under the mattress. It took years to work my way out of the hole, but as soon as there was enough cash I split for South America to write my novel. It was now or never. I would leave the film industry behind for a while, forgetting about the relationship between image and cost, and would concentrate on unfettered creativity through the written word, which knows no constraints.

The entire trip would be dedicated to writing my novel. An idea had been gestating for a couple of years; it was time to write it. The last thing I wanted to do was take hold of a camera.

But on that first training day, Jarle brought his little camera out and handed it to Manuel, who pointed it in my direction. For a moment, I hesitated. I wanted to tell him right then and there to fuck off, that I did not want either to be filmed or to do any filming at all. But I realised that this was part of the deal and to offer resistance would be futile, would only cause unrest on board ship. Begrudgingly,

I tripped over a word as the light switch flipped on in my head and I answered his question. Whenever he brought out the camera thereafter, whether to film me or have me film him, I was not happy about it, but played along as part of the price of getting to Antarctica.

We turned the Horn that day before settling back in a private anchorage in the bay of a small island. Jarle whipped up a hearty sailor's stew of cabbage and potatoes, tossing in the smoked salmon given to me in Punta Arenas, and we laughed and joked and relaxed, and were delighted when Jarle gave us the next day off to explore. We were in no rush to get back, since the wind pilot wouldn't be ready for a few days anyway.

We rowed to shore for a look around. There were wild birds everywhere: geese, ducks, sea birds. Manuel was particularly fascinated by the little gardens created by the local flora growing underfoot and wandered the beach, staring down at the little flowers, touching them gingerly. I don't think it hurt that he had smoked a joint on shore, either.

Jarle and I returned to the boat while Manuel took the dinghy back to the shore. He tiptoed along the beach for hours. 'What's he doing out there?' Jarle asked. Manuel wandered from one end of the horseshoe-shaped bay to the other and then back again, staring down in stoned concentration. Later, when he returned, Jarle scolded him about the dope, considered contraband by maritime law. While they argued, I took some notes in a small notebook, remarking: 'The weather changes like a woman's mind; sun one minute, rain and hail the next. Is this what Antarctica holds?' We may have been on the same boat, but we were still all off on our own trips.

Two days later, after being forced by fierce, howling winds to remain at bay for another day, we finally set sail for Puerto Williams again. By then we'd had a chance to get used to the ship a bit. As soon as we cleared the island we were hit with wind in the face and were forced to go on a hard tack.

Suddenly, like a bolt of lightning out of nowhere, Manuel and Jarle began to argue about a rope. A seemingly insignificant matter, how to roll it, where to stow it, something along those lines, blows up into a full-scale screaming match. Jarle instructs Manuel where to put the rope five times. When Manuel asks a sixth, he flies off the handle. The high tension, along with a period of introspection, remained in the air for the next two days, until we finally made it back to Puerto Williams.

As we spent our last few days preparing in Puerto Williams, Manuel spent most of the time on the wood dock deck sewing and repairing sails. It wasn't the sewing part he resented; he claimed he had helped design and construct golden metal costumes for a Red Hot Chili Peppers rock video and crowed like a rooster about it. But when Jarle handed him an old safety vest and told him to use the material to fix one of the small holes in the sail, Manuel balked.

Bertrand, the captain of the *Balthazar*, brings the video from his camera back to Jarle and joins us in our little cabin for a sip of whiskey. He looks around at the quaint innards reminiscently, and tells us a story of when he too was a young intrepid sailor.

It was on his maiden voyage with his prized new ship, heading with charter tourists across the Atlantic from England to Canada, when they hit a monster storm, a storm that panicked both he and his guests (this was the area that felled both the *Titanic* and the crew in *The Perfect Storm*). Desperate, they sent out an SOS – and unexpectedly received an answer. A Danish military helicopter picked up their call from a base in Greenland and just happened to be in the area. It miraculously found them in the storm and hovered overhead while the boat rocked back and forth precipitously, knocked about by the sizeable waves. The helicopter lowered a rope and the guests, only too glad, scampered up with their lives intact until Bertrand, the captain, was the only one left on board. 'Last chance,' they told him. 'We have to leave now – and we won't be able to come back.' Bertrand looked around at his beloved boat. He thought that he could survive the storm – but he just was not sure. He took a last loving glance around and joined the others in the helicopter. The boat was never seen again.

'I still think I could have saved the boat,' he told us wistfully. 'But I just wasn't certain.

'There are two places in the world where the seas act like that,' he continued. 'There, in the North Atlantic – and where you're going. But… you could get lucky.'

I stared wide-eyed at the old curly-haired salty dog and relished my last slug of whiskey like a true sailor. When he left, Jarle told me that earlier Bertrand had told him that going out to sea was like playing Russian Roulette, only instead of six holes in the chamber there are a thousand, and if you hit the wrong one…

Then, affable Manuel returns from one of his afternoon sojourns along with Hank – and a large, old-style radio distress box. We don't have a long distance radio on board, only a VHF with a signal radius of 25 miles. This metal distress box, about the size of a large stereo speaker, would emit a longer signal for the rescue ships in case we went down, and Hank generously offered to let us borrow it until we saw him next.

But Jarle does not want to bring it on board. It is large and cumbersome, and would occupy too much room. Besides, we are heading to South Africa after Antarctica, and Jarle would feel responsible to get it back to him. He sends a gruff and angry Hank away with the box.

Manuel turns to him. 'What are you doing?' he shrieks. 'That box could save our lives!'

'If we had such a radio we would be more likely to use it,' he explained. 'And if they sent out rescue ships, they would send us the bill to charge us. We would spend the rest of our lives paying it off.'

Manuel and I were repairing sails on the dock one day when an elderly Chilean tourist in a baseball cap wandered down to join us. When we tell him where we are going, he raises his outstretched arms and offers up a benediction for us in Spanish. 'Always remember,' he tells us: 'When you are out there and things are at their most desperate and you need help, at the moment when everything appears to be lost, open your hearts and look up at the sky, and He will always be there for you.' He kindly tells us he will pray for us, and he leaves.

Manuel looks over at me. 'We're not going to die, are we?' There is a moment of deafening silence. By now we have both heard repeatedly about the Drake Passage – the most dangerous water crossing in the world.

I set our odds of death at 30 per cent.

That night, the captain brings up Manuel's up-and-down attitude. We are set to leave the next day. As we lie in our bunks, we debate whether or not we should bring him along.

I want Manuel to go with us. I'm excited as hell, but have no idea what to expect out there on the ocean. I've never been on the open seas before and honestly want a third person to make our shifts easier.

But we've all noticed Manuel's change in attitude. It started with the rope incident and got worse. Now, even he admits he's not sure if he should go with us or not. He reads aloud two entries of florid prose from his journal, one describing his glee, the other his dread. Eventually he decides to leave the decision up to the captain.

We debated in our bunks for hours. Finally Jarle announces that he will make the decision – in the morning.

We awaken to the captain's decision: Manuel will go with us. We will leave that afternoon, as soon as final preparations are made. By now we're almost ready to go. Jarle has picked up the wind pilot and we have attached it to the back of the boat. He told us that with this wacky contraption, the boat would steer itself, giving us all a break. We have loaded the *Berserk* to its gills with fuel and food, lugging 50 litres of gas by hand from a station a mile away. The day before, Jarle ordered 400 English muffin-sized breads from the local baker. They fill three large white rice sacks to the brim. We carry them back to the boat and stow them in the bow, in the spare bunk across from me.

Manuel and I go into town one last time. He's begging me to buy chocolate and cigarettes. We stock up on all the items we can afford, but he becomes a bit miffed when I opt for suntan lotion over more chocolate. It does seem a bit ridiculous – but my fair skin burns easily and I did not want to get caught on the way to South Africa without any. I sport him a last pack of cigs, even though he vows he will stop.

That afternoon I treat myself to a final can of Coke in the town square. I savour and enjoy every sip, knowing full well it might be my last. The townspeople keep calling us *valientes* – though I'm not really sure why. We're doing what any red-blooded dreamer in their right mind would. People have been calling us crazy the whole time now, but as Jarle used to say often: 'Crazy, but not stupid.'

That afternoon we're just about ready to leave when Jarle tells me to go down to the gas station and buy a new flashlight. He shows me the one we have, which runs on D batteries but works only intermittently. 'We need a new one,' he explains succinctly, adding how vital it is, and off I run.

But when I get to the gas station, it is closed for siesta. The attendant is nowhere to be found. I return empty-handed and continue to help Jarle load the boat.

Right before it closes for the night, Jarle sends Manuel back to the gas station to get the last item on our list: the flashlight. Manuel bounds off and returns an hour later, pleased as punch. 'We didn't need a new flashlight,' he tells us gleefully. 'All we needed was some new batteries.' He holds up the old beat-up black flashlight proudly, along with 12 new D-cell batteries. Exasperated, Jarle tells him that yes indeed, we needed a new one – Manuel should have listened to him.

I knew right then and there, felt it deep in my soul and bones, that Manuel's decision would come back to haunt us.

Indeed, it would.

CHAPTER THREE

"Bersek"

LEAVING FOR ANTARCTICA

We waited for three days, anchored 500 feet off Isla Lennox, a palpable excitement in the air, a proverbial calm before the storm. We had no type of satellite communication or fax machine; we were completely reliant on *Hugo*, the larger sailing vessel anchored a few hundred feet away. Twice a day the captain radioed over, inquiring as to the latest conditions they received by fax on their Intelsat. The replies never varied: low pressure systems hovering, with big seas and big winds.

We were waiting for the right moment to head out into the Drake. It made sense to me: I'd heard the tales. That night in the Country Pub, John and the other American sailors from the *Lawrence M. Gould* had spun wild stories of the Drake, of boiling seas and 40-foot monster waves that tilted their 300-foot vessel well to the side. You could see that my new pal John had the 'thousand mile stare' that a sailor gets after seeing such storms. All it did was excite me. I wanted to see it for myself.

On Sunday 16 January that wish became reality.

LEAVING FOR ANTARCTICA

Manuel was on shore. He had run out of cigarettes the day before and had rowed the dinghy onto the beach in the hopes of bumming one off of the Chilean armada officer who manned the lone house/base/radio station along with his wife and two young children.

This was the last outpost in South America – further out than the so-called 'lighthouse at the end of the world' found on a remote island to the north-east. The only reason for having a base here was to establish territorial control in the ongoing battle with Argentina.

While the captain and I waited for *Hugo*'s six o'clock report, making final preparations in the cold wind, Manuel was sitting inside a warm house, stuffing his face with a home-cooked Chilean dinner and smoking cigarette after cigarette. We knew it, and we even joked about it.

We already were on tight rations, eating two meals a day. The morning meal consisted of four or five breads – little tightly-packed hamburger roll-type biscuits, covered with your choice: *manjar* (better known as *dulce de leche*, a caramel-like spread); honey; or jam (the captain preferred strawberry preserves in a bag, so that's usually what was found on the table). My preference was the *manjar*. Manuel preferred everything – as long as it was in large quantities. A couple of times we would be sitting around eating and the captain would scream out: 'That's too much, man. That's enough for two.' I would reduce my ration, barely covering the stale crust with the tiniest sliver of flavour. I would look over at Manuel and see his bread covered with heaps of topping – probably four times the amount on my bread. But we knew Manuel was the weak link, and for this reason the captain gave him the benefit of the doubt and stoically allowed him to gorge himself at our expense. Still, it was irritating, made all the more so because he still thought he wasn't getting enough to eat, yet we were actually making an effort to stick to rations while he didn't really care. Even more irritating was the look he would get on his face, as if he were savouring the last morsel of food he would ever get. He would shut his eyes after rolling them up into his head and chew rhythmically. Distinctly, loudly and repeatedly.

The days were long. At that time of year the sun didn't 'set' until around 11.30 p.m., when a dull purplish-orange gloom pervaded the dark air. At the right moment, sometime around 1.30 or 2.00, you could actually see a stunning sight: the sun rising and setting at the same time. At these times, when the glow from the great orb wrapped around the bottom of the earth, peace and serenity reigned.

Shortly after six o'clock we looked out and saw the *Hugo* hoisting anchor. Jarle picked up the radio handset and called over.

'We got the latest report and the weather is good,' the voice on the other end crackled. We could hear the muffled sounds of activity on board. 'We're leaving.' In a flash, the anchor was up and the *Hugo* was gone.

Jarle wanted to keep pace. Having another boat heading in the same general direction is always a sailor's comfort, and this was no exception. Our first baby steps into the Drake would at least be mirrored by another, more seasoned vessel.

Immediately Jarle got into the 'go' mode that he reached anytime he wanted to leave. When he wanted to set off, it was five minutes ago, not now, not five minutes from now. He began racing around like a madman, scrambling to get everything battened down for the long haul ahead. 'Call Manuel and tell him to get his ass back here,' he screamed in the middle of securing the galley table on my front bunk.

I got onto the VHF and radioed the base, asking for Manuel. He was right there, probably sipping a warm cup of herbal tea. You could hear the smile on his face over the airwaves. He was enjoying a cigarette by the warm fire.

'We're leaving,' I told him. 'Get back here now.'

He was hesitant. 'Are you sure the weather's OK?' he asked.

'Tell him to get his ass back here!' Jarle shouted from the bow.

'Yeah,' I said. 'The *Hugo*'s going, and we're going too. Hurry up.'

I started to help stow things away while we waited for Manuel to row back. We could still see the dinghy abandoned on the beach.

'Where the hell is Manuel?!' Jarle would ask every so often.

'I guarantee you he's in there eating a sumptuous feast,' I answered bitterly. 'I can guarantee you that. He's probably not done with his flan yet.'

Finally, about half an hour later, we saw Manuel walking down to the beach, dragging the dinghy to the water's edge and then finally rowing back toward us through the cold, grey mist. When he reached the *Berserk*, I grabbed the green dinghy rope and helped him aboard.

'Get ready – we're leaving,' I explained with a wry smile.

Manuel climbed on board and ran up to Jarle, who was busy stowing material away for the long haul ahead of us. He was holding a sheet of paper in his hand.

'Look,' he said, shoving the paper in Jarle's face.

It was a report that had just been received by fax in the Chilean base. On it was the Chilean armada's latest updated six o'clock report. Jarle glanced down at it.

'What's that?'

Manuel pointed out that the Chilean report still contained warnings: winds over 30 knots and continuing low pressure.

'What do they know? It's the fucking Chileans,' Jarle scowled. He was angry – Manuel had already kept us from heading out immediately with the *Hugo*. Now it would require quite an effort to catch up.

I had to agree. I never placed much credence in weather reports. To me, a weatherman is a step above a politician – and a small step at that. Any clown can look at a chart and guess what's going to happen. What's amazing to me is the extraordinarily high percentage of times they're wrong. Call me a cynic, but it's annoying as hell living according to these so-called 'meteorologists'. There was no way I was going to give credence to a report from a Chilean base on the edge of the world. In the best-case scenario, they were clueless. Who knew how old or outdated this latest info was? Even though we were uncertain of the conditions we might find out in the Drake, my vote was to go on with the *Hugo*.

Of course, we had already been forbidden from leaving by the Chilean armada. Jarle was furious. He had spent two months in Puerto Williams repairing and preparing the *Berserk* for the voyage, and had developed good relations with the port's commandant. He had even gone to eat dinner and get drunk at the commandant's house with the officer's family.

But a new captain had recently come to Puerto Williams. In the little hillside office overlooking the harbour below – a sort of central command post where all ships entering or leaving the harbour are required to register both their vessels and their crews – Jarle was told that the *Berserk* did not have permission to cross the Drake.

'It's too dangerous. Your boat's too small,' he was told by one of the new captain's underlings. 'The captain is just trying to save your life,' I heard them say later.

As we busily sewed sails on the wood dock next to where we were moored, Jarle came back. He was irate. He explained what had happened, threatening to bust the new man's balls by going over his head to his pal the commandant.

'What are we going to do?' Manuel asked.

'We're going to go anyway,' Jarle said.

Manuel looked over at me, then back at the captain. 'But we don't have permission. They won't let us.'

'They can't stop us. We'll tell them we're going to the Falklands.'

We were the crew of the *Berserk* and we didn't really care if we had permission or not. True, we would not be cleared to leave port with a destination of Antarctica on our manifesto. But there was no way they could keep us there in Puerto Williams. We were going to list the Islas Malvinas – better known in the English-speaking world as the Falklands – on our log as our destination (even though Manuel, with his Argentinian passport, would not be admitted). To hell with them if they believed us or not.

So when the bad weather report came to us from the Chileans, it was taken with the same grain of salt that we took any news from them. Jarle felt that the *Hugo* had the latest info from their satellite fax receiver; there was no way these backwards Chileans could possibly have the same up-to date information. We were ready to head out; we'd been waiting there for three days already. We were anxious to get going.

But Manuel pleaded and pleaded. 'Please Jarle, let's wait,' he begged, but the captain would have none of it.

'Get ready, Manuel,' he snarled. We were getting used to 'harmonious' Manuel's whining about every little thing. This was to be no different. The decision had already been made by the captain; now it was time to get ready to go. The young captain's frustration had only mounted as we waited those 45 minutes for Manuel to get his lazy ass back from the shore.

Manuel held out a plastic bag filled with a few warm baked rolls that had been freshly prepared by the Chilean officer's wife. I quickly began to devour them as I told Manuel my theory that he was over there the whole time enjoying a nice hot meal.

He smiled and explained that he had been enjoying a nice cut of meat, some potatoes and veggies – a whole sit-down dinner. To be honest, I was more than a little jealous. But he generously had brought back the warm buns, along with an unopened gold box of cigarettes for himself that had been given to him in the greatest of hospitality by the officer and his family. He was happy as a clam – except that it was, in his opinion, not the proper time to leave.

He was outvoted. Despite his protestations to the very end, the captain ordered him to pull up the anchor while we quickly lifted the dinghy onto the deck and lashed it down to the wood rails in front of the mast. He tossed the sheet of paper into the cabin and started to get dressed in a hurry. It all happened in a blur – the scramble to get into wet gear, get the right clothes on and get ready for the long trip ahead.

Jarle started the small 7.5 horsepower Suzuki engine jerry-rigged into the back hatch (there are lawnmowers with more power), and kicked the boat into gear, propelling us along the same path that *Hugo* had taken earlier. While Manuel stowed the anchor and the ropes – we wouldn't be needing them again until we landed on the seventh continent – I ran to the bow in my yellow Gloucester fisherman rain slickers that had been worn by Norwegian fisherman in ages past and prepared to pull up the mainsail. The sail went up easily.

After the main sail came the jib. I grabbed the rope from the mast, readied the halyard by attaching it to the sail, and with the boat bouncing along the calm water, pulled it up quickly.

'Tension, I need tension!' Jarle screamed. Using my weight as leverage – and making full sure nothing was wrapped around any of the metal stairs used to climb the mast in emergency or necessary manoeuvres – I tightened and secured the rope.

'Get back here and take the helm,' Jarle said as he handed over the tiller. He ducked down inside to look at the charts and to try and raise the *Hugo* on the radio. To no avail. We didn't know it at the time, but *Hugo* wasn't heading out into the Drake at all. They were simply taking their charters around the Horn.

Manuel stood at my side as he finished tucking the anchor and the ropes under one of the two hatches on either side of the small cockpit. He knew that seasickness was a possibility, but for the moment that potential was quelled as he lit up another cigarette.

'Don't you think you should save those?' I asked. He just looked at me, as if to say, 'I want one now.' We had a long trip ahead of us; he was broke, and these were the last cigs he would get, possibly until we reached South Africa in three months. Even though he claimed it was a perfect time to quit, I secretly wondered how an addict's irritation would compound on the high seas. In the back of his mind, undoubtedly, were the two cartons of Marlboro reds tucked neatly beneath the spare clothes in the captain's portside panel above his bunk.

We watched the Chilean base, and Lennox Island, fade into the distance as we passed through several islands on our way to the open sea. To our right, in the way distance, we could see the vague shadow purported to be Cape Horn – the last island connected on the ocean floor to the great land mass of South America.

'I don't think we should have left,' Manuel said to me quietly as the ship cut through the serenity of its last sheltered waters before venturing out into the great and ominous Drake – the Drake we had heard so much about.

By around eight o'clock all the excitement of leaving was settled and we were legitimately heading out into the great unknown. There was a relaxed and eager atmosphere on board the *Berserk*. With two sails up, we moved slowly but surely between two distant island masses, on the other side of which lay the beginning of open water. But then, as we moved between the two small islands, after three days of howling, screeching, screaming winds, the wind simply... died.

With a flutter, the sails began to flap, not from strong winds but because there were none. The *Berserk* began to move slower through the water. The *Hugo* was nowhere in sight. Jarle looked around for ripples in the water, then scampered up to the bow and lowered the front sail. We were practically halted.

But we were still only a short distance away from land, still but a couple of hours' sail back to the safety of the small harbour at Lennox. There was still time to turn back.

This was not quite what we had expected. We knew the weather patterns prevalent in the Drake Passage and the area surrounding Cape Horn. Lows, lows, and more lows – followed by even more lows. Jarle had explained that the weather patterns were lengthier in Antarctica, meaning they would settle in for greater periods of time. A storm down there could last a week. This became an even greater worry toward the end of the season, at the beginning of March when the long Antarctic winter began to announce its presence.

Here, around Cape Horn, the systems behaved differently. There were many storms but also significant periods between them. Our goal would be to 'chase a low' right out into the Drake; we wanted to set sail as closely behind an exiting storm as we could, to try to shoot the gap between them and hopefully, in the best case scenario, reach Antarctica before the next one hit.

At that moment it looked like we had timed our departure a little too accurately. Not only had the latest front left, but it had taken all the wind with it. Now we were stuck without any. We were barely moving.

'Should we go back?' Jarle asked, surveying in a complete circle. He was more thinking out loud than asking for advice, though he always would welcome an opinion, whether he listened to it or not. He never did. He was strong enough to trust his own instincts. Or foolish enough.

I had already determined that Jarle was a good captain who knew what he was doing. The last thing I wanted to do was head back. That meant two hours sailing the wrong way, then two hours more retracing our steps when we finally headed out.

But there was no wind. None. Soon we even took down the main sail. We didn't want to waste our gasoline by using the engine here, but it was coming to that point just if we wanted to get back to Lennox.

While we were debating our course, we felt a slight breeze on our cheeks. Just as suddenly as it had left us, the wind was back. This was the art of sailing: waiting in pockets of still air for the next blow, not knowing from which direction it will hit. First up went the main sail; before long, the sail in front, the jib. We were back underway, heading off into the grey twilight dusk that existed when there was no sun.

There was no turning back now.

At around midnight Jarle called for Manuel and told him they were going inside to get some sleep. I was at the helm and was to remain there until they relieved me four hours later.

Like always, I had drawn first watch. But more annoyingly, like always I had drawn the night watch – the most brutal shift. Not only would there be very little light (if any) during the middle part of it, making it impossible to see anything that might wind up in our path, but it was therefore also the coldest. And it was cold. We may not have been in Antarctica yet, but we were south of the southernmost tip of South America. It was wet to boot.

As they crawled inside and into their sleeping bags on the stern bunks, I held the steel tiller, bundled and ready for the long night ahead of me. Through my foggy glasses the compass was barely visible; before they shut the hatch for the final time, Jarle turned on the red light that illuminated the dial at night. We always waited until the last possible instant to use electrical items, since we were reliant upon solar panels to recharge our batteries and were heading to a part of the world where direct sunlight was uncertain.

As the light of day faded into the twilight grey which accompanied every evening, the *Berserk* lost sight first of the distant ghostlike glow of Cape Horn, then of the small land masses we were passing through when the wind died. After a while I stopped craning my neck and looking around, back over my shoulder. There was no longer any point. The midnight dusk had obscured any land. For the first time in my life, I was truly out to sea.

The quiet of our night-time sojourn, broken only by the occasional soothing ripple of a sail or the tranquil bubbling of our wake, was relaxing. So far Hank's premium bartered 'half-wol' clothes were holding up, leaving me feeling warm and comfortable, poised and excited.

Slowly, though, the swells became bigger. The boat began gently rocking from side to side as it was lifted, then dropped, by these big undulating balls of water underneath. Still, the *Berserk* maintained a steady course, ever heading due south, 180 degrees. But by now it was dark, as dark as it was going to get, and outside the little cockpit, it became difficult to see anything.

Soon I felt the first wet mist of rain hitting my cheeks. The mist transformed into stinging pellets as the rain grew in strength and intensity. The seas too became a little rougher, rocking the boat more and more, a cradle gone awry. I began to look not only at the compass but also out to the sea, where rolling waves were swelling toward the boat from the right, increasing slowly but surely in size.

LEAVING FOR ANTARCTICA

For the first time it truly dawned on me that we were free of the bonding constraints of land and were now in open sea, unfettered or sheltered by any more land masses. I thought to myself, 'Holy shit.' Here we are, only a few hours into the voyage, and already the waves are bigger than any waves seen in my life. The swells were ranging from six to eight feet by now, but if anything, that would be on the conservative side. When you're out in the middle of the ocean, with nothing to gauge yourself against, you lose perspective of both size and distance.

But one thing became apparent: these swells were not getting any smaller. And the rain was continuing, meaning, in my book, we were in the middle of some kind of storm.

Maybe we caught the very tail end of the one we were chasing; who knew. It didn't matter. What did matter was that my entire body was wet and my feet were starting to get cold, the same kind of numb feeling you get when you walk through the snow for too long. Even though I was wearing black rubber boots that went up most of the shin, I had decided to wear only one pair of socks. Wool, especially full wool, was at a premium, and I didn't want to waste any clean or dry wool socks on the first few hours of our sail.

At around two it had started to get light again; by four, I could really see what was going on around me. Instead of looking down at the horizon, as I had imagined it would be, I was crouched in the open cockpit, holding onto a steel tiller with fingers frozen through the gloves, with slightly numb feet, sopping wet even under my raingear, staring up at rolling swells as they lifted then gently dropped our little bobber.

The first sounds of movement emanated from inside. Jarle lifted the top hatch plank and leaned his head out, looking around.

'How's it going out here?' he asked with a smile.

'OK,' I smiled back. 'It's raining.'

'What's your course?' He leaned over, trying to get a look at the compass.

'One-eighty – due south,' I answered.

'Good, good,' he said. 'We'll be up soon. We're getting dressed.'

Manuel started to pull on his gear as Jarle slid the wood hatch back into place.

By the time the two of them crawled out from inside about 15 minutes later, I was more than ready to head in. As we passed each other, Manuel gave me one of his patented head-lowered, eyes-up glares. This dilettante certainly didn't want to do his first full shift in the rain, that was certain. His glance let me know it.

My first task was to 'take care of business', or relieve myself, for lack of a better phrase. The *Berserk* had no toilet facilities; in still waters, that doesn't really prove to be a problem. But on the move, tilting and bouncing on waves at such extreme angles, well, it can get a little tough. Hell, it was tough just standing up.

It was even harder walking to the bow, avoiding what the captain called 'elephant steps'. No matter how gently a person walked – a ballerina in slippers could've tiptoed gingerly to the bow and done a pirouette – to the captain, it still would've been elephant steps. I don't think anyone made louder elephant steps than he did, but for me to say that would be not only blasphemy but mutiny.

For me, the most difficult thing was crawling in and out of the cabin through the hatch. First, you had to push back the fibreglass 'lid' that covered the opening. Then, you had to slide out the wood planks one at a time. The two wooden steps down became slippery from the moisture, so you had to hold on tight when going in or out. We were going to try to keep the inside of the boat as clean as possible by removing all wet gear and boots at the bottom of the steps. Easier said than done. This would result in a logjam of monstrous proportions, piles of wet and slimy clothes stacked right in everyone's way. Once inside, with the boat pitching from side to side, it was necessary to hold onto whatever you could grab. Often it was hard to grab hold of anything before the boat lurched and my body was thrown forcefully into some hard, protruding object. Sometimes the object gave; sometimes my body did. Pretty soon, I earned the unwarranted reputation as 'the clumsy sailor.' This undeserved accolade solidified even further when my shoulder speared into our one aluminium cooking pot during a particularly violent pitch, putting a huge dent in the side of it.

As I tried to take care of business, eventually relieving myself into the metal plate which we had used to bail out the leaking water in the dinghy but which now became our piss pot, Jarle and Manuel took their positions outside. I awkwardly slid the boards back into place and shut the lid, holding on to the bunk while slowly taking off the rest of my clothes.

The cabin stank like spilled gasoline. Somehow as the boat began to tilt, one of our makeshift jerry cans had spilled and was still leaking. The stench would continue to become stronger and stronger until eventually it was so terrible it would sting the eyes. My undergarments were soaking wet. This half-wool crap Hank had sold me was useless. Luckily, Jarle had given me an old, ripped, full-wool Norwegian sweater to wear that, combined with the blue pullover hat remaining on my head most of the time, made me look like Richard III. But I had no underwear made of full wool; these had been given to Manuel. My practical solution inside when drying out was to wear no underwear at all, instead walking around nude from the waist down, a ridiculous caricature while still wearing my hat and sweater.

I stripped down and climbed into my sleeping bag wearing no bottoms or socks. My feet were frozen and soggy. It would take two hours just to dry them; forget about getting them warm. They wouldn't be warm for another three months.

The bag rolled back and forth on the starboard stern bunk. During the rollicking evening, Jarle had rigged up the built-in constraints, tying the ropes to the wooden banisters screwed into the ceiling. Now there was a only a thin wisp of strained burlap sack standing between me and the floor. As per our previous arrangement, whoever was not working would sleep in one of the two stern bunks on a rotating basis. I pulled the bag over my head, my body starting to warm up as it pitched around Manuel's bunk.

But I wouldn't sleep. Not a wink. What I heard outside was enough to keep me awake forever. Or at least until the moment of my death. Whichever came first.

CHAPTER FOUR
THE FIRST STORM

I curled up in the fetal position deep inside my sleeping bag, pulling it over my head in a feeble attempt to foster an atmosphere of dry warmth.

The boat was rocking much more furiously now as the storm picked up. I tried to doze off, but there was no way. It wasn't going to happen. Not with things banging around, myself included. My body was tossed from side to side, hitting first the cushioned panels on the right, then rolling into the burlap sack on my left. Pots and dishes rattled as they spilled from the counters onto the floor or simply within the cabinet. If it wasn't lashed down, it was going down. Simple as that.

As I huddled in my sleeping bag, waiting for some semblance of feeling to return to my toes, I felt and heard a loud crash underneath me. Eyes wide open, I wondered what it could be. It wasn't long before I found out.

Up on deck, Manuel and Jarle began to go at it. Manuel had gotten sick on our trial run around Cape Horn, when the seas were calm; there was no doubt what was going on up there now. Jarle told Manuel to grab the digital video camera from inside to get some storm footage, but it was all Manuel could do just to stand up.

Up on deck could be heard lots of clanging and banging, constant elephant steps, the sounds of someone walking to the bow, the sails clattering down.

Inside the boat, water cascaded in through the cracks in the hatch and through the wet wood beneath the mast. The cushions became soaked with the moisture of the sea; to be expected, but not to such an extent. The cushioned panel above me on the side crashed off, poking sharply into my lower back. I was too horrified to creep out of the sleeping bag, even for an instant to put it back.

Suddenly I heard Manuel shout at the top of his lungs: 'Oh my God! Watch out!' There was a loud crash into the side of the boat, along with a hard impact. It felt like the *Starship Enterprise* being hit by a Klingon photon torpedo. The whole boat shook and listed far to the side before finally righting itself.

My eyes were now fully open.

Up on deck, the sounds of panic and movement. 'Jarle! Jarle!!' What the hell was going on up there? 'What do I do? What do I do?!?'

'Hang on!!'

Another impact jolted the *Berserk*. The burlap restraint barely kept my body from spilling out onto the floor.

The wood-creaking, metal-scraping roars reverberating throughout the cabin were terrifying. A deafening deep bass echoed beneath our feet each time a wave crashed into the side of the boat. I had been accustomed to being on boats, but the sounds I heard now made me think, 'Can this ship handle this? Will this little boat hold up under the stress? Will we hold up under the stress?'

Less than 12 hours from port we were deep in the middle of our first storm, a severe one at that. The wood boards holding the mast to the ship began to creak like wood does before it fractures from stress. Jarle had spoken repeatedly of masts snapping; he had assured me that that's when the real adventure would begin. We would then have to create a makeshift mast using the remaining steel spinnaker boom, something desperate sailors do in desperate situations – like when their boat's about to sink. It wasn't something I wanted to try now or ever. I didn't even know how the spinnaker boom worked.

Underneath me, the ocean began to make gurgling noises like a mean-spirited, overgrown baby. It heaved and gurgled as the ship rose and fell. On the way up, the water coated the sides and slid down like an off-kilter musical instrument making discordant tonal sounds felt deeply in the soul; on the way down, the crash was like a percussive cymbal. After a sleepless night, these disjointed noises began to take on mysterious 'shapes' of their own.

There was no time to dwell on them. Up on deck, things seemed to be getting worse. I lost track of time, deep in the bosom of hopeless fear, shivering beneath my bag in a mixture of cold and utter horror.

'Jarle, where's the harness?!' Manuel screamed. The sheer terror of an unseasoned sailor could be heard in his voice as he frantically searched for the belt used to tether himself to the rail during emergency situations. 'Where's the fucking harness!!?'

'I showed you before!' Jarle screamed back.

'I don't remember!' Manuel wailed.

'It's under the fucking hatch – where I showed you!'

'Fuck you, Jarle! Fuck you!' Manuel was screaming at the top of his lungs – a volume necessary to drown out the crashing of the giant waves toppling into the side of our boat and the constant din of the steady pelting rain.

The two – who had gotten along so famously, like brothers, at first – were now going at it like two enemy birds in a cockfight.

Manuel hurled open a side hatch, rummaging under the ropes to get at the white harness belt, lodged next to the rusty can of axle grease at the very bottom.

'How do I put it on?!' Manuel screamed.

Jarle's exasperation was reaching the boiling point.

'I fucking showed you, man,' the long-haired boy shouted at his green, inexperienced crewman.

'Jarle, how do I put it on?!!'

'I showed you!!'

'I DON'T FUCKING REMEMBER!!'

'Watch out, man!!'

BOOM!

Shouts and screams blended seamlessly with the crashing waves to create a true symphony of terror – just like the beginning of the television show *Gilligan's Island*, when the tiny ship the *Minnow* is tossed around haplessly in a blinding, raging torrent.

Barely audible above the din of nature could be heard Jarle screaming at an indignant Manuel, leading him through the steps of getting the tiny harness on one arm at a time as torpedoes continued smashing our ship with increasing frequency and regularity, no rhyme, reason, or pattern to their attack. The whole time I crouched in the fetal position inside my sleeping bag, wondering if the boat would hold.

Then I heard some words I definitely did not want to hear: 'Skull, start getting ready.' The words slithered through a crack in the top hatch. I pretended not to hear, looking down at my watch: 7.45 already? Didn't I have more time? Where did it all go? Hell, I did a four-and-a-half-hour shift. What gives? I was procrastinating.

'Skull!' I didn't answer. 'Skull!! Get dressed and get your ass up here!' the captain shouted down again.

I finally capitulated. 'OK,' I shouted back in a mixture of aggravation and exasperation. I'm sure I sounded less than enthusiastic to go back up there. I was.

THE FIRST STORM

I flipped the sleeping bag off from over my head and slowly began to get my clothes back on. The inside of the boat was soaking and the smell of gasoline was awful, as bad as it had been. It was no easy task getting dressed as the boat continued to pitch from side to side. You had to hold on and put your clothes on at the same time. More than once the crashing waves knocked me back into the bunk, forcing me to grab onto anything just to keep from slipping onto my butt on the wet floor.

The hatch slid open and Manuel crawled slowly back inside.

'What the hell's going on up there?' I asked him.

He just rolled his eyes back up into his head, too aggravated, too horrified to utter a single word.

'Did you get sick?' I asked him as I started to ascend the wood steps.

'Yeah – and so did Jarle.'

It was the first time in his entire life that our young captain had ever been seasick. That did not bode well.

'We lost the wind pilot.'

'What do you mean, we lost the wind pilot?'

'The wind ripped it right off the back of the boat.'

I was beginning to get more of an inkling of what had been going on up there.

'This is fucking madness. It's suicide. We've got to go back.' He started to scream. 'Jarle, we've got to go back!!'

Manuel turned back toward me as he undressed, grabbing me by the collar of my sweater.

'David, he's just a boy.' In between the lines, he was saying something else: we should have listened to the report that he ignored. As I climbed up, I was sure we would see Manuel again soon enough: the choking odour of gas inside was so intense it was hard to breathe. Manuel was repeating this mantra out loud as I finally reached the deck and looked around.

It was madness. I looked into my young captain's face and saw something I had never seen there before.

His face was literally green. There was the dull, glazed look in his eyes of a man who's drunk too much cheap alcohol over a period of many years, leaving him unable to understand what another says. Comprehension just doesn't register on the face.

It was a young face without a smile, making Jarle look somehow older underneath the brown fur hunting cap he always wore. This was no boy, but a seafaring captain – and it was the sea I now saw reflected in his eyes, in all its grim, shimmering glory. He was sitting at the back of the boat, holding onto the tiller.

'How's it going?' I asked. What else was I going to say?

'OK. We lost the wind pilot.'

'I heard.'

I looked around me at the rough seas. The swells had become full-fledged breaking waves, topped with whitecaps of froth. I thought of what toothless Boris had told me in Ushuaia about the giant breakers on the open sea. Then I looked over Jarle's shoulder to where the wind pilot used to be. The entire top half was gone.

'What happened?' I asked dumbly.

'The wind took it. It snapped off.' I had filed the nut too far. I knew it. But I wasn't taking the rap for this. The winds were howling and strong, well in excess of 50 knots, as was to be expected in the so-called 'furious 50s', the legendarily difficult seas found at such latitudes. We were passing through them, on our way from the 'roaring 40s' to the 'screaming 60s'.

'I took the sails down.' Jarle explained that we were now riding the storm out without sails. We were just trying to hold on. There was no course. We'd worry about that after the storm.

'What's that?' I asked, pointing to the green line spooled off the back of the boat.

Jarle whirled around and explained it was the sea anchor, a dull weight used as drag to slow and steady the boat in rough conditions.

'Well, we just lost the sea anchor.' A strong gust literally ripped the sea anchor right off the rope before my very eyes. I was aghast.

Jarle momentarily tied the tiller between the two back rails with an old rope and stood up, talking to me face to face as I started to put the emergency harness on.

'How's the gas smell?' he asked.

'Bad.'

Beneath us a 20-litre metal paint can filled with benzine was bouncing around, crashing from side to side at our feet. In the throes of the storm it had lost its hold on the deck and had now become a nuisance every time the boat rose and fell on the swells.

Then a change came over Jarle's face. Deep in his eyes all colour drained – even the green – leaving him a pasty white. His eyes were looking past me, over my shoulder.

'Oh my God,' he whispered.

I followed his gaze and slowly turned around.

A giant wave had begun to curl as it approached the boat. My head tilted up for what seemed like an eternity until I finally saw the top of the breaker, aiming down toward us from a height well above our 30-foot mast.

'Hold on!' Jarle screamed, bracing himself.

I turned back around quickly and reached out my hands, grabbing for anything as the wave crashed down over the boat. It soaked me and threw me against Jarle. I struggled to stay on board by grabbing at the wires, eyes shut against the icy cold clobbering me in the neck, until the wave abated and I finally regained my balance.

'Are you OK?' Jarle asked as the wave's residual water began to slowly drain from the cockpit. I could only wonder what Manuel was thinking inside, experiencing the reverberating echoes of the inner hull for the first time.

'You don't have to stay out here,' Jarle explained. 'There's no reason. There's no point. There's nothing you can do. We can tie off the tiller and you can come back inside with us.'

I stood on the deck for a moment, horrified, looking around me at the great silver sea. The prospect of staying out on deck and getting soaked to the bone and frozen did not appeal to me – but then again, neither did going back inside with the smell of spilled gas and two seasick people. Both stern bunks would be occupied: where would I go? I decided to stay outside for the duration of my shift.

Another wave crashed into the boat, rocking our world. The paint can jostled loose again and started to bounce around at our feet. Jarle became frustrated. He lifted the irritating can over his head with both hands and, holding it like a keg of beer, tossed it into the sea.

'I'm sorry Mother Nature,' he said as it sank.

We were completely opposed to such an action on many accounts. We didn't believe in either littering or dumping gas in a natural environment, and our supplies were limited. We might very well need that gas in Antarctica. But this was not the time to argue. Decisions – life and death decisions – were being made. I was still green, inexperienced. I had never sailed before. I knew we were in a severe storm, but had no idea how severe. In my book, I was in no position to make these decisions for the crew. That was the captain's responsibility, even if he was only 21 years old.

I opted to remain on deck. In steering the boat, the tiller man sits on the high side, the side from which the wind blows, affording him the best view of what's in front of the boat. We were expecting icebergs – we just didn't know when. Still, it was important to keep your eyes peeled. If we whacked into anything we were going down. We had no lifeboat. In these conditions it wouldn't matter anyway.

I took my place on the left side of the stern, propping my black rubber boots up and across the cockpit, bottoms flush with the right wall – they almost fit perfectly since this was the width of the boat. Jarle explained to me: keep the back of the boat toward the wind. This would hopefully ensure that we would coast down the inside of any potential breaking waves, surfing our way to safety. Jarle often described how fun that manoeuvre was; it sure didn't seem like any fun to me. But it beat the alternative. Using both tillers in unison, the wood one inside the cockpit and the metal one on the stern, would be the best way to control the boat.

I clipped my harness to the rail and took position, watching as Jarle clambered inside. I was now left on deck alone.

I looked around me. The swells were enormous – at least 30 feet. Whitecaps topped almost every wave, which seemed to approach the boat from every direction all at once. It was hard to tell where the next one was going to come from.

The sky was cold, grey and moist. I had imagined the ocean extending blue into the far horizon, the world bending at my feet as I sailed gleefully along under a warming sun in the fresh sea breeze. Instead, the whipping wind pierced with such intensity it was almost difficult to breathe, and when the pelting rain didn't sting your cheeks or eyes making it difficult to see, you were not looking down at the horizon but rather up at the next crashing silver wave – and your boat was the beach.

Manipulating both tillers, I tried hard to keep the wind at my back. The best I could manage was to keep it approaching consistently from our left flank – behind me.

I wanted to keep the swells coming from behind me. I didn't want to see them. It was too intimidating.

Watching the curling wave approach before it crashed on top of us was more terrifying than the impact itself. First, from a lost, vague distance, it would begin to take shape and form. Before long I would notice that it was taking a general course in our direction. Powerless to manipulate the vessel, with absolutely no control, I was simply chained to the rail bracing for impact. On each occasion I was frightened that if, God forbid, the boat did flip, it would be difficult for me to unleash the harness and I would drown. Only by pulling both tiller handles toward me with full strength, as hard as I could – and then hanging on for dear life when the wave hit – could I make sure there would be consistency, and that we would maintain our general direction after the impact. In truth, there was only one direction I was really concerned with at the time: staying upright.

We bounced along, the torpedo shots ricocheting off our hull repeatedly. It reminded me of a Mickey Mouse cartoon. Mickey is standing at the wheel of his faithful tugboat, whistling gleefully. Suddenly he sees a wave coming and his eyebrows pop off his head. 'Whaaa?' he gets out before the giant white-topped wave curls and forms a hand. As it nears the little tugboat, the 'hand' forms fingers that gently tap Mickey on the back of his shoulder from behind; when he turns around, the middle finger hauls back and flicks the little tugboat, spinning it like a tornado high into the air. A second 'hand' comes along and flicks Mickey into his own spin, only he spirals in the opposite direction like a speeding corkscrew. With a splashing thud the tugboat crashes back to the sea, followed by a dizzy Mickey landing feet first on the deck, dazed and trying to regain balance. Before long the entire cycle begins again.

Off in the distance, the birds were playing with the waves, dancing in the surf. For them it was one big party. Albatrosses would circle our boat, soaring around and over our dilemma, watching with detached spectacle before landing nearby.

THE FIRST STORM

Occasionally, smaller birds, little black and white wren-looking creatures called storm petrels, would gather behind us in groups of up to 20, landing on the slimy swells left behind in the trail of the *Berserk* before picking up to follow us and land again.

As these random thoughts ran through my head, I looked around me and saw a particularly big wave approaching. I pulled on the tillers hard, desperate to turn the back of the boat to the approaching wave. It was not to be. The curl lifted the boat inside its arc and turned us sideways. I looked straight down at the ocean and screamed as the right side of the boat plunged into the water at a 90-degree angle with tremendous force. The wave pushed us forcefully downward, trying its best to put us under. I was virtually standing on the ocean looking down when water began to spill into the cockpit, filling it before the boat slowly bounced back up thanks to the buoyant air trapped inside the cabin.

'Jarle!' I screamed. 'Jarle!!'

'What?!' He slid the top of the hatch back and looked out, seeing the cockpit full of water. Quickly he threw off the rest of the hatches and leaped out barefoot, grabbing a nearby bucket and beginning to bail. The automatic drainage system did the rest. When the *Berserk* was 'back on course', he climbed back inside again to try to get some rest.

I was left alone on the deck again, waiting for the next wave to crash, not sure that the next time we would be so lucky. This wave did not break directly on top of the boat. A direct hit would put us under, dooming us to the much-bemoaned fate of many a sailor throughout time.

I did not think I was going to die in that storm. I was certain of it. It was not a question of 'if' but of 'when'. I stared out at the horizon resignedly. The storm was still raging and intense – at its peak – and penguins were swimming all over the place, playing leapfrog in the frothy surf of the giant waves. I did not think: 'Wow, penguins. Cool. I'm at one with nature.' I thought: 'Fuck you, assholes.' They were mocking our plight, playing nearby and watching us die. They dodged in and out of the nearby silver surf before finally disappearing.

By now I did not dare look behind me over my shoulder. It was too terrifying watching the approaching waves, like watching an aeroplane landing on top of you. Instead my eyes focused off into the horizon, picking a point far in the distance. By now, lack of sleep, lack of food – we still hadn't eaten since we left – and a sort of bizarre sensory deprivation caused by the ocean started to kick in.

I began to think of everyone I knew in my life. I couldn't help it or control it. The first thoughts were of my family. I heard my father's infamous words ringing inside my head: 'Being soaking wet and getting bashed around in a small boat for three months doesn't sound like fun to me, but if that's what you want to do...' I thought of my sister; God, how I tortured her when we were younger. I began to think of all my friends – thoughts of every friend held dear over the course of an entire lifetime sprang up randomly and uncontrollably.

Another wave hit, dousing me. It landed flush on the back of my head, nearly snapping my neck. Again my knees were deep in icy water after the cockeyed boat regained its bearing. This time I didn't even bother calling for Jarle's assistance. I bailed with the white Mobil bucket, letting the boat's drainage system do the rest.

Soon the boat and I were both back in position, fighting off more wandering thoughts. Try as I might, I could not control them. My mind began to think of the strangest people, acquaintances unremembered for years – people like my third grade teacher's curly-haired brother, who had visited our class but once with his pet boa constrictor that went to the bathroom in the sink. I became certain of the cause of this: I am going to die. Soon. It all makes perfect sense.

Waves hit from all angles. It's difficult to tell where the next wall of water will come from. Each one gets me wet in an innovative way, a few drops eventually winding their way through every layer down to my bare skin. The wet gear has already begun to sprout holes, like Swiss cheese. It's too late to do any more patchwork. I just hope the boat will hold up. I'm not sure.

Fuck Antarctica, I think. Fuck my dream. I don't give a shit if I never see that godforsaken wasteland. I just want to live. I just want to set foot on the safety of dry land again, and kiss it. I want to go home. I want to apologise to my father for all the awful things I did to him as a kid. They didn't seem so bad then, but now, by god, now do they ever.

I pray to every god I can think of. I remember the Chilean who gave us the spiritual benediction on the docks before we left. He held his arms out and told us that if ever we were in a time of need, we should look to the sky. Christ would be there for us always, listening even when things were at their worst. I look straight up, thinking of the Chilean.

I don't want to die. But I'm not going to cry. There's no point. I don't feel like crying. My eyes are wide open. If Death knocks on the door to greet me, I'll be wide-awake to answer.

I think about how cold it will be when I finally go into the water, grateful the agony will only last four minutes if I'm lucky. Another monster wave slowly forms, curling toward the boat, and I think deep down in my soul: this is the one. Here it comes. Here it comes.

I scream for Jarle's help. The entire cockpit is full. He leaps out again, grabbing the pot and helping me bail.

'I'll be right out,' he says. I look at my watch. My four-hour shift is coming to a close. I'm more than glad. I'm ecstatic.

I hand off the tiller to Jarle and climb down through the companionway into the boat to find Manuel waiting. Immediately he grabs me by the collar and starts shaking.

'We're going to die!' he shrieks repeatedly. 'We have to go back!!' His ranting goes on and on, as bad as the storm, and he shakes me furiously, like I'm some kind of human martini.

Up on deck, the captain finally breaks his long silence. 'This is a democracy. There are three of us. If two of us vote to go back, we'll let the majority decide.'

All the thoughts run through my head at once: Death, Antarctica, Manuel's desperation, my father's plaintive plea. Finally, that's the deciding factor.

'Jarle!' I yell up. 'I think we should go back.'

'What?' my disbelieving captain yells down.

'I think we should go back and regroup.'

There is that long moment of silence as Manuel smugly nods his head, with that closed-mouthed I-told-you-so grimace of satisfaction.

Finally Jarle calls back down: 'Skull, get dressed and come back up here.'

The three of us were on deck. It seemed as though perhaps the storm may have been abating ever so slightly. Only occasionally were we swamped by the freak wave.

The captain sat at the tiller, holding us steady. I sat on the left, looking back, Manuel across from me.

'Are you sure you want to go back?' Jarle asked.

'I think we should regroup,' I reiterated.

'Turn the boat around, Jarle,' Manuel ordered.

Jarle stared away from me, straight over the starboard side and out blankly to the sea. His lips were pursed in tight Scandinavian strength, his steely-eyed complexion as colourless and grey as the sky and sea enveloping him.

'We can't turn back,' he explained, looking both of us squarely in the eye.

'Why not?' Manuel wanted to know.

'We wouldn't make it.'

'Jarle, if we don't turn back, we're certainly not going to make it,' Manuel continued, trying to be reasonable.

'We're sixty miles south of Cape Horn – the roughest seas in the world,' he went on. 'The water is shallow here. That's why the waves are so big. If we turn around now, we'll have to go back into the face of this on the tack. It will take us two and a half days just to make it back – if we're lucky. We could miss land entirely and wind up in the middle of the Atlantic.'

The prospect did not seem pleasant: riding sideways at a 45-degree angle on the tack, sailing right back into the teeth of this monster. I knew what Jarle must be thinking. He had fought the Cape once before. For three days he didn't move. He was alone, fatigued just keeping the nose of the *Berserk* pointed in the right direction. The timeless legend of the Cape was well known. Many a good man had fallen prey to its snare.

'This is the Drake Passage, man!' Jarle said, voice raised. 'What did you think it would be?' He reiterated that these were the roughest seas in the world.

'We're getting hit by a storm, man,' Jarle argued. 'In the worst place in the world. It doesn't get any worse than this.'

I sat and thought silently. Manuel held firm; his eyes shone a cocktail of fear, anger, hate and regret. I looked over at the captain. Sure, he was 21, but even though others thought he was reckless it was simply because they envied his freedom of spirit. They would never understand what made such a great man tick, a man who had a *National Geographic* map of the world's great explorers taped over his bunk. It didn't matter what age he was. We had never sailed before; he had come down alone from Norway. He had prepared for months for this expedition; we had just wandered on board at the last possible minute. It wasn't my decision to make.

'OK,' I said. 'Let's go on.' Listening to the captain's reasoning had made me a little less panicked, leaving me feeling a little more tranquil and calm.

The captain smiled. His eyes reflected a bond between us that from that moment would never be broken again. His first mate, when ultimately confronted, had supported his leader.

But Manuel lost it completely.

'What do you mean, let's go on?' he shrieked, standing.

'I told you Manuel, once we started, there's no turning back,' the satisfied, smug Norwegian smiled.

'You're both crazy! This is fucking nuts!!' Manuel threw open the hatch, screaming indiscernibly something about suicide and death and Shackleton as he crawled back inside to get away from both of us as quickly as he could.

The captain and I looked at each other.

'Are you sure the boat can handle the pounding?' I asked him.

'Of course, it can, man,' he said. 'It's a boat. That's what it's made for. Now go inside and get some rest before your next shift.'

I nodded and went inside, saying nothing to Manuel as I undressed. He was already curled up inside his sleeping bag, facing away from me. The smell of gas was as awful as ever.

I decided that from now on, I would sleep in my own bunk, in the bow. I didn't care how much the *Berserk* bounced or how wet the cushions were. I told them before: I've never gotten seasick. I never did. They did.

As I lay in my sleeping bag, my body below sea level, items tumbling down on top of me, leaning uncomfortably against the bottom of the upside-down galley table stowed underneath me, bouncing against the boat and bruising myself against first the side, then the top, then the table, the horrible gurgling of the sirens of the ocean lapped near my ear, separated only by an eighth of an inch of questionable fibreglass.

When the next wave crashed, a horrendous, thundering roar reverberated throughout the inner hull, quaking the *Berserk*. After that I was not certain that the boat could take the pounding of the next wave – much less an entire three-month journey into iceberg-infested waters. And Manuel had emerged as a major problem, worse than an iceberg. If we didn't get rid of him now, he would surely only get worse.

'I think we should go back,' I shouted again half-heartedly from beneath my bag, to myself more than anyone else, to no one in particular.

'We've got to go back, Jarle,' Manuel chimed in.

The young captain above held firm. 'We're going on.'

The next day we saw our first ship, a huge yellow Chilean naval vessel. We pulled out the binoculars and saw the word 'Armada' written on the side.

For the first time, there was no rain. The storm had abated. Jarle took a reading on one of our four GPS's: we had been blown 60 miles off course to the east. We were now heading directly due west hoping to slowly get back on course. The sails were up.

Jarle hurried inside to raise the ship on the short-range VHF, beckoning Manuel to join him for translation. I stayed at the helm.

Soon the captain came running out, pumping his fists into the air.

'Force-Twelve! We were in a Force-Twelve!!' he screamed with glee and delight. 'Fucking Force-Twelve!' he shouted, looking up at the sky, shaking his fist in triumph and using the 'is-that-all-you've-got-motherfucker' line I taught him from *Forrest Gump*.

'What's a Force-Twelve?' I asked. I had no idea.

'I told you, man,' he explained. 'It's the worst storm you can get. We hit the worst storm possible in the worst place possible.'

Jarle was beaming. The Chileans had told him that we had just come out of three days of a Force-12 front.

'It doesn't get any worse,' he smiled. 'And they said that we're heading into more settled weather systems now.'

'That's not what they said!' Manuel said, poking his head up out of the hatch. 'They said we're heading into more weather.'

I didn't know whom to believe. They were both, in their own eyes, telling the truth. But Manuel did speak Spanish as a native language.

The two of them began to argue about what they heard while I went inside and looked up 'Force-12' in one of the many damp sailing manuals. Indeed, it was at the top of the Beaufort Scale. A storm so rated includes waves in excess of 30 feet and hurricane strength winds in excess of 70 knots. The severity of our dilemma had indeed been confirmed by the Chilean Navy.

Later that day I pulled out a piece of bread and slapped together a ham and cheese sandwich, eating for the first time since we left. Jarle sat near me inside the cabin. Manuel was just starting his shift alone at the helm.

'I can't fucking take it anymore!' he screamed.

Jarle and I looked at each other.

'Shut up and do your shift, Manuel,' Jarle yelled back between bites.

'I'm going to jump!' Manuel screamed. 'I mean it!'

We kept eating.

Then we heard the loudest scream of all, a bloodcurdling 'Aaaaaaaaaaaaah!'

I looked at Jarle. 'Is he still out there?' I asked. I stopped chewing.

Jarle stood and peered through a crack in the hatch. He sat back down, nodding his head.

Then, on the upper deck, Manuel began sobbing. He was a grown man crying from the gut, his lungs heaving like a bear that can't breathe properly.

I looked at Jarle. 'He's crying,' I said quietly.

'I know,' Jarle responded.

'What do we do?'

'Let him cry,' he said.

I repeated softly. 'What do we do?'

Jarle took a bite of his sandwich. 'Let him do his shift.'

We ate in silence for the first time in three days, on our way to Antarctica. We had no idea when we'd see our first iceberg or whale, or what we'd even encounter. Only God knew what lay before us.

But an irreparable rift had developed between us on the *Berserk*. I didn't know it at the time, but it was only just beginning, and would get far, far worse. I remembered Manuel's statement, the one he had heard from his friends on our sailing boat neighbour, the *Voyeu*: 'Three's a good number – unless two turn against one.' In Manuel's eyes, Jarle and I were the two.

He was the one.

CHAPTER FIVE

"Berserk"

WE GO ON:
THE CROSSING

A couple of days later we were back on track, dead-set on Antarctica again. The sun finally decided to make an appearance after hiding for nearly a week and we hung our soaked clothes and socks out to dry everywhere, over the boom, on the wire rails, on anything that could be used as a makeshift hook. Everything in the boat was sopping wet, and the cabin permeated with the residual faint aroma of mildew, spilled gas and sea salt.

Even Manuel began to show some signs of life again after his 'mutiny'. For days he had eaten nothing at all and now, when he did put something into his mouth, it was either chocolate or a cigarette. Both made him sick like clockwork. Jarle, in pity, had given the begging crewman a couple of packs out of the cartons he had brought with him to use as trade bait. I knew – it did not take a rocket scientist to figure out – that Manuel would not either be capable of or desire to quit smoking when his packs ran out. The storm had put the fear of God into him and now he was smoking as if his very life depended on it. And, like clockwork, as soon as he would finish his cigarette, he would lean over the edge of the boat and puke.

'Have you ever noticed that you throw up every time you smoke?' I asked him.

He simply nodded his head and stared at me. 'Why don't you mind your own business?' he scowled. I shrugged. So be it; if he wanted to puke all the time, that's his business – as long as he kept it out of the boat. At first, he had been a good sport about his seasickness. But as the trip wore on and it became apparent to him that he would never get over it – he threw up every day – he became increasingly unenamoured of the process, as if he were tossing out the baby with the bathwater, heaving up all his good will with whatever else came up from within.

These were some good days. We were racing as fast as we could go across the passage and the wind favoured us. Still, the size of the sails limited our speed to around 5 knots an hour, 6 if we were really lucky. We had been blown 60 miles off course by the first storm, so we still had about a week at sea ahead of us.

We began our shifts in earnest. Jarle had it the worst; any time the wind shifted even the slightest bit, we would call out 'Jarle!' from the cockpit and he would pop his head up for a peek at the situation. If it warranted any change whatsoever, he would get dressed and come out. He did not get much sleep.

Neither Manuel nor I knew the slightest thing about sailing. By now, with plenty of turns at the tiller, I was able to hold a steady course and feel the boat's movement beneath me. But whenever the wind changed, I was incapable of tacking, or switching its direction in our front sail, without Jarle's direct assistance or instructions. The process required loosening the ropes that held the sail taut on one side, while turning into the wind, thus changing its direction, and pulling the ropes tight on the other side – all while steering. A simple manoeuvre for an experienced sailor – but for me, well, I might as well have been asked to design a rocket for moon launching. If I tried it alone, I would fumble with the ropes; they would get caught on something, and I would be forced to let go of the tiller, like a man letting go of the wheel to deal with spilled coffee. Chaos would ensue. The boat would spin in a horrific circle, our course would be stopped, or worse yet, as Jarle warned, the boat would be in danger of immediate swamping, especially if a sudden burst of wind caught us flush in the main sail and knocked us down, the worst possible scenario. For Manuel, simply steering held the same possibilities – and thus, the few times he was actually left alone at the helm filled me with greater dread than any Force-12 gale ever could.

Jarle had long forewarned us that any time we were not on our shift we would spend cocooned inside our sleeping bags and he was right. The chill in the air became colder and colder, thicker and thicker, as we headed further and further south, and as the water beneath us cooled, the bottom of the boat absorbed the lack of heat. We could feel the chill through the bottoms of our rubber boots (mine had actual holes in the soles) and through our soaking wool socks, even once we started wearing two pairs. Within 15 minutes of walking out for a shift, my feet would be completely numb – and the remainder of the time would be spent trying all sorts of tactics to keep them from getting worse.

The decided shifts were three hours on, six hours off – but that was with three. Manuel copped attitude when we decided to go on, only this time he never went back, like a snapped rubber band. He balked any time he went on shift, complaining within minutes that he was cold. Jarle, like a dutiful father, told him repeatedly to just do his shift, but soon it became easier to simply cover for him than to argue.

Even when he did manage to hold the tiller down, it was more horrifying than if he wasn't even there at all. We never knew what he would do, what impulsive act would propel him, if he was even paying attention or simply smoking a cigarette. We were worried about when we would see our first iceberg and vigilant watch was required; with Manuel at the helm, I was scared we would first see it when it plunged upward through the bottom of the bow. As the course wore on, he began to spend more and more time wrapped up in his sleeping bag, and as we grew tired of his antics, we began to let him.

From the very beginning we were soaked to the bone from head to toe. Jarle had been right: the only substance that kept us warm in the wet was wool. But in that first storm I had discovered one thing: the tags inside Hank's raggish green duds read 'Half-wol' for a reason. Indeed the material was some sort of hybrid between wool and some other fabric; instead of keeping me warm when wet, it simply became wet and cold. I stopped wearing the shirts altogether, but had no choice with the pants. Without them, my bony, bare legs would be exposed beneath the yellow wetgear. I was reduced to stripping off the wet underwear between shifts, curling up nude below the waist, and stuffing the wet togs in the crook of my stomach, hoping my excess body heat would evaporate just a bit of the dampness before I had to put them back on, never a pleasant experience since they greeted whatever warmth my body had mustered with the frigid cold of steel.

When I realised Hank the pious had ripped me off, I was furious. At the end of one of my shifts I stripped the wet clothes off of my soaking, blue body and hurled the underwear at the bulkhead. 'Fucking half wool bullshit!' I screamed impulsively. Manuel and Jarle laughed heartily, enjoying the spectacle. From then on, we used the phrase 'half wool' to represent anything of inferior quality that displeased us and 'full wool' for anything we liked. Whenever we needed some instant camaraderie, we would shake our heads at how I had been rooked by good ol' 'Half Wool' Hank.

Our precious cocoon time never lasted the full six hours; even so, it took the entire respite simply to thaw the numbness out of the feet. I would try to exercise my toes as much as possible within my boots while on my watch, wiggling them, standing up and walking around the cockpit like a tin soldier to keep the blood flowing, but it was like the veritable plaster on the broken arm. Often while under the damp bag, hat and wool sweater still on, breathing heavy hot air from my lungs into my sealed space waiting to warm up, I would wonder whether my toes actually would ever thaw out at all. I would wait an hour, maybe two, expectantly, hoping to feel that first slight tingle announcing the arrival of feeling once again. Even after the toes began to tingle and my fear a bit relieved, it would take hours until my feet were merely cold, wet, and pruned rather than frozen. By then it was time to suit up again.

As the trip wore on, the feeling returned to my toes later and later. Eventually they turned white, like a bleached bone found on the beach, and became hard as wood, so hard you could rap on them like knocking on a front door. I began to fear that incipient frostbite had begun to set in and that it was completely within the realm of possibility that one or all of them might fall off, but other than do my best to keep them warm and dry, there was nothing else to do but wait.

Days later I got my first sleep. I dragged our wood galley tabletop on top of the wet cushion and lay on top of it to keep me dry, separated from the soaking cushions that had become more like sponges filled with melted ice. I knew if he caught me sleeping on the table Jarle would have been upset, afraid it would warp – so I didn't bother to mention it. In the smoothest of seas the severe bounce of the bow would send my cocooned body spiralling up into the ceiling, then pounding back down onto the wood again – making it difficult to sleep. Two solid hits, two bruises for the price of one. Still, it was much better than rolling around in the stern bunk restrainers, which swung back and forth like hammocks in a hurricane. Eventually as we finished the bread I covered the wet cushions with the empty rice bags that once held the by-now mouldy green rolls and slept on top of them, softening both the dampness of the cushions and the constant blows.

Eventually, it became time to go to the bathroom for the first time. A monumentous event in the annals of polar exploration, no doubt, but literally a bare necessity. The seas rolled along behind us, moderate swells that dipped the back of the boat up and down. Left with no recourse, I found the most solid position on the rail – which happened to be in the back of the boat, near the tiller – and pulled down my gear, hoping to dispose of matters as quickly as possible. It was extremely difficult to simply hold on without spilling back over the edge; after becoming comfortable and somewhat balanced, I then had to overcome my shyness, being only inches away from a smirking Manuel. But just then Jarle emerged from within the cabin with his video camera and in my haste to cover up I panicked, dropping the precious roll of toilet paper into the Drake. I was left immobilised, bare-assed, hanging my better half over the rail while a horrified Manuel shrieked 'Get him some toilet paper!' to our chuckling boy captain. Eventually I took care of business, more out of necessity than pleasure.

But Manuel was like a camel. He did not go to the bathroom 'sitting down' for the entire crossing. To this day I don't know how he did it without rupturing an intestine (I suspect eating only chocolate had something to do with it) and consider his achievement among the trip's most worthy.

I am drawn to the night like a moth to the flame, and more often than not, by fluke or fate, I drew the coldest shift.

It was on one such shift where the wind died completely in the middle of my watch. Jarle and Manuel were in their bunks getting warm and sleeping.

'Jarle, the wind died,' I called out. Experienced with the sea, he peeked his head out of the top of the wood hatch and assessed the situation. 'Pull down the sails and come in,' he said.

'What about steering?' I asked.

'There's no wind. Tie off the tiller and we'll all get some sleep.' He popped his head back down.

The wind had stopped completely out there on the sea and the sun began to rise. The boat bobbed from side to side, swinging like a pendulum back and forth. I awkwardly walked to the bow and lowered the flapping front sail, tying it up as best I could, then ambled back to the mast to drop the main sail. I untied the rope and lowered the sail, but the instant I unhooked it, the boat lurched then pitched and for a moment I lost my balance. I reached out awkwardly to hold onto anything I could grab but found it difficult to hang on. I clutched the mast with my arm but like a fool dropped the halyard and watched in horror as it scampered halfway up to the top. The boat rocked back the other way and I lunged for the clip on the end of the rope, but it eluded me again, scampering further up the mast and wrapping around the other way.

This went on for an hour as my frustration mounted. The sky became a bewildering orange and pink cherry sherbet and the *Berserk*'s rocking obscured all other sound, and I held onto the mast securely so I wouldn't fall, occasionally attempting to grab the swinging, teasing rope and clip, hoping to time my lunge accordingly but always just failing, leaving just enough room to grab hold of the mast again before I slipped over the side. While inside my shipmates were catching up on the sleep we all so desperately needed, I was utterly powerless and could feel the frustration welling inside me, like a kettle right before the water boils.

Suddenly, out of nowhere, an exhalation of air escaped a blowhole. I looked over to the mercury sea and, saw the very thing I thought I'd heard: a dolphin, rising to the surface and breathing out of its blowhole to say hello, there in the middle of the sea, in the middle of the Drake Passage. My heart felt calm and serene and as the soothing creatures rose next to the boat, I somehow knew inside that everything would be all right, the entire trip destined to be fortunate. These empathetic creatures had felt the hopelessness of my plight and had risen from the depths at this very instant to reassure me; from then on I would feel even more of a kinship with them.

As the boat continued to bounce on a beautiful sea I relaxed, enjoying the peace of the moment while the dolphins swam around. Eventually, an hour later, Manuel popped his head out of the hatch. 'David, do you need some help?' he asked with a smile. I nodded my head sheepishly, still clinging to the mast and the rope. 'Yes,' I answered. 'I'll be out in a minute,' he said before ducking back inside to get dressed.

Manuel came out to the deck a few minutes later and helped me grab hold of the elusive rope and tie everything up. He was jovial and friendly, and I was grateful. I never liked him more than at that very moment.

We crawled back down into our bunks as the boat bobbed on the windless, silvery sea and for the first time in the entire crossing we all managed to get some real sleep. I dreamt that we were passing land, a mysterious, smouldering, volcanic island in the middle of nowhere right off our starboard side, like something out of *King Kong*, and I could not fathom what it was doing there or why we were heading east. The dream expanded and overlapped into a hallucinatory reality, and in that half state between slumber and consciousness, beneath the unreal orange sky, I was not sure where I was.

When we finally hit the Antarctic Convergence Zone, I figured it would be a bit like walking through a dark tunnel from the parking lot on the way into a stadium, or passing through a nebulous, cloudy boundary at the edge of the galaxy. Jarle had told us what to expect: we would pass through a zone of fog, and on the other side we would encounter icebergs. We had kept a sharp lookout for icebergs since the very first watch – but from now on they would be a legitimate threat.

The *Berserk* crept along slowly through the eerie, surreal Zone. The wind almost died, the sails flapped and we chugged along slowly, like a coal car on a train track that starts with each tug from the little locomotive, then coasts on inertia till the next tug comes along. We kept a sharp lookout from the bow, hearts bumping inside our wet sweaters, waiting for the first sign of ice. Visibility dipped to under 50 feet for long stretches, sometimes worse. We were draped in a blanket of fog and somewhere on the other side lay Antarctica, shrouded in mystery and destiny. As our time in the Zone increased, it ratcheted our tension up notch by notch, for we knew not what to expect on the other side, but we knew well that whatever it was, danger lurked beneath the surface.

Everything I knew about the ice I learned from the movie *Titanic*. The flick had captured the public's imagination, bursting into popular consciousness and making people as scared of icebergs as the movie *Jaws* did of sharks. To me, not quite a rocket scientist, the lesson went something like this: big boat cruising along and then wham! It hits the ice without warning and goes down hard. If the unsinkable

Titanic on its maiden voyage could be brought to its knees, our little plastic bathtub could too. But Jarle smugly believed that our small boat had its advantages; the *Titanic*'s hefty size limited its ability to manoeuvre quickly. The *Berserk*, on the other hand, could be steered away from a giant iceberg more easily – if we spotted it in time. Therein lay the problem. The *Berserk* was so small that the swells eclipsed our mast. When we rose to the top, we would have a clear view – but when we plunged to the bottom in the natural path of our course, all we could see were walls of water.

We had no idea what the ice would actually look like. We figured, of course, that it would be massive and readily identifiable, practically its own country, and that we would have plenty of time to avoid it. But we had heard that little bits called 'growlers' broke off from the larger bergs and these were more difficult to spot, they camouflaged themselves darkly in the sea as sharp, flat, black ice, waiting patiently for unsuspecting victims to impale. The fate of the *Titanic* remained a constant at the back of all our minds. So we watched and we waited, and we waited and we watched, and the longer it took, the more the pressure increased.

But still the majestic ice made no appearance.

When things were good on the *Berserk* and the crew in jovial spirits, there was always lots of laughter. We used to talk a lot about our ultimate destination, Capetown, and joke about the special treats we would reward ourselves with once we got there – especially regarding women. Jarle preferred women of cocoa colour, while I promised myself a big, blonde Afrikaaner woman. The lure of the elusive 'toothless hookers of Capetown' kept us going on more than one lonely watch beneath the storm-swept stars.

We made a couple of other vows and promises to be fulfilled when we arrived in Capetown. First, we all promised to go and get brotherhood tattoos together – it seemed like something sailors would do. We bandied about our designs, though none stuck out or caught our imaginations. I was the only *Berserk* crewmember currently without one. Jarle had a large, fully-maned lion's head emblazoned in green ink on his right pectoral, back from his days as a teenage punk rocker with a Mohawk, while the ironically discordant Manuel had the aforementioned 'Harmony' stretched across his shoulders.

I also made one other promise to myself. Falling rapturously under the peculiar influence of a certain brand of literature, I had often reread a short story by Edgar Allan Poe entitled 'A Descent into the Maelstrom'. In the story, the hero is a fisherman whose ship meets disaster in the form of a monstrous whirlpool that chasms open in the middle of the great vast ocean, destroying everything in its path, including the fisherman's ship. As the fisherman watches his crewmates get sucked one by one below the waves to their deaths, he realises, upon observing a simple plank of wood, that the only chance he has to escape the swirling vortex is if he can remain perfectly still at the very moment he reaches the bottom. Ultimately, he gambles and survives – but emerges so petrified from the experience that every single hair on his body turns completely white. I vowed that once we reached Capetown, I would dye every hair on my face completely white – beard, moustache and all – as a symbol of the voyage's power of transformation.

'Only then will you know what you have done,' Jarle would tell us repeatedly of the open-armed welcome our arrival would inspire in the legion of sailors awaiting us in Capetown. I was not sure what he was talking about, but he seemed confident the world-renowned international sailing community in South Africa would herald our arrival.

It seemed absurd. Manuel and I had absolutely no clue about what to do with the sails, leaving all decisions in Jarle's hands. The same went for navigation. Though it has been said before that all a person needs is a 'tall ship and a star to steer her by', in this case we needed a little more. Jarle brought along with him not one, not two, but four, count 'em four, portable GPS or Global Positioning Satellite systems. The little devices, about the size of mobile phones, used orbiting satellites to triangulate a signal and deliver an accurate readout of latitude and longitude so that we could calculate our position on the charts Jarle had copied from other sailors who travelled the region. He had previously had his GPS's conk out on him in the middle of the ocean and was not taking any chances this time. He stored them, along with his camera equipment, in a waterproof silver case that he kept bungied to a shelf near the bow, and he brought them out only long enough to take sporadic readings to chart our position.

We knew, therefore, approximately where we were – or at least we thought we knew – as we inched closer and closer to Antarctica and the ice.

CHAPTER SIX

ARRIVAL

We were only about 80 miles from the Antarctic coast when our ninth morning at sea broke and another storm hit. By now, Jarle and I had stopped bothering to ask Manuel to even do his shifts unless we needed a break from the cold in the long night. On this last morning, I took the tiller and stayed there throughout the day. I desperately wanted to be at the helm when we first spotted land – like a little kid, I desperately wanted to be the one to call out 'Land ho!'

The seas kicked up a bit and icy rain pelted down, stinging like little flicks of a whip. The mist and rain made it difficult to see the compass, but steadily the *Berserk* churned along like the Little Engine That Could fighting its way uphill. Throughout the day, Jarle and I took turns steering the boat toward her destination as the wind held steady. 'You can go in if you want,' Jarle said, but I shook my head. I didn't want to miss it for the world.

By the end of the day, my clothes and half-wol undergarments were all soaked and sticking to my wet skin. I was beginning to turn blue and my body started to shiver convulsively with the onset of hypothermia. Inside were no remaining dry, warm clothes to replace them with. I wanted more than anything to be outside when we spotted land but simply could not hold out any longer without freezing.

At around one in the morning, after Jarle cooked up a warm treat of his house speciality, spaghetti with onion, I begrudgingly turned over my post – to a complaining Manuel. 'Shut up, Manuel,' said the captain. 'You've been inside your sleeping bag all day. Now it's time to do a shift – if you want to eat.'

Though Manuel had spent most of the trip scarfing down chocolate, he got the point, and after dinner both he and Jarle went out for the run in toward Antarctica. I had been outside for fourteen-and-a-half hours. I made Jarle promise to alert me the second anything at all was spotted.

I stripped the freezing, wet clothes from my body and crawled quickly into my sleeping bag in the bow, ice cold and shivering. It would take hours for the heat to creep back into the bones. The sooner it started the better.

'Iceberg ahoy!' I heard the exultant scream through the groggy, semi-conscious daze that passes for sleep in the bow of a bouncing boat. It had emanated from the mouth of Manuel, and he followed it up with another gem: 'Land ho!'

My bones and meat not yet thawed, I lifted my wet, naked body to the small portal window above my bunk and took a peek out. Sure enough, through the haze, barely visible off our starboard side, passed what looked like the black outcroppings of a small rocky island covered with a mountain of snow.

Instinct took over. I looked at my watch, it was about 4 a.m. I shrugged my shoulders and wrapped myself back up in the sleeping bag, craving each additional second of blessed warmth.

'David!' Jarle called out.

'Yeah, I saw,' I screamed back from inside my comfortable cocoon, basking in the humidity of my breath like a lizard on a rock in the sun.

'David, get your ass up here!'

'I saw!' I repeated.

The argument seemed to hold no merit with the boy captain. 'David, get dressed and get your ass up here!'

I was fighting a losing battle. I peeked out from under the sleeping bag.

'Dressed to see, or dressed to work?' I asked, sitting up and pulling on my wet socks.

'Dressed to work! Hurry!'

I quickly tossed on the rest of my wetgear, not even bothering to layer up as normal. Forget that half-wool crap. It was still soaking, like it had been sitting in a bathtub full of ice. It would be a quick in and out anyway; I'd take a gander at Antarctica and be back down in the bag before you know it.

I was wrong.

I walked up through the cockpit. Manuel looked at me and rolled his eyes; by now it had become his signature move. I turned around toward the bow – and saw a huge, baby-blue, monolithic tower of ice hovering directly in our path like a grand cathedral. My first iceberg. 'The engine won't start,' said Manuel, dumbstruck with awe.

'David, take the tiller,' Jarle shouted.

I whirled back around, no time to absorb the enormity of the baby-blue ice spire looming directly in our path, and grabbed the iron bar. 'Where do you want me to go?'

Dead ahead were two huge icebergs. We were heading toward both of them. The boat bounced high up on the waves; even though we were closer in toward shore, the storm had left bubbly seas, the water pushing up from under the ice, making manoeuvring the vessel difficult.

ARRIVAL

'Go right in the middle of them,' Jarle said. He turned back toward the little outboard engine tucked beneath our back hatch and started pulling on the rip cord furiously, like an irate, middle-aged suburbanite trying to start an old out-of-petrol lawnmower. '*Fey fa-aaaaaahn!*' he shouted, cursing furiously in Norwegian. I still don't know exactly what it means, but I got the point. '*Helveta*!!!!!' That means 'fucking hell', or something along those lines; that one I understood clearly.

'You want me to go down the middle?' I asked curiously. 'What if one of them topples over?'

Jarle was too busy ripping at the engine cord and muttering in Norwegian to answer.

'It's pretty damn huge,' Manuel moaned as he tried to point the video camera at the walls of ice.

He stumbled around the boat toward the bouncing bow. 'We've got growlers!' he shouted, a bit like an expectant mother whose long-awaited contractions had finally begun for real. We had long expected to see these little pieces of floating ice. They were a great worry, since they often blend with the dark silvery waters and are invisible – until they put a hole in the boat. Lucky us: we saw our first icebergs and growlers at the same time.

These weren't merely small icebergs – these were freaking mountainous pillars of ice, deadly, leaning, top-heavy towers threatening to calve and topple at any instant.

'What if there's an avalanche?' I asked dumbly.

'Just stay in the middle,' Jarle explained, ducking into the galley to grab the charts.

I grasped the tiller firmly, tasting the cool blue in my nostrils and feeling it graze my cheeks as we held course straight down iceberg alley, no more than 25 feet wide, like a bowling ball trying to avoid the gutter.

Jarle emerged from below, pointing out our new destination. Our first anchorage lay somewhere over there, off to the left, on the other side of the ice giant, but without an engine, we couldn't cross swords with the ice – so instead we would shoot the gap and head to our second planned anchorage, an abandoned Argentinian base on another small isle in the archipelago.

I could feel the air throbbing as we cleared the walls of the icebergs – much to our relief without avalanche – and spotted the small island off the starboard bow.

'Head for that island, David,' Jarle told me as he lifted the anchor and rope from beneath the tangled mess the crossing had left underneath the hatch.

As we neared the snow-covered island, a jutting white peninsula slowly became visible through the mist, revealing on the high ground a grey wood structure that looked something like a large, square storage barn: the Argentinian base, abandoned. It was boarded up like it hadn't been used in years.

Next to the base, on the near side, flowed a little inlet. We would be able to sail downwind into the ice-cube-filled inlet – but would get only one chance at it. Without the engine, there would be no way to turn the boat around. We would get one crack; if we messed up, we would wind up on the rocks.

With great consternation, we readied the dinghy and dropped it overboard. It floated behind the boat, waiting. On Jarle's command, Manuel tossed the anchor off the bow. I clambered down into the little yellow corncob mini-rowboat, taking hold of the wood oars and squeezing the thick green rope tightly between my knees.

'Good luck,' Jarle shouted, casting me off and away from the boat. I was on my own. I began to row, looking awkwardly over my shoulder at the abandoned base as it got nearer and nearer, hoping beyond hope that the choppy waves ricocheting off the rocks in the inlet wouldn't swamp my boat.

I managed to navigate the little boat over to a series of rocks at the base of what looked like some sort of concrete loading dock, complete with a big rusty iron cleat obviously used to tie up bigger boats in the golden days of exploratory drop-offs, back when the Argentinians could afford to man the base themselves.

The final approach to shore would be tricky. While Manuel and Jarle were busy on board keeping the *Berserk* from smashing into anything, trying desperately to hold just enough wind in the sails to keep us off the rocks, I looked over my shoulder and approached a break in the wet, black boulders I had chosen as my landing point. I would have to time my jump perfectly in order to catch the right tide; if not, the little dinghy would either be slammed onto the rocks or immediately swamped.

As the dinghy neared the shore, the ricocheting bounce increased in intensity. I waited for my moment, timing the move to the water's cadence – and then stuck the oars deep. With a final, unexpected thrust the inlet's waves tossed me onto the rocks and I leapt out of the dinghy, trying to hold onto oars and ropes and boat all at once like a frenzied shopper with an armful of bargain clothes on the first day of a clearance sale. In my excitement I mistimed the first step and went into the drink up to my knees. Instantly, my rubber boots filled with pure, chilly, clear, light-blue Antarctic water and I could feel its grip circle underneath my feet, but I didn't have time to give a damn. I quickly dragged the little boat up over the rocks and secured it from the tide as in the background Jarle's muffled voice screamed for me to hurry up.

I climbed up the slippery rocks slowly and carefully, dragging the green rope over to the rusty cleat where finally my intensive training would be put to the test. Could I tie a proper knot? What if my life depended on it? It did. I had not faced such a knot-tying challenge since first lacing my own shoes on the first day of primary school. I wrapped the rope around the cleat and successfully tied first one, then two knots – and then added a third for insurance.

I looked around, pleased as punch with myself, out over the snow-covered peninsula, and noticed a dark blot on the surface across the inlet: A large blimp of a seal basking in the doldrums of its afternoon nap – at four o'clock in the morning.

'Get back here now!' I didn't have time to chill. I ran back down to the dinghy and splashed back into the water, my boots filling again, then set off, timing my descent back into the waves precisely so they wouldn't crash me back onto the shore. I frantically rowed back to the boat and picked up another rope, heading for the other side of the inlet.

On this side there was no loading dock – I had to determine a landing spot and find a big rock for the rope, all on my own. As the dinghy circled past the boat to grab the next rope, Jarle tossed a hammer and a bag of metal pitons – the kind used by mountain climbers to secure their lines – into the dinghy. He told me to use them if necessary – but I was morally opposed to destroying any aspect of the environment here and was uncertain as to whether they were considered valid or not according to Hank's Antarctic Treaty. Manuel and I wholeheartedly agreed regarding ecological matters, amidst any and all past and future disagreements; not once did I see him toss so much as a cigarette butt overboard. Here I was determined to tie the rope to a rock come hell or high water.

Landing on the far shore would prove to be both. Looking over my shoulder, I awkwardly headed for the best landing spot, fighting my way through the high waves toward a gap in the pounded rocky shore. Again I timed my leap and planted my foot firmly in the water – and again my boots filled. This time, the jolt out of the dinghy snapped the single remaining strap on my yellow Gloucester-fisherman overalls, and my pants literally fell down to my ankles, exposing my spindly legs as I scraped the dinghy up onto the rocks and quickly scanned the hill for a suitable boulder on stable high ground.

I clambered my way up the icy, slippery slope and reached the rope under and around a boulder big enough to hold the *Berserk* against the wind. Once again, I tied a methodical knot and tripled it – I would not be the one responsible for the *Berserk* bobbing into the rocks in the dead of our sleep.

I looked up proudly and for a moment the inlet stood in the peaceful serenity of quiet, like a painting come to life. I drank it all in. A few penguins dotted the icy peninsula across the way; the sleeping seal, only a few feet away, moved not. My hairy legs, exposed, tinged with blue, tingled to the slight Antarctic breeze; water sloshed inside my boots. The firmly anchored *Berserk* bobbed, suspended between the two tautly-stretched green ropes, the waves and the wind playing with the little boat in nature's ongoing relentless tug-of-war that momentarily had been declared a draw.

Shortly after four in the morning, in a place where light and shadow mix like the Twilight Zone, where blue and grey commingle seamlessly in their collision with ice, we had made it to Antarctica, and we were secure.

Manuel called out to me from the boat. 'David,' he said to me, smiling, 'congratulations – you made it to all seven continents. You're standing in Antarctica.'

I smiled broadly – and then I bent over and fixed my pants.

CHAPTER SEVEN
ANTARCTICA

Somewhere in the last part of the voyage we had misplaced our matches. They were nowhere to be found. The inside of the boat was soaking. Every cushion, every article of clothing, quite simply everything. And we were damn cold.

Jarle had packed along a small kerosene heater and had promised that the first thing we would do upon landing would be to turn it on and dry out the inside of the boat. Now he and I turned over everything to search for those damn missing matches. A Drug Enforcement Agent searching for clues in the biggest career-making bust of his life could not have undertaken a more thorough search than the one we were performing at that very moment.

Meanwhile, in the midst of our frantic upheaval, Manuel immediately announced that he was going to shore. We did not have time to argue with him as we lifted every cushion and tossed wet clothes aside in our frantic search. We emptied hatches, unpacked well-wrapped plastic bags filled with supplies, even sorted through every ounce of food and still no matches. The more we searched without result, the colder it seemed to become, and the more our search intensified. We didn't have time to deal with him at the moment.

'Aaaaah!!! Aaaauuuugggghhhhh!' Whimpering, from outside the boat. 'Help! Help!' Manuel, in trouble. Jarle and I quickly leapt out of the hatch – only to find Manuel desperately clinging to the side of the boat, up to his neck in icy water.

We fished him out of the inlet and asked him what happened. 'I fell in,' was not the response. Jarle grabbed the rope of the dinghy and heaved upward, dragging the submerged boat above the water, where he could spill out its icy contents.

Manuel ran inside and changed his clothes and immediately set off again. He now had an assignment: go to shore and search the abandoned base for matches. This time, Jarle helped him on his way. I watched Manuel row the little dinghy with great difficulty toward the rock outcropping and awkwardly land it onshore, where he proceeded to immediately bend over and on his knees literally kiss the ground. I shook my head in disbelief and went back inside to look for the matches.

Eventually, with Manuel on shore and out of our hair, we managed to locate a single box of matches wrapped in a plastic bag somewhere beneath the wet cushions. Jarle – who blamed Manuel for losing the rest of them, since he had been smoking the whole time after swearing he would quit – rigged up an aluminium pipe chimney for the kerosene heater, which he stuck through the roof of the little fore cabin after unscrewing the plastic air vent. Without too much ado he lit the kerosene heater and the drying process began.

'Aaaaaaaah!' Another scream. Not again. We rushed to the deck and saw something straight out of a cartoon: Manuel, rowing back from the shore, with the boat sinking beneath him, now up to his neck in icy water once again. 'Aaaaaaaaaaaah!' I couldn't believe it. The dinghy was going down right out from under him and still the guy was rowing furiously.

'Get back to shore!' Jarle screamed. By now, Manuel groped desperately, trying to keep hold of the boat even though he was sinking. 'Don't worry about the dinghy!' He might not have been worried about it, but I certainly was. Without it, we were in trouble, with no way to leave the boat save for jumping in and swimming. Still, Manuel gamely hoisted the submerged dinghy back to shore with him, and eventually he managed to rejoin us on the *Berserk* where, finally, we were going to get some much-needed rest – or so we thought.

Manuel and Jarle returned to shore together to break into the abandoned snowbound base. The objective: to raid and ransack the place in search of more matches. Above the barricaded, locked wooden door, they found a glass jar containing the key – but for some reason, they couldn't get the rusty lid of the frozen jar open. Eventually they simply broke it, unlocked the door and busted their way inside, where they found a veritable treasure trove of supplies tucked away neatly in the sparse, clean, bucolic setting which resembled nothing less than a charming holiday cabin in the woods.

It is the Antarctic way – the Way of the Explorer – to leave easy access to life-saving materials for all who may stumble upon them in their time of great need. The harsh landscapes of both Arctic regions are dotted with way stations constructed for that very purpose: to save lives, in a 'there but for the grace of God go I' scenario – they all knew that they might be next.

For the next several days, the debate would rage on the *Berserk* as to what exactly determines 'need'. Manuel, obviously, needed to help himself to the stash of chocolate bars he found nestled firmly at the top of the crate containing emergency food supplies. He basically cleaned them out. But when Jarle pilfered some kerosene to replace what we had lost at sea, Manuel became indignant. Being Argentinian, he felt the supplies belonged to Argentina. A couple of days later from the deck of the *Berserk* I watched the two of them walk out of the base and turn the corner when suddenly Jarle lunged for Manuel's throat, tossing him up against a tall snow bank piled up near the side of the building. A tangle of bodies, they disappeared around the corner and I did not see them again for hours while I guarded the boat, pondering what the hell had happened.

After returning successfully from shore – an accomplishment in and of itself – Manuel brazenly announced that he wanted to spend the night on land, in the base. He would sleep on the bare floor if necessary, but come hell or high water, he would be on land that night. He would use some of the base's piled wood and logs to light a fire in the old pot-bellied stove and he would curl up in front of it like a cat and dream of being home.

After warming our guts with a hot pasta dinner, I rowed Manuel back to shore with his sleeping bag and dropped him off. Jarle agreed that he could sleep in the base, but in case of emergency, we would have the dinghy with us on the *Berserk*.

That night, while Manuel raided the base and fell asleep on the wood planks of the cabin floor before a crackling stove fire, Jarle and I celebrated on the *Berserk*. To my delight, Jarle pulled out the booze and concocted his speciality, a mixture of ginger wine and spiced rum. We laughed and smiled the true camaraderie that only comes to sailors after surviving a storm or negotiating a crossing like the Drake. We listened to by-now familiar Norwegian heavy metal tunes and our favourite AC/DC on the boom box, and got toasted inside the *Berserk* as our little makeshift kerosene heater chugged away, slowly evaporating the moisture from the insides of our home – and unbeknownst to us at the time, melting away the plastic ring that housed the air vent it replaced, adding another leak to the boat.

And when we finally fell asleep that night, in the gloomy, perpetual twilight that looms shroudlike over the seventh continent, we felt warm and happy and excited – the best was yet to come.

'Jarle! Jar-le!' Our short-lived reverie ended early the next morning with Manuel, standing on shore and shouting at the top of his lungs, anxious to come back to the *Berserk* – obviously ready for breakfast. In a land where the sun doesn't set, the time on the clock loses its meaning; from here on in, for us night and day would merge seamlessly.

As we warmed our remaining stale bread over the stove and prepared hot drinks for the morning, our first sound sleep in ten days over, we awakened to the harsh reality and beauty of Antarctica.

What now?

That indeed seemed to be the question that permeated the crew of the *Berserk*. What were we going to do now? Why were we there?

Jarle felt that Manuel's discomfort at the first storm would pass as soon as we hit land and that our voyage would continue as planned, but the jury was still out. Certainly his attitude had brightened upon hitting shore.

We decided to stick around our first stop for a few days, giving us all the chance to explore the shore while Jarle tried to fix the engine. I wanted to get close to the penguins: I vowed to touch one. We went ashore, hiking out to the end of the peninsula to get a closer look at the cute little birds. Lord, did they ever stink!! Everyone immediately understood Nature's lesson not to eat or drink snow turned pink by penguin excrement.

While checking out the penguins, I looked out toward the horizon, my distant gaze revealing a long-awaited sight. 'Thar she blows!' I shouted with glee. 'Whale ahoy!' Sure enough, the high spout of whales broke the stillness of the water in the iceberg-laden cove on the other side of the peninsula.

Jarle set out with Manuel to sail amongst the whales and icebergs while I remained behind with the video camera and a tripod on the tip of the snowy peninsula. I wanted to enjoy the spectacle of the quiet land and landscape in solitude, using the camera being the necessary price to pay. I focused in on the whales as they sounded, their broad tails slapping the surface as they sank; they were long gone before the *Berserk* rounded the peninsula.

Finally, the *Berserk* made her way to the giant iceberg stuffing the cove and sailed around and around it, in front of and behind the big, blue block of ice, like a little white fly in a giant baby-blue drink, and by the time they returned we had frittered the afternoon away.

Manuel returned irate. 'We ran aground!' he shrieked, regaling me with a tale of how Jarle had stubbornly chosen a path that took the boat above a shallow series of rocks when they rounded the corner. He had tried to argue with him, he told me, then called him reckless, complaining that they were a hair's breadth away from being stuck without means of escape for all eternity. Jarle shrugged it off, claiming that they had merely scraped the keel on the bottom and were never in any real danger, but an indignant Manuel claimed that they had for a moment actually been completely stuck – another example of the many dangers that lay ahead.

Like the Kiwi man we had heard about who took an ice bath each and every morning, swimming buck-naked to the consternation of his bewildered and ultimately appalled shipmates, Manuel too began to demonstrate wackier and wackier behaviour. He continued to relax and ease his tension by bringing out a bevy of yoga moves whenever he became stressed. Often we would see him on the foredeck performing the 'downward-facing dog' manoeuvre, a sort of flexible worm push-up. He also brought out a book that he always carried with him, a red-covered mystical tome of Eastern spiritual writings, and read it often in the hope that it would quell his anxiety and give him some kind of inner peace.

But when it came time to finally leave our little paradise, Jarle and Manuel went at it again. Manuel demanded that a note be written and left in the abandoned base for the next Argentinian expedition, explaining who we were, why we were there, and what had been taken. Personally, I had taken nothing. Both Jarle and I felt it to be unnecessary, part of the unspoken bond between explorers, but Manuel would hear none of it. He concocted the lengthy epistle to which we all signed our names – I made sure to sign mine with the flourish of John Hancock – and he left it sitting on top of a makeshift desk for his Argentinian brothers to find the next time they entered the base, whenever that would be. Since we were at the heart of the Antarctic summer, it did not seem likely to be that year.

And just like that, once again we were off.

Without much incident, we sailed across the little bay to our original first anchorage destination, a small glacier-surrounded cove on the other side of the Melchior Archipelago.

To our surprise, when we arrived we found a couple of other sailing boats – and Jarle knew them all from his stint at Puerto Williams. Once again we went through the landing process, but this time it proved more difficult – the rocks were brittle and we barely avoided using the dreaded pitons, which we all agreed were not ecologically preferable.

Jarle went over to visit his fellow sailors, a bald Italian man and his wife, and returned with a boxful of fresh red apples and other supplies, a veritable bounty. Thus began an odd tradition: from here on out, whenever we encountered someone down there, they gave us something. I was never quite sure why, but of course I have my theories. They felt sorry for us, in our bare-bones, cold and wet boat; they felt compassion for the boy wonder, the prodigy, the special sailor bred from youth to follow in the long line of tradition they shared; or, most likely, they thought we were going to die. They supplemented our meagre rations so that we would at the very least be able to enjoy our last meal, however imminent that was going to be.

But we really didn't care why. We simply enjoyed the luxury the new food gave us, the occasional scurvy-inhibiting sliver of a shared fresh apple, the ever-so-slight loosening of rations that had begun to take its toll on all of us, Manuel most of all.

Meanwhile, Jarle continued to pull apart the engine. Our new anchorage left us in the middle of a quiet cove, completely surrounded by mountains and ice. I took the dinghy out on my own and rowed and rowed and rowed, leaving the vicinity of the boat to explore, passing closely to basking seals on ice floes and icy cliffs dropping chunks into the summer sea.

It was there, in the serenity of the little dinghy, on my own and away from the troubles brewing on the boat, that I began to soak in my surroundings. The colours in Antarctica are remarkable, and I felt like I was travelling in a painting (albeit a chilly one). It was as if each colour was mixed in a bucket of white, so subtle were the shadings; one part blue, and nine parts white, and *voilà!* the pale, soft colour of the ice. It was the same whether pink, or orange, or red, or purple, a land of sherbet that you wanted to swallow in your soul.

Jarle reconstructed the engine and decided that the whole thing must be due to the damp and cold – and therefore we needed to dry the engine out. A sunny day would help, but we couldn't afford to wait for one – in fact, there would be only three the entire voyage. Instead, while Manuel voiced his concern, he took our little military kerosene kitchen stove and placed it in a cleared-out space beneath the back hatch, right next to the little engine. He stuffed the sails and other debris to the side and leaned down to light it. 'What if it explodes?' Manuel asked, worried it could sink the boat. I must admit: I was a little concerned myself. It certainly doesn't take the brightest bulb in the box to imagine that possibility.

'It won't explode,' Jarle assured us, 'because I've removed all the petrol and the line to the tank. Besides, it must be done.' He lit the little stove and turned it on, then shut the hatch to allow the cold engine to soak up the heat and dry out.

On deck, we went about our business, periodically checking on the drying-out process, which seemed to be going quite smoothly, but reluctant to check too often for fear of letting the accumulating heat escape. Eventually, Jarle walked over and lifted the back hatch. An eight-foot wall of flame shot upward like a thick, fiery geyser, as if all Hell had been unleashed. As the engine blazed, a momentary panic ensued. Our worst fears had been realised. The imminent explosion and fireball would leave us mere mortals but a cinderful of frozen ashes, and we would get our own little funeral cairn, just like all the other explorers who went down for one reason or another.

Manuel shrieked like he had just seen a spider, turned and grabbed a bucketful of water. He reared back, desperation in his eyes. 'No!' Jarle screamed at him. Water would only spread the petrol-inspired inferno.

For an instant, my soul was taken over like one of the pod people from *Invasion of the Body Snatchers*. Without thinking, I calmly turned and walked down into the boat, grabbing the little red fire extinguisher from its nesting place on the far wall. I walked back up and calmly handed it to Jarle, who quickly extinguished the flames. I did not consciously know of the extinguisher, knew even less about operating the damn thing, and, honestly, even if I did, under those seriously imperilled conditions am shocked I did not react less surehandedly. But the fire was out and all was well.

Jarle surveyed the damage. Luckily, we found no hole in the boat, though one of the sails was singed.

But Manuel rolled his eyes yet again. For him, this was the last straw. He had long ago reached his limit; now he exceeded it. Right then and there he became convinced that the *Berserk* was a death trap, an accident waiting to happen, and that yes indeed, her captain was as reckless as everyone had said. All self-doubt within him vanished, and for the first and perhaps only time on the trip, he became confident and determined. Only one thing mattered to him, and nothing would stand in his way. From here on in, whatever it took, he was going to get off the boat as soon as possible.

Manuel's presence on the boat became downright unpleasant. He announced that he no longer wanted to continue with us to South Georgia Island, where he would be met with antagonism from the British soldiers with whom his land still smouldered regarding the Falkland Island War in 1982. He wanted to go home. And most of all, he wanted off the *Berserk* as soon as possible.

Most of the friction up till now had been between Manuel and Jarle. Like Larry, the third stooge, I simply turned my head and, as if spectating at a tennis match, silently watched the verbal jousting bounce back and forth between the two of them. But the boat being small, it would not be long before I would be dragged into the fray.

Manuel demanded that Jarle ask his Italian friend if he could ride back with him. The Italian flatly refused. In the small world of Antarctic sailors word quickly got out, and the story of the little boat with the seasick sailor spread like an engine fire.

Knowing we would be questioned, Jarle concocted a story: perpetually seasick Manuel needed prompt medical attention, and his condition excluded him from continuing with us on our long voyage. Jarle knew that no one would bring this kind of troublesome crewman on board their peaceful ships; convincing them it was a medical emergency would be our only hope. Basically, we would be pulling a bait and switch operation – but by now Jarle and I wanted him off the ship as much as he wanted to leave.

But until we found a way to get rid of him, we were stuck with him.

Our next anchorage established a pattern that would be repeated throughout our sojourn. Each night, throughout the night, our fragile boat would be pelted with large blocks of ice. First, a chunk would tap the boat, a light knock on the door. Inside my bag my eyes would open. Praying it would go away, the second tap came, a little firmer, a little harder, trying to find out if someone's home. By now my eyes were wide. On the third crash, Jarle would scream 'David!' and out of the hatch I would pop, often not bothering to dress at all, grabbing an oar or a stick and pushing the ice out of our way, away from the brittle bow or the anchor line, to be washed away to the other side of the current. This procedure, much like exhausted parents awakening periodically to deal with a wailing newborn, would be repeated each and every night until we left Antarctica.

ANTARCTICA

Fractured sleep became the norm for all of us as we took turns freeing our ship from harm's way. Each tap of the ice portended doom, like the knuckle of the great Grim Reaper rapping raven-like on our chamber door – and each night held all the horrors of Hallowe'en. Never in my bunk would my mind be settled. Animal instinct overwhelmed reason, and we were always one tap away from a permanent ice bath.

As we sailed our way through Antarctica, we first crossed a passage known as the Gerlache Strait. Here we witnessed sights that could have never been imagined. The sun made an appearance that day; the engine started, miraculously, and we determined that the warmth cleared the dampness. Baby-blue icebergs floated everywhere, thousands of them, dotting the horizon. The clear clean water, pure and placid, looked like a mirror, and not a cloud hovered low in the sky, which matched the water's colour precisely – creating the illusion of a world without boundary, without horizon. The icebergs simply hung suspended in time and space, like something out of a surrealistic Salvador Dali painting. And in the midst of such incredible, breath-defying beauty, which my soul drank anxiously in bewilderment, the whales surfaced, everywhere.

Spotted from the bow with a cry of 'Thar she blows!' they were drawn to our boat by my vocal 'whale call'. What had worked with the dolphins proved even more effective with the whales. That day alone we saw nine pods, or family groups, of humpbacks and Minkes – and never once tired of seeing them. They were everywhere. And there we were, floating through their timeless playground as if we were riding on a magical hot-air balloon.

I called them over to the boat. Curious, they swam under us, around us, checking us out. We pulled out the camera and when the whales surrounded us Manuel ducked inside and brought out his little plastic recorder. He knew only one song and played it again and again and again throughout the trip; within minutes the whales were as sick of it as we were.

Jarle popped a tape of whale music, recorded underwater by marine biologists, into the cassette deck to see if the whales would react. They did not – but the party really started to rock when we popped in the AC/DC tape. We had along with us one of the hard rock group's earlier efforts, *High Voltage*, and we played it constantly throughout the trip, enjoying it all the more because Manuel hated it. That day, the whales rocked out in a manner never before seen in Antarctic waters. They loved it. Who could ever possibly claim they are not fully intelligent creatures?

This emerged as one of the greatest days of my life, sights unimaginable in their wonder, breath-taking beauty and serenity. And throughout it all, Manuel maintained a surly countenance of malcontent. Though he had indeed pulled out his little pan-like flute and bombarded us with his single, off-kilter, wheezing, odd, Frankenstein-like melody, the rest of the day he simply moped, unable to appreciate the wonderment that surrounded us as we drifted in suspended animation through the heart of the colourful Antarctic summer. I knew then and there that we had to get Manuel off the boat if we wanted to enjoy the rest of the trip.

Later that day as we crossed yet another strait, the winds kicked up in our face and forced us on the tack. The boat lurched to the side, the angle extreme. Constantly we would tack, switching the angle of the wind as it hit our sails. The crossing proved difficult. Manuel turned to me in the cold wind of the afternoon and said simply: 'If there was any chance of me staying on the *Berserk*, it just ended.'

That night in anchorage, Manuel announced once again that he wanted off the *Berserk* – with a new twist. He no longer desired to continue with us as we sailed our way further and further south. Instead, he wanted to return to the abandoned Antarctic base, which he considered to be 'sovereign Argentinian soil'. He would wait there until his Argentinian brothers arrived to rescue him.

Jarle and I tried to talk some sense into the guy. 'Who's going to tell them you're there?' we asked. He answered that we would. We reiterated that the short distance of our radio precluded contact with any base until we were practically within shouting distance. He heard none of it. We told him we were heading south and were not even planning to turn north again for another month, during which time he would be required to take care of himself. Still, he demanded to be let off, claiming it was his right as a human being.

Jarle balked but Manuel persisted as I sat the argument out. But Manuel became increasingly belligerent. Finally, as he and Jarle screamed back and forth, he turned slowly toward me.

'And you – I hate you most of all,' he said, slowly and deliberately, catching me completely by surprise. I was shocked. What had I done? I had been sitting out the fight the entire time – but now he was dragging me in. He stared at me coldly. 'It takes you five minutes to decide whether you want to go to the bow or not.' An apparent allusion to my flip-flop during the first storm. Still, I said nothing. I gave him one freebie, but he didn't stop there. He persisted. 'You're exactly the type of person I left Hollywood to get away from.' I may be a lot of things, but one thing I'm not is a Hollywood phoney. He was trying to bait me. This time he succeeded.

'You know what I think?' I asked, staring back at him as I spoke for the first time during the argument. I let the moment breathe with dramatic pause before continuing: 'I think you're a traitor and a coward.'

The arrow hit its mark. Evidently wounded, he pursed his lips and nodded silently up and down, not saying a word in reply. For the first time in a long while, he was speechless. We would never be on anything resembling friendly terms again. I hated him.

He turned back toward Jarle, reiterating his demand to be set off on the island. 'You'll die!' Jarle barked back. 'I don't care,' Manuel answered, stubborn as a mule.

By now I was irate. 'I'd rather you died on Melchior Island than continue with us!' I shouted. The cabin became silent. Immediately after I said it, I felt awful about the comment; it's a horrible thing to say to anyone, and I didn't mean it. But by the time days later when I would apologise, ashamed, permanent damage had already been done.

After sleeping on it, Jarle made the most difficult decision of his young life. Manuel's stubborn persistence had left him with no choice. He would accede to his wayward crewman's wishes and reluctantly set him ashore on the abandoned base, almost certainly putting the man to death. But his reasoning was certainly understandable. He simply could not hold the man hostage.

By now Manuel and I were not speaking to each other at all. I turned to Jarle. 'We have to get Manuel on tape saying that he is going ashore of his own free will,' I said, 'so that when he dies we are not held to blame.'

Fire raged in Manuel's savage eyes as Jarle agreed. I set up the camera and focused in on Manuel as he faced Jarle, who began the interrogation captured for all eternity on what we would later refer to as 'the hostage tape.'

'Juan Manuel H--------, how did you come to the *Berserk*?' Jarle started.

'I hitched a ride to Ushuaia, and I just kept going. It took ten minutes to decide our fate,' answered Manuel.

The interrogation continued. Manuel, on tape, appears visibly bereft of energy. He looks like the original Terminator when the red light finally faded from its defeated eyes. When Jarle mentions that he had let Manuel borrow the best clothes, the obstinate crewman answers: 'Still, my feet are numb.'

'It is Antarctica,' Jarle responds. 'You have cold feet.'

Manuel has no answer, simply tilts his head in exasperation.

Eventually, Jarle got around to the meatier questions. 'We have offered to take you with us and drop you off at Port Lockroy (the British base), where you can find a cruise ship; we have offered to drop you off at the American Palmer Station; we have offered to take you with us and drop you off at the occupied Argentinian base on our way north; we have offered to sail you back to Ushuaia and South America on the *Berserk*. What is your choice?'

'I choose to remain on Melchior Island,' Manuel answers defiantly, reiterating that he considered the land to be 'sovereign Argentinian soil'. The interrogation over, I stop the tape.

'Jarle, you have to get him to say he exonerates us in the event of his death,' I explained matter-of-factly. Manuel became immediately incensed.

I switched on the camera again.

'Manuel, do you hold the crew of the *Berserk* free from blame in the event of your death?' Jarle asks.

'Yes, I do,' he answered curtly – immediately turning toward the camera and snapping: 'Is that OK, David?!?'

I switched off the camera. The interview – and whatever remained of our relationship – was over.

That night it was decided. The next day, we would return to the abandoned base and solve our problem once and for all. Jarle announced that when we managed to get close, I would take Manuel in the dinghy and set him ashore while he waited on the boat.

But again, Manuel balked. 'I don't think David should take me to shore,' he said. 'He and I will get into a fistfight.' He looked over at me snidely. Though it was the farthest thing from my mind, when he said it so awkwardly, it brought to mind the old wives' tale of the sailor calling up a storm, and it became a legitimate possibility.

That night we all went to sleep without saying a word.

When we awoke the next morning, Jarle announced that he had changed his mind after sleeping on his decision. He could not wilfully send a man to his death – and as captain had made the decision to keep Manuel on board until we could find another solution, another way to get him off the boat that would not require him to sacrifice his life.

Manuel, frustrated beyond belief, balked. But Jarle held firm: he was the captain – the decision was his. What happened to the boat and the crew was his responsibility. We all knew Manuel wanted to get off the boat, and we wanted him gone as much as he wanted to be. But he could not knowingly leave him on Melchior Island because, quite simply, he was likely to die there.

I stood by and listened silently, seething on the inside. My feelings toward Manuel had turned and I could feel the bloodlust inside me swelling up into my throat. All consideration had been given to Manuel: he had the warmest clothes, took more than his fair share of rations, drew shorter shifts, complained incessantly, stayed in his sleeping bag, and sucked all joy out of the ship. He had become a far cry from the jovial, smiling ventriloquist's dummy sitting on the park bench. I wanted to set him ashore and be rid of him once and for all, and by now, I frankly didn't give a damn what happened to him – and I said as much. Manuel's gaze cast daggers in my direction.

But Jarle held firm. Manuel would continue with us, and we would get him off the *Berserk* as soon as possible.

So onward we sailed, we unhappy three. Manuel curled up inside his sleeping bag and stayed there, emerging only to eat or smoke whatever cigarettes he could scrounge. Jarle and I stayed outside in the cockpit and guided the *Berserk* along her course.

Jarle and he had argued about cigarettes from the get-go. Jarle had brought along a couple of cartons of Marlboro reds to use as trade bait and Manuel knew it. As soon as he ran out of cigs of his own, he harangued Jarle to give him a pack or two. At first, the captain resisted firmly. 'You said you were going to stop,' he would respond. But Manuel remained persistent, like a bird pecking at a corn stalk, until finally the kind-hearted captain relinquished, gave in and tossed him a pack just to get him off his back.

As Jarle and I sailed the *Berserk* through narrow channels filled with ice and wildlife, I turned to him. 'Now I know why they used to slice the throats of pirates on pirate ships and toss them overboard,' I said quietly. We looked each other in the eyes and many more words remained unspoken as we sailed onward. The sad thing was, I meant it.

Things on the *Berserk* got worse before they got better. There were no more whale days, just lots of grumbling as ice slammed into the boat at every anchorage. Manuel let it be known that though he remained on the boat, he did so against his will – and therefore would not work. So, he stayed in his sleeping bag, day and night. For us it was easier to have him do so since at least he wasn't getting in the way, but whenever we really needed a third hand, Jarle would roust him with a rousing rendition of 'If you don't work, you don't eat.' Begrudgingly, Manuel would then join us to toss the anchor before silently creeping back into his sleeping bag to curl up with a dog-eared copy of Stephen King's *Needful Things* that he had found rotting on one of the shelves.

Meals were eaten in silence. The tight rations began to take their effect on Manuel. Occasionally Jarle would admonish both of us for putting too much topping on our bread, reminding us that our supplies would have to last us many more months. We would then all look at the others, each of us silently believing that we alone were getting the short end of the stick, believing that the other two were certainly getting more spread on their bread than we were.

Manuel would take a bite of bread and shut his eyes, as if he had just tasted nectar from Heaven, and he would chew slowly and surely, savouring every bite. We were allotted a ration of four or five breads in the morning; we could put whatever topping on it we wanted, provided it was used sparingly. By now, our choices had grown to include honey, cheese-spread from a toothpaste-like tube, and 'kaviar', a Scandinavian fish egg-spread also from a tube. We had plenty of powdered milk on board, and chocolate milk mix to add to it, but I preferred putting it in the always-welcome cup of coffee along with a spoonful of sugar. Before bed, we would always warm up with a hot drink, the water prepared in our single dented pan – and always flecked with the residue of pasta, onion, and rice – and we would drink heartily until the lukewarm water ran out. After pouring enough coffee with caffeine down my gullet to power the graveyard shift at a factory, I still managed to fall asleep right away – after the standard humorous and joyful pre-sleep ship's banter, followed by a trip or two up through the little pop-up hatch to heed nature's call and gaze in wonder at the splendour of the cool, metallic blue of the white Antarctic night.

But with Manuel's renewed mutiny, the banter fizzled, and all the joy of sleep along with it.

We endured our course, steadily making our way toward Port Lockroy, an old British whaling station with a large collection of giant beached bones that has become something of a stopping point for cruise ships and a playground for its passengers.

On the back of the *Berserk* Jarle had attached a small solar panel. The panel picked up the sunlight, converting it to energy which charged our batteries. But there simply was not that much sunlight in Antarctica, and we had to conserve our energy. So a couple of times a day, we would turn on our little radio and scan for chatter, to see if we could pick up some of the sporadic cruise ships or small sailing boats cruising Antarctic waters.

Manuel was desperate to contact the ship *Voyeu* – where the girl who had given him flowers was to be found. He was convinced that his French friends on board the ship would understand his plight and would take him home with them. 'We must find the *Voyeu*,' he would say repeatedly, like a mantra from his yoga book. The *Voyeu*, Manuel felt, was his last, best hope for escaping the doomed fate of the *Berserk*.

As Manuel's gloomy pallor descended over the boat, we made our way to a little bay near a place called Cuverville Island. As we rounded the corner and made our way into the calm little bay, lo and behold, we noticed another ship at anchor. It was yellow in colour and we all recognised it at once: the *Voyeu*.

Manuel instantly became giddy with glee upon finding they shared our harbour. He was beside himself, bouncing up and down like a joyous little kid. 'Hallo, hallo!' Jarle bellowed into the radio, refraining his by-now familiar friendly greeting. They quickly reached us by radio and invited us to join them the next morning for breakfast.

That night, we established a plan. We would enjoy the sumptuous warm meal we so eagerly desired, without so much as broaching the subject of Manuel's return whatsoever. But at the end of the meal, Jarle would bring up the subject of Manuel gingerly, like a firewalker on coals, springing it on them with the suddenness of a pouncing panther.

Until then, anxious Manuel would say nothing. He was convinced that here was his best opportunity. He knew the *Voyeu* was touring Antarctic waters, and he knew they were heading back soon. He was convinced that the woman who once gave him flowers would hold sway and persuade her boyfriend, the captain, to take her dear Argentinian friend home with them. They alone would understand his plight; they would seal his fate.

The next morning, the three of us stuffed into our little dinghy looking very much like the Three Stooges, laughing as we awkwardly rowed our way over to the nearby *Voyeu*, while the French captain snapped photos from the mast. The captain, his brother, and his American girlfriend greeted us with smiles and the delightful, wafting aromas of a warm egg breakfast and fresh real coffee.

After gobbling down the warm meal in the boat's plush heated galley on our best behaviour, Jarle mentioned over coffee that Manuel – who grinned coyly with delight throughout the meal – was having some difficulty handling the sea. Immediately the French captain shot back, cutting him off before he could finish his sentence: 'Yes, we have heard you have some problems – but unfortunately we cannot take Manuel back with us.' He had been laying in wait. And he had ended the debate emphatically, before it had even started.

Like a deflated helium balloon, all colour drained from Manuel's face and in an instant his smug smirk was gone. The woman batted her eyelashes apologetically as her French boyfriend explained that the camaraderie on the boat between the three of them balanced delicately, on a tightrope; adding a fourth would throw it off. They were still in the midst of their tour to boot and were planning to hit some of the northern Antarctic islands before turning for home. They had spoken to the Italian captain by radio, who told them that Manuel was looking for a way back. They were sorry, but they would not be able to take him with them.

'The balance of a crew is a delicate thing,' postulated the captain, 'and we can't take the chance of throwing ours off.'

They loaded up a box of goodies for us to take back to the *Berserk*, and watched as we hauled our kitty back to the boat. Later that morning, they lifted their anchor and set sail toward home without Manuel on board their ship.

Manuel, crushed, beyond hope, awakened to reality like a child discovering there is no Santa Claus, crawled into his sleeping bag and pulled it over his head. He vowed to stop eating – later on, he told us he was going on a hunger strike, though I'm not sure what point he was trying to prove. It didn't matter to me whether he ate or not. He determined that he would not lift another finger in the aid of the *Berserk*. For all intents and purposes, we now had a two-man crew – and a sackful of dead weight.

Manuel and I had long ago stopped speaking. But now, not even Jarle cared to speak to him. Manuel would no longer be allowed to taint our trip. We would continue on our adventure, with or without him.

Later that day, Jarle and I headed for shore to explore. We left Manuel behind, to 'guard' the boat. I was uncomfortable. 'Are you sure it's safe?' I asked Jarle as we paddled to shore. 'What can he do?' he answered.

I knew damn well what he could do, and had a pretty good idea he would be doing it. I was convinced that Manuel would raid our food supplies and gorge on our rations. He would quickly open a can of meat and stuff it down his throat as quickly as he could swallow, then toss the container overboard, disposing of the evidence. His hunger, his need for food, his sea madness, would overwhelm his basic sense of decency, and he would pollute the ecosystem, justifying it in the name of his own precious survival. He would scrape whatever rations he could from open containers, leaving not a crumb behind as evidence. His so-called hunger strike would continue, as much a façade as ever. And he would certainly pilfer for an extra pack of cigarettes as well.

But the threat to our immediate well-being did not stop there – the danger posed by Manuel ran much deeper. Without the ballast of reason, driven to extremes of desperation, Manuel was capable of much, much worse, and there was no telling what he might do. What if he decided to drill a hole in the bottom of the boat? If we had problems staying afloat, we would be forced to head for the nearest base – and this would be one way for him to ensure that we did. We had no idea just how far off the deep end he had really gone – and there were any number of ways for him to jeopardise our expedition, whether by taking his own life or even threatening both of ours. No possibility, however irrational to sober thought, was out of the question. His lack of reason had become potentially more combustible than our little kerosene stove ever would be.

So with one nervous eye always firmly cast toward the boat, Jarle and I landed ashore and set off in search of... in search of what? That was the real question. What were we actually looking for? We had spent so much time dealing with Manuel and trying to fix the engine that we seemed to have lost sight of why we were even there.

We clambered up onto shore, secured the dinghy and started to hike up the small hill in front of us, where an enormous penguin colony made its home. It was the largest penguin colony we would see the entire trip. There are lots of different types of penguins – but they basically all looked the same to me.

Jarle wanted to get some pictures and some video footage, so he brought along some accoutrements – and handed them to me. Of course, instead of carrying it, in prototypical lazy-sailor fashion I nonchalantly tossed the little plastic Viking helmet onto my head and walked around with it, like a Viking warrior of old.

We climbed through the mountainside colony as the little waddling birds whirred and chirped all around us, enjoying the spectacle. When we reached the high ground, we were suddenly attacked from above by large hawk-like birds known as skuas. We had inadvertently wandered into their nesting ground and they would protect their island at all costs. They dive-bombed precariously close to our heads; we were forced to cover our scalps with our forearms lest we lose a chunk of hair.

Soon, Jarle and I split up to explore on our own. I was wandering through the colony by myself when I looked below to check on the boat and noticed the spout of a whale moving left to right through our little harbour. The faint shape of the long, thin whale glided smoothly beneath the rippling water – accompanied by a little baby whale swimming closely by its mother's side. This whale appeared different than the others; likely a Southern Right whale. As it moved across my field of vision, I cupped my hands around my lips and called out to it, using my patented whale call. The two whales continued, and I called out again, the sound echoing across the lonely divide. Suddenly, the mother turned back and uttered its response with the trajectory of a large spout. It was listening! I called out again – and again it responded with a spout. It was playing with me! I called out yet again, only this time I varied the call, cutting the tone short and repeating it, like a truncated oral Morse code. The circling whale answered exactly in kind, with two short bursts from its spout, the sound of the spray carrying on the wind up to my position high in the hills.

For an hour we carried on like this, the playful whale far below in the grey mists of Antarctica, me above the penguin colony in the skua nesting area, calling out in a succession of tones while the whale below answered directly in kind, three blasts, four blasts, a short blast followed by a long, and on and on. We were communicating with each other; there were no two other creatures on earth. It understood me, and I it, and only God knows what its pup was thinking. Eventually the mother turned back and resumed its route, its course taking it around the corner and out past the island into the next bay as the two of us communicated our farewells.

After a great day on land, Jarle and I returned to the stony silence of Manuel on the *Berserk*, thankful to find the boat in one piece. Left with no choice, we would leave the next morning and continue our journey with Manuel begrudgingly on board.

We awoke the next day to find ourselves in the midst of a blizzard. Large chunks of soft snow dropped all around us, leaving the penguin colony draped in a chilly blanket of white icing. While we ate our customary stale, mouldy breakfast, Jarle turned on the VHF radio to briefly monitor for chatter. Only this time, to our surprise, we picked up the communication from a nearby cruise ship. Manuel's dull ears perked up like a vampire bat's as Jarle picked up the handset. 'Hallo, hallo!' he called out, identifying our boat with his familiar 'lima kilo' call-sign-followed-by-a-set-of-numbers refrain.

A voice on the other end responded as Manuel and I listened intently to the crackle of airwaves. Jarle spoke to the cruise director, a low-ranking officer on the ship. He explained who we were, what we were doing and that we had a problem: we had a seasick sailor on board who wanted to return to South America instead of continuing on with us to South Africa. The cruise director, a young man, hemmed and hawed, but ultimately admitted there were some empty berths on board the cruise ship, which was going to head back to Ushuaia in two days. They were available – but he would have to check on the price. Manuel became giddy and glassy-eyed while we endured the radio silence as the young voice sought out the authority to bring him on board the ship – and the cost. The excitement on his face became clearly evident; the spark of life returned momentarily behind his eyes.

After what seemed like an eternity in the galley, the voice crackled on the other end once again. The young man announced proudly that his cruise ship would indeed be able to take Manuel – his eyes alight – for the paltry sum of US$1,500. He explained that the ship still had two and a half more days visiting the Antarctica Peninsula, followed by a two-and-a-half-day crossing of the Drake Passage back to Argentina. Five days at $300 per day. Fifteen-hundred US dollars, price non-negotiable. It was the best they could do.

There was only one slight problem. Manuel did not have a cent left to his name.

Jarle signed off to discuss the matter with his crew. Immediately Manuel pleaded and cajoled. He tried every trick in the book: my mother will send you the money, I'll wire it to you, I promise I'll pay you back. Of course, Jarle had the cash stowed away in his precious metal case. But it was his entire nutbag and would wipe us out. He shook his head. He simply could not afford it. 'We will find another way,' he told us, turning back to the radio.

Tears formed in Manuel's desperate eyes, but it was a battle he could not win. He simply had no leverage, no cash. He sulked, lower lip quivering, as Jarle picked up the radio and rejected the offer apologetically.

The young man on the other end understood. 'There is another cruise ship due to arrive in the area later today,' he explained. 'Maybe you'll have better luck with them.'

Jarle thanked the man for his help and signed off. Manuel remained silent, an impenetrable brick wall, belligerent to the last. Eventually he crawled back into his sleeping bag and covered himself completely, defeated and abject.

Jarle looked at me. 'OK, let's get ready to go,' he said. We suited up thoroughly and walked up through the hatch into the blizzard, which had intensified. The thick flakes fell through the wind with greater density as he and I lifted the anchor and began hoisting the sails. We did not even try the engine, by now resigned to the fact that if it worked at all, it would require the Antarctic version of a sunny tropical day.

Slowly, in the midst of the blizzard, wind rippled through the sails and *Berserk* slowly turned and headed away from Cuverville Bay. Suddenly, Manuel leapt up through the hatch shrieking at the top of his lungs. 'What are you doing?' he screamed. 'Are you crazy?!? We're in the middle of a fucking blizzard!!'

Jarle told him to shut up and go below. 'Didn't you hear him? There's another boat coming!!' he wailed. 'We have to wait!!!' But both Jarle and I thought it would be ridiculous to wait for anything; there were no schedules in the Antarctic. Manuel had sabotaged our adventure long enough. There was no more room for negotiation.

'You can't see anything!! It's a blizzard!!!!' he shrieked.

Jarle answered calmly. 'Manuel, you do not do any work – so you do not have any say in where we go.' In our opinion, he was lucky to still be eating on board. He had long ago refused to lift a finger as a working crewmember on the boat, leaving Jarle and I a virtual two-man crew.

'You're both fucking crazy!!' he caterwauled at the top of his lungs, practically in tears as he begrudgingly crawled back inside once again, slamming the hatch down behind him.

The snow speared down at a severe angle as the blizzard intensified. Jarle and I sailed the boat along Cuverville, persevering through the ice until the island ended and the passage dog-legged to the right between a series of significant mountain peaks. The sailing proved time-consuming and difficult, our course necessarily angular to take advantage of the sparse wind.

After a few hours of sailing, suddenly and without warning, all traces of the wind died completely. The *Berserk* stopped amidst the ice, frozen in its tracks.

'Get out the oars,' Jarle called to me. I fished the dinghy's wood oars from beneath the debris in the hatch and walked out to the bow to row as if the *Berserk* were an overgrown, fibreglass canoe. I had to lean over the edge and dip the oar as deep as possible, and still, even utilising all my strength, the boat barely moved. But due to the ice and lack of discernible current, it proved the only manoeuvre possible.

My forearms grew heavy and tired, my biceps aching dully in the cold. I wanted to stop before I started. I seethed inside, hating Manuel, whose lazy ass was wrapped warmly in his sleeping bag cocoon while I plunged the oar into the water time and again like a galley slave straight out of *Ben Hur*.

Jarle tried the engine, but it did not start, would not start, and eventually, frustrated, he tossed his hands in the air and gave up. With nothing else to do, he turned on the radio, at Manuel's behest, and sent out the 'limo kilo' identity signal to see if he could attract any boats.

'Go ahead, lima kilo,' came the response, surprising us all. I walked back toward the stern to row and listen to the conversation at the same time. The speaker identified the ship as the *Disko*, a Danish cruise ship operating for the southern-hemisphere summer out of Argentina.

'This is the *Berserk*,' Jarle answered. He explained our situation. 'We have a seasick sailor on board. We are going on to South Africa, and he is looking for a way to go back to Ushuaia.'

The voice on the other end responded: 'Wait a moment.'

Down through the hatch, Manuel began to stir; his eyes popped open.

'This is the captain of the *Disko*,' the radio rang out.

Jarle identified himself.

'Yes, we have heard about you.' The captain's Danish accent came through loud and clear. By now, Manuel sat bolt upright.

'We have a seasick sailor on board. We are going on to South Africa, and he is looking for a way to go back to Argentina.'

'We will take him.'

All sound stopped. We were frozen in time. Manuel's eyes popped open wider than the Grand Canyon. I ceased rowing completely and leaned in further.

Jarle raised his eyebrows and clicked the handset. 'For free?'

An eternity as we waited expectantly.

'Yes, for free.'

At that moment all of our hearts skipped a beat. On every face, through the stoic mask of cold, crept a clear-cut smile.

'We are leaving here at exactly four o'clock,' the Danish captain continued. 'If you have him on board by then, we will take him with us.'

'Where are you?' Jarle asked, but all of us already knew the answer.

'Cuverville Island.'

As Jarle signed off, I looked down at my watch: it was already well after noon. We had been sailing for over four hours, through a wicked blizzard. The wind had been at our backs until it died completely. Now we were ensconced in the sort of bathwater calm normally found in the Sargasso Sea or the Bermuda Triangle. We would have to turn around completely and head back the way we had just come, only this time with the wind, if any, directly in our faces.

'Manuel, get your ass up here and start rowing!' Jarle called out, leaping out of the hatch and taking the tiller as I turned the boat around slowly with the oar.

The clock was ticking and inside all of us felt a sense of complete panic. Finally, Manuel emerged and took hold of an oar. But the work was difficult and hurt the muscles through the cold, and after a few meagre strokes, he tired of it.

Meanwhile, I stood on the bow and rowed as if my life depended on it. I looked over at Manuel; he barely dipped his oar in the water. He might as well have been dipping a teabag, sitting down for parlour games and butter biscuits. My frustration mounted. I rowed harder in anger. The boat began to turn away from the direction of my oar stroke, toward Manuel's side. Biting my lip to suppress the anger, I ran to the other side and kept up the pace next to Manuel. 'Come on, damn it, row!' I shouted. I wanted to toss him overboard. Daggers darted in my direction from Manuel's bloodshot eyes.

In the cockpit, Jarle, sensing the desperation of our situation, had begun to take apart the engine. 'Manuel, we want you off the boat as much as you want to get off,' he called out. 'So if you want off, you will row.' His admonition did no good. After less than a half hour of jockeying back and forth across the bow, plunging my oar desperately into the water, I ceased, sweating profusely in the snowstorm. Manuel had long ago given up even the gesture of helping us out. We were being teased by Mother Nature, a cruel trick of fate laid directly in our laps – so close, yet so far. We had found a solution to our problem, but we would never get the chance to experience it. We would be stuck with Manuel forever. A profound sense of complete and utter hopelessness overwhelmed me.

Jarle yanked the rusty spark plugs out of the engine. He had developed a method of 'cooking' them by heating them in the flame of our kerosene kitchen stove. Using needle nose pliers, he would lay them down directly over the blue flame, heating the steel plugs until they turned branding orange. Then, using gloves as makeshift potholders, he would yank them out of the fire and snap them directly back into the top of the cherished little two-stroke 7.5 HP Suzuki lawnmower engine given to him by his grandfather, immediately yank the starter cord and hope that the molten contact points would create enough of a spark to catch.

Early on, in our first experiments with the dead engine, this method had sporadically provided enough spark to start the engine – but only in direct sunlight, and rarely at that. The method had failed so often that it had come to be completely disregarded in all but the most dire of situations. Even at that, the method proved futile at such a significant rate that Jarle had stopped using it altogether. In the dark, grey afternoon mist of that blizzard, the odds against us would be astronomical.

But desperate times call for drastic measures – and for us, this was the most desperate of times. While Manuel and I bickered silently on the bow, reaching a complete spiritual impasse, Jarle heated the spark plugs again and again and again, to no avail. Without wind, we were left with no other alternative, and each began to silently resign ourselves to a doomed fate together.

I wish I could tell you that suddenly a strong gust of wind blew up from behind and filled our sails magically, coursing us back directly to our little Cuverville Bay, that the blizzard stopped and the sun came out and warmed not only ourselves but our little engine, giving it the spark it needed to kick in. But this is the Antarctic, where many a better man than I has fallen prey to the vagaries of Nature, and in the depths of our souls rang out the despair befallen their lot as we were seemingly destined to join their coterie.

Futility set in. Manuel simply stopped rowing and sat looking out at the snow. I joined him and exhaled, blowing the most recent icy snowflakes from my beard and moustache, gazing out at the pristine mountains and calming my sweaty self with the clean cool air of the South. Game over.

Suddenly, a click. A repeating click. Ears perked first, we turned; eyes perked next. For a moment, the engine had caught. Jarle ripped the spark plugs out and heated them again, snapped them back in immediately. Like holding the winning lottery ticket, that little engine started – and Jarle kicked it into gear immediately. We couldn't believe it, but nor did we question our fortune. The *Berserk* cut through the calm water, avoiding the ice and cutting her way on a direct course back to Cuverville.

To this day, we refer to that moment and the trip back in one precise, profound way: we call it simply 'The Miracle of Cuverville Island'.

Shortly before four, we rounded the corner and sighted through the snowy haze a vague outline of the large red cruise ship *Disko* anchored outside Cuverville Island. Almost immediately, as if dictated by Fate, the little engine stopped and would not start again. By then we weren't complaining. Jarle bellowed the command and we raised our sails valiantly.

A crowd of tourists gathered on the deck of the cruise ship, bundled in their bright, out-of-place tourist clothes against the cold. We cut a starboard tack and then pitched back to the left, swooping smoothly, gliding serenely to a perfect stop on the starboard side of the huge ship, sweaty and relieved that we had indeed arrived in the nick of time.

We fastened our lines firmly, secured the *Berserk* against the side of the bobbing monster, and looked up against the wall of looming red steel to see a rope ladder unfurl from the topside like something out of a movie.

Manuel couldn't wait; he immediately grabbed hold and scampered up the ladder, first off the boat. The *Berserk* secure, I grabbed hold and climbed up into a wild throng of flash bulbs and excited old tourists, who gaped in awe as I set foot on deck looking every bit the vintage Antarctic explorer, with full icicle-laden beard and patched yellow wetgear. I felt a bit like a zoo animal. Jarle joined us on deck and there were smiles all around as we shook hands with the crew.

'How would you like a hot shower?' the baby-faced purser asked. A hot shower?!? How long had it been since we'd had any shower at all?? I couldn't remember.

The crowd gasped and opened like the parting of the Red Sea, giving us passage to a door leading into a plush, heated, humid interior. He led us through the cavernous, carpeted hallways to a little steel door and a public crew shower, where we were handed clean white bath towels, fresh bars of deodorant soap, and small containers of shampoo (thankfully, the crowd did not follow). 'I'll be back in a few minutes and we'll get you something to eat.' We peeled off our soaking clothes – we had been wearing them for at least a month steady – and climbed into the hot, steamy spray. It felt like a dream. My eyes reflexively began to tear.

As we showered, the three of us, Manuel, Jarle and myself, laughed and joked and splashed amongst ourselves like happy kids at the neighbourhood pool. We were back at the beginning, all ills forgotten. If indeed we were in a film, this would have been the part with the rousing, rising musical score and the cheesy slow motion.

I could have stayed in the reverie of that shower forever. I could actually feel the entirety of my body thawing out beneath the wave of warmth. Suddenly, I knew what the Ice Man must have felt like when his block wedge of blue ice thawed him back into civilisation. I wiggled my numb toes in the run-off above the drain, soaking as much feeling into them as possible, in a desperate race against time before having to put my heartless rubber boots back on.

'How would you like something to eat?' the purser asked, returning to pick us up as we wrapped ourselves back up in our soggy gear.

Manuel and I both grinned. But Jarle had other ideas. 'Can I talk to your chief engineer?' he asked. 'We are having some problems with our engine.'

Jarle walked off to see the ship's chief engineer. Manuel and I were led into the crew's galley and handed off to a burly ship's cook in a paper hat.

'What would you like?' the burly cook asked. We were speechless. 'How does fried chicken and chips sound?' he added.

I beamed. 'That would be great,' I answered.

'Make yourselves at home and it'll be ready in a few minutes.'

The cook walked back into the kitchen to whip up our order while Manuel and I plunked ourselves down into the warm, padded kitchen chairs of the working crew's small yet comfortable pink galley. The area was sparsely populated with a few scattered Indonesian and Filipino room-service busboys and waiters kicking it on their afternoon break. One of them walked over, friendly and inquisitive. Manuel immediately bummed a cigarette off of him and lit it up; his face contorted, all heaviness lifted, and for a brief instant an observer might have believed he was in the process of reaching enlightenment one puff at a time.

'Have a dessert,' our new friend said, pointing to the counter where eight leftover bowls awaited. Inside the bowls stood the most delicious concoction ever devised by man: a graham cracker-crusted sweet cake immersed in thick creamy vanilla custard and topped with a maraschino cherry. You could almost hear the angels singing just looking at it. Manuel ate his spoonfuls between puffs of smoke; I devoured my first one in its entirety and headed straight for the second. After gobbling down my share rapaciously, I turned toward a smug Manuel.

'Do you mind if I keep eating?' I asked.

Manuel smiled, amused. 'No, go ahead,' he answered, well aware that he would be eating like this for the next few days. I downed the remaining five bowls one after the other without blinking like they were served up on a conveyor belt – and then the big cook with the paper hat walked out with two heaping steaming aromatic platefuls of golden fried chicken piled high on a mountain of savoury crispy chips, setting the delicacies gently down in front of us. I didn't know whether to cry or bury my head into the chips like an ostrich and go to sleep.

We became friends again, Manuel and I, as we savoured each bite of that sumptuous meal, reawakening our taste buds to the sensational delights of cuisine after a month of green bread and spaghetti with onion. As we ate, a crewmember with an apron – a bespectacled waiter from the dining room – burst into the galley with a little disposable camera and excitedly began snapping pictures of us. He was ebullient, giddy with delight – like a country cousin who heads to Hollywood for the first time and stumbles into Tom Hanks eating lunch at Denny's.

'I just had to see the craziest motherfuckers on the ocean,' he gushed, snapping away. 'You guys are legends.'

Legends? I was astonished. How did this guy even know about us? I asked him.

'A guy named Boris told us to watch out for you,' he answered with a smile. 'He worked as a dishwasher on our last voyage.' Boris – the toothless Russian-Spaniard who drove the camper van, who had first pointed out the looming mast of the *Berserk* in the dark harbour of Ushuaia – the guy who said we were going to die – had worked as a dishwasher in a windowless dungeon below deck, scrubbing suds with rubber gloves for eight hours at a pop in exchange for five brief days in the Antarctic, the bulk of which were spent scraping somebody else's scrambled eggs into the sink.

'Did he ever make it to shore?' I asked.

'I think he got onto one of the rafts once,' our new friend answered. 'I think so.'

He shook his head again and laughed. 'You guys are crazy!'

'As my captain says: crazy – but not stupid.' I smiled.

Our friend pointed out that in the galley, tables and chairs were nailed to the floor, and ropes abounded so they had something to hold when things got rough. When crossing the Drake, the nearly 300-foot *Disko* had often been racked to a 45-degree angle by mountainous seas that crashed over its looming deck; during such storms, it became necessary to batten down the hatches and secure everything that moved. 'I can't believe you guys came across the Drake in that,' he guffawed, invoking the spirit of Boris yet again.

So good ol' Boris had outlasted the waiting list after all – and had made it to Antarctica. Good for him. Now, Manuel would head back the same way, scrubbing pots and pans with steel wool and peeling potatoes in lieu of payment for a ticket. He would certainly complain – but no longer would it be our problem.

Jarle rejoined us briefly for a bit of chicken but rose up again almost immediately. 'I must go check on the engine,' he said. 'David, be ready to go in a few minutes.' He walked out, leaving Manuel and me to enjoy our hot coffee.

For a moment, Manuel and I were alone. He looked up at me, his soulful brown eyes reflecting genuine and sincere compassion and concern. He spoke softly.

'David, you cannot tell me that you are not thinking of getting off the boat.' His eyes prodded silently for an answer.

It was one of those moments that span time. I delved deeply into my own thoughts. What was I thinking? Thoughts ran rampant. I had just soaked in a hot shower and for the first time in months felt warm. The inside of my stomach was coated with cream custard, coffee and chicken – a mere snack compared to what lay before Manuel. Heat bellowed from the vents; no stinging, whipping rain pelted my face, the absence of pain euphoria in itself. Momentarily dry, I could sense feeling creeping, crawling, slowly re-emerging back into my toes, certainly a pleasing alternative to the incipient frostbite which must inevitably come next. The comfortable cruise ship, replete with dry bunks, sheets, and blankets, would soon chug northward toward the sun.

On the other hand, what lay ahead for us on the *Berserk*? Without Manuel, we would be two. That would mean I would be forced by necessity to undertake not only all of my own responsibilities, but Manuel's as well. Not only would I still row the dinghy to shore, I would also be forced to heave and lift the anchor, wash all the dishes, clean the galley, and, of course, in the tradition of all great sailors, swab the deck. And that did not include the gruelling sailing duties: raising and lowering the sails, taking the tiller while Jarle made adjustments, the constant sleep-depriving up-and-down to fend off the icebergs – and round-the-clock three-hour shifts without respite. To reach our final destination of Capetown, we would need two weeks to sail to South Georgia – followed by at least another four to reach South Africa. The final leg would consist of at least a month at sea, three hours on, three hours off, for what would feel like an eternity. As soon as I stepped onto the deck of the *Disko* again, cold would begin to creep back into my bones, hovering around like one of the great southern seabirds on the wind, threatening to leave behind a chill that would remain for a lifetime to haunt me. Without a third person, suddenly the task seemed extraordinarily daunting.

And then, in that very same instant, I thought of Jarle. Only 21 years old, he had already accomplished more than many would in a lifetime. He might very well be a world-class sailor, but I didn't care what he said. There was no way he could do this alone – certainly not if he wanted to enjoy any of it. It would simply be too brutal and devastating, each manoeuvre more stressful and agonising than the last but not quite as overwhelming as the next.

Without my help and companionship, he would be left completely alone to withstand the harshest of elements in the most severe region in the world, victim of a scurrilous, mutinous crew – just like Captain Bligh. A month across the South Atlantic alone might very well drive him mad. Tough as he was, he could not help but become embittered; the deep scar would last a lifetime, even if it lingered well below the surface. And if something happened and he died, it went without saying: I would never forgive myself.

But the plain fact of the matter remained: all else said and done, I simply still wanted to see Antarctica, as badly as I ever had. My enthusiasm had not wavered a bit.

'David, you cannot tell me you are not thinking of getting off the boat.'

The nanosecond ended. I looked Manuel dead in the eyes and spoke matter-of-factly: 'Not for a single instant.'

The purser came back into the galley. 'Your captain wants you to go back to the ship,' he announced. 'We're getting ready to leave.'

I stood and picked up my hat and neck sock.

'We brought you some things from the kitchen,' the purser announced, handing me a big box full of goodies: instant milk, Milo nutritional drink mix, Kaviar, cheese spread, tubes of flavourful meat topping, bottles of red wine. The welcome ritual had by now become rote, but we never tired of it.

I followed the purser, carrying the box through the dining room, where well-dressed, freshly-shaven tourists had begun to gather at tables for an early supper. They began to whisper and murmur amongst themselves, taking in the spectacle of the odd, wizened Antarctic sailor ambling awkwardly down the middle of the banquet hall in full cold-weather wetgear.

Back down on the *Berserk*, Jarle, Manuel and I gathered in our little, damp, freezing-cold galley and poured ourselves three shots of spiced rum.

Manuel lifted his glass. 'Godspeed to the *Berserk*!'

We clinked our cups and drank. We stood as Manuel prepared to leave.

'Manuel,' I said, 'if you're getting off, you're leaving your underwear.'

He darted me his dagger gaze – then slowly began to strip, tossing the precious home-made wool long johns onto his bunk.

In a flash he was gone, standing on deck on the *Disko* as the ladder furled upward once again. The matter of the engine still unresolved – the chief engineer had been unable to solve its bizarre riddle, claiming that the adverse conditions were likely to blame – we cast off under sail from the side of the looming cruise ship.

'David – put on your Viking helmet!' Jarle called out. We both put on our plastic horned helmets and stood out in the cockpit, raising our arms victoriously as the gathered crowd once again snapped our photos, flash after flash, while Manuel stood happily on the deck, leaning over the rail and grinning from ear to ear.

A few minutes later the *Disko* pulled up her giant anchor and began her long trek north toward home with a deliriously happy Manuel on board. As she turned to leave sight, her

Danish captain uttered the command – and two loud peals of the foghorn echoed over the mountaintops, an homage, one single blast each in honour of the two remaining crewmembers of the *Berserk*. With her, she took the third one home.

It was the last I ever saw of him.

CHAPTER EIGHT

"Berserk"

ANTARCTICA II: SNIFFING OUT THE WIND

Without the luxury of a nearby dry cleaners, I had been wearing Manuel's filthy wool underwear all day, and for the first time all trip my buns were warm – as if I had spent nearly a whole game sitting on a rigid aluminium bench when suddenly a hot cheerleader had slid an oven-warmed seat cushion beneath my butt, smiled and batted her eyelashes at me. Manuel also left behind his green Chilean jumpsuit and his watertight black rubber boots, items immediately introduced into the rotation with great glee.

We had been ceremoniously unencumbered of our very own lead albatross that had been destined – seemingly pre-ordained – to bring us down, and now our glorious adventure was only just beginning. We found ourselves awhirl in a bewildering beauty and splendour one could only drink in one pastel at a time, one spot more beautiful than the next.

We spent our first night without Manuel in our old Cuverville anchorage, too wiped out physically and emotionally to move any further. Excited beyond belief, we fell asleep playing a game of one-upmanship with the phrase 'I hate Manuel' the lead-in. The next day, we retraced our steps, this time without the pleasure of blizzard, and wound up the next night by ourselves in a secluded, walled cove on the night of a full moon, as if Mother Nature herself was rewarding us for our penance.

Late in the evening I popped out of the bow hatch to take care of business. I hung my bare bottom over the rail, looking up at the icy canyon walls as they calved and avalanched around me, the cold quiet of the gorgeous canyon ringing in my ears. A shrill snort broke the still silence. Swimming amidst the ice chunks, two eyes and a whiskery snout peered up furtively, watching my every move – and quite obviously seeing something it had never seen before. A bit abashed, I was delighted for our new friend and immediately dubbed him, due to his serendipitous fortune, 'Lucky'. Lucky swam around the boat all the thankfully calm night, snorting and keeping us company as the moon cast its glow over the blue dim eternal dusk. This was the world into which we had been cast, only a day after Manuel's departure.

Antarctica, the world's largest desert, far from being desolate, teems with life – both natural and unnatural. The world's war for wealth found its way to the free continent, as we all knew eventually it would, and here the powers of the world, past, present and yet-to-be, sent their minions and scientists further and further south in the name of peace and prosperity, leapfrogging each other and staking claim to whatever parcel of glacial ground they could lay their hands on.

We had been forewarned: people who go to Antarctica are strange. We were about to begin running into them. Then again, they were about to run into us.

BERSERK IN THE ANTARCTIC

The Chilean base sat at the end of a long peninsula off the Antarctic mainland, situated at the mouth of a wide bay that proved to be a gathering point and a rapid water funnel for large blue chunks of broken-off glacial ice that would move en masse in and out, depending on the tide. It being a shallow anchorage, we were forced to tie up to a large boulder situated near the edge of the water. Unbeknownst to us, we arrived at the dearth of an extremely low tide – it never receded to that low level again during our stay.

We rowed the dinghy ashore and were greeted with smiles and handshakes all around. The Commandant, a bulky, full-haired, cigar-smoking loudmouth, brash and arrogant with a heart as big as his smile, and a resemblance to Jackie Gleason as well as quite a Napoleon complex, immediately welcomed us with open arms and invited us to join them for dinner.

When we returned later that afternoon for supper, Jarle carried with him an uncracked bottle of Chivas Regal, knowing that such a fine whiskey is hard to come by in such a remote station. He presented the pristine bottle to the pleased Commandant, who ushered us in to join the eleven members of his outpost regiment at a long banquet table in their dining room, which had been arranged with what appeared to be their finest china and cloth napkins. As was rapidly becoming our tradition, we joined the party in the same musty clothes we had been wearing for two months straight.

Throughout the meal, the entire complement was waited upon hand and foot by a well-dressed, stuck-up maitre-d', whose sole responsibility seemed to be to cater to every one of the Commandant's whims. The Commandant sat at the head of his table and bellowed out his jokes, feeling an immediate kinship with the other commandant sitting right next to him: Jarle, the boy captain of his own ship, his own private empire. They were like warlords over the spoils. But Jarle's fiefdom was only one; I, his only loyal subject.

On that base, the Commandant lorded supreme. His right hand man – his hatchet man – was a young guy too, also in his thirties, with straight black hair greasily combed to the side and a thin black moustache. He seemed to be the brains of the bunch, intelligent and friendly. The next day we found him wearing pink spandex and hustling in place doing jazzercise to the strains of tinny disco blaring from a small boom box in the base's cramped, humid workout room while a female penguin counter pedalled furiously on a stationery bike nearby.

We were exceptionally grateful to discover that two of the base's residents were female – two Chilean women who had been sent down from their university in Santiago to work as penguin counters. During the summer months, they would undertake a census of the enormous penguin colony based just on the other side of the encampment.

When the wind kicked up the wrong way, it blew the cold pink essence of penguin across the ice and over the encampment itself, the very borders of the colony spilling onto the outskirts of the base, so that it always smelled of the colony's fishy aroma. The women – one tall and thin, the other short and squat – walked out every day into the colony like C3PO and R2D2, where they spent eight hours straight counting the penguins one head at a time, mountain by mountain, nest by nest, day after day. Immediately I thought we had a chance with them, if for no other reason than for a variation in routine.

One afternoon, while walking on the outskirts of the colony, a young adult penguin waddled along with its eye dangling out on a cord. Blind and in agony, it bleated helplessly as the hawkish skuas made bombing runs one after the other, ripping the eye further and further out piece by piece, chunk by chunk. I was overwhelmed with sadness for the poor bird and wanted to fend them off, to save it from its inevitable doom. But I knew in my heart: I could do nothing. I turned away. It was against all rules to interfere, stood against all Laws of Nature. Thus existed the cycle of life in the Antarctic, an event witnessed hour after hour, day after day, by these fresh, young, smiling faces. How could they do it?

That night, flush after a good meal and wrapped in my faithful sleeping bag, I tried in vain to describe to Jarle the truly vintage American concept of Ginger and Mary Ann – the two women from the classic sixties television show *Gilligan's Island*, a show by now passing into the distant recesses of pop-cultural memory but to this very day an oh-so-relevant, primal breakdown of the appealing essence of woman: one, Ginger, the voluptuous va-va-va-voom sex-bomb actress, the red-lipped, swinging-hipped, painted seductress; the other, Mary Ann, the pigtail-wearin' farm girl in jeans, nice to the core with the most pleasant of smiles; both, desirable beyond belief. He had never heard of the show and had absolutely no idea what the hell I was taking about. I tried to tell him about how the Skipper and Gilligan and the rest had set off on a three-hour tour but had been sidetracked by a hurricane and marooned on a desert island with a millionaire, a whacked-out professor and these two hot babes. To no avail. Eventually, I gave up trying; he would simply have to see the show someday. Then he would get it. Here we were deep in the Antarctic and all we could think about was *Gilligan's Island*. Yet, when out at sea, a man is likely to contemplate such things – they strike without warning – and since we were living out our boyhood fantasies, we were no different.

The next day, I was sent ashore to pick up my favourite Chilean: Mr Spock, the base's engineer. Jarle had invited him aboard so the two could discuss the little engine that couldn't.

ANTARCTICA II: SNIFFING OUT THE WIND

Mr Spock, an affable man from the south of Chile, had a leathery, tan face etched with deep weathered lines, as if chiselled by a woodworker, along with quite the pocked proboscis. I loved the man immediately. He was one of those guys that emanate humanity with every word, your favourite uncle, the guy puttering in the barn, whistling and even-keeled. As engineer, he was responsible for every technical aspect of keeping the base running, surely he would solve our dilemma.

He ambled on board, and I stuck around to translate. The two poked and prodded around the engine, hypothesised, discussed, yanked the thing apart. Mr Spock held the engine's pieces up to the sky and studied them, squinting to focus in the haze. They talked about bad gas, they argued about the spark plugs, they debated the coil, but they still could not get it to work. Eventually Mr Spock shrugged and I rowed him back to shore.

For the entire length of our stay, I was Mr Spock's personal chauffeur, ferrying him back and forth from the shore to the *Berserk*. He always brought a smile to my face. Every time I rowed him back to shore, Mr Spock said to me, with great resignation and sorrow, 'The engine is old; its time is done.'

After setting him ashore, I would return to the *Berserk*, and Jarle would always say the same thing: 'He doesn't have any idea what the hell he's talking about.'

The next day, Jarle and I were invited to participate in a mysterious, special ceremony with the Chileans. Shrouded in secrecy, we gathered in a large group on their rubber Zodiac and set off, kicking the high-powered outboard into high gear, holding fast to the outer ropes and bracing against the friction of the wind. All available hands joined us including Mr Spock, the jazzercise first officer with the moustache, and, of course, the Commandant, but unfortunately the penguin counters couldn't make it, because they were out counting penguins.

We sped along the choppy inlets for about half an hour, until we found ourselves surrounded by glaciers and mountains in the centre of a beautiful bay. Suddenly, the driver cut the engine. The dinghy bobbed, the water choppy, as the group broke out a bag of plastic cups and started handing them out. Jazzercise leaned over the edge and used an oar to drag a big growler of light blue ice over toward us, and hacked a chunk out with his Rambo knife, hauling it on board and breaking off little pieces, filling the cups.

'We have a tradition,' the Commandant announced proudly. 'We share a special drink together with the same ice, and we become Antarctic brothers.'

He pulled Jarle's bottle of donated Chivas. 'We already had this bottle before you came,' he demurred, cracking the seal and filling all of our glasses. I chuckled to myself. The tradition began right then and there.

We lifted them all high. '*Salud!*' Down the hatch they went.

On the cold, bouncy ride back, Jazzercise told of us of their earlier comrades who had gone down on the very spot we drank. The story began a pattern that would repeat itself throughout our trip: unimaginable tales of horrific fate, resulting in tragic death again and again and again. We would hear about them or come across their memorial markers or cairns constantly, small piles of rocks with a hand-carved nameplate at the top. They could pop up anywhere, like crosses on the side of the road, the nationalities of the names emblematic of the wide swathe of explorers who had conquered the land. In this case, their comrades' raft had hit a chunk of ice and popped on the spot, dropping them down into the icy water. Within minutes they were dead.

From then on, it became more apparent: Death became our constant companion throughout the trip, hovering over us, around us, within us. But we always seemed to be one step ahead, ushered along by an even stronger ally: Life.

I dreaded leaving the Chilean base, not because of our newfound friends, not because we had received such grand hospitality, not because they gave us two heaping boxes of supplies to take with us, but because the tide never dropped to a level at which the rope securing us to our boulder could be properly removed. Jarle adamantly refused to leave the rope for the Chileans, claiming we would need it when things got rough. I would simply have to jump into the chest-high water, lean down and untie us. As soon as we were free, I would hop back on board and immediately change all of my clothes before hypothermia set in as Jarle sailed us toward our next destination.

The instant I jumped into the water, I felt a stinging in my nerves like I had whacked my funny bone smack into the corner of a table. Immobilising paralysis shot throughout my body like an electric current of needles, straight to the bottoms of my feet and to the side of my neck. The reaction time of my limbs instantly dropped in speed like an automatic transmission downshifting toward neutral.

The Chileans who had gathered on shore to wave goodbye gasped audibly and the tall Chilean penguin counter clasped her hands up to her face as I leaned my cheeks down into the ice water and reached out desperately toward the knot. I stretched to my limit; it felt like a meat clever cut into my neck. I could not reach.

I leaned back up. Time was running out. There was no choice: I had to go completely under. I took a breath and submerged myself, grabbing the knot and starting to work it out with my numb fingers. After going under three times, I finally managed to free us.

Overwhelmed by numbness like a mummy swathed in bandages, I groped for the nearby boat and clambered back on board. The Chileans called out and waved goodbye, but I was too cold to care. I jumped down through the hatch and tore off the soaking gear, waiting for the accompanying warmth of the new wool. By the time I re-emerged, they were gone.

On a day destined to be ruled by clouds, a low wet mist hung over the water, occasionally broken by snow flurries. We were making our way slowly to Port Lockroy, the old British whaling station, and hoped to be there by 'nightfall', which occurred around midnight. Dodging large chunks of ice had become the norm; hitting a piece was never a pleasant feeling. Echoes lingered constantly. The reliability and sturdiness of the fibreglass remained to be seen. Each chunk of ice we hit could easily be our last.

Conditions worsened as we headed south and before long we noticed a thick, white obstacle across our path: our first major ice belt. We were having problems with the wind and the ice was getting thicker and thicker; with our useless engine, we were at the mercy of the elements.

Avoiding all the ice became impossible, and the further south we travelled, the thicker it became. Complete concentration was required for long stretches at a time, and with only two of us onboard, we had few respites. Whenever I inevitably hit the ice, Jarle would become annoyed, tell me to 'watch out' and be more careful, making matters worse until I simply preferred not to steer in the ice – an option completely out of the question.

Jarle read the charts, took readings and navigated, while I held the tiller firm. Up ahead through the clearing mist, a line of ice stretched directly across our path. We had become accustomed to the minefields of ice dotting the waterways, but here, blockading our route, floated our first serious ice belt. And we had no choice: we had to plow straight through it.

With the wind at our backs, Jarle took the tiller and I stood on the bow, calling back the location of the ice as snow fell around us. Hitting each chunk of ice rattled the hull and reverberated loudly below deck like the rapid bongo beating of a timpani drum. We rammed the belt at full speed; chunks of ice scraped the bottom of the boat, raising us up out of the water nose-first. At any moment, one wrong turn directly into a chunk and we would be stuck. The thick belt taxed our nerves dearly and I stood on the bow, trying to shove the chunks out of the way with a large, thick wooden plank. With great consternation, we plunged through the 50-foot barrier like a tanker rumbling over an unpaved stretch of rough road, rocking the entire time like the rattling victim of a great earthquake.

Breathing a huge sigh of relief once we reached the other side, we resumed our course. But then, suddenly and without warning, in the dead calm still of afternoon, all wind simply ceased as the snow and foggy mist thickened. The afternoon sky took on the dark grey hue of storm and an early nightfall rapidly encroached. The *Berserk* waffled aimlessly, at the mercy of the Fates, and the current began to push us back toward the thickening ice belt, now curling around slightly to encircle us.

We were crossing in the middle of a strait far from land and my heart began to pound heavily with the dawning realisation that without wind, we would not only be stuck adrift for the night, but that we were being sucked quickly right back toward that thick belt of ice that we had only narrowly escaped an hour earlier.

Jarle calculated our position with the charts and tried desperately to start the engine, to no avail. Eventually, he dropped the sails and we floated backwards toward the belt. I tried to keep the tiller steady and to point our nose toward our destination, but without wind we might as well have been caught in a whirlpool. Suddenly, that great vortex in

Poe's 'Descent into the Maelstrom' made a bit more sense. I might not have to bother dyeing my hair at all. Nature might take care of it for me.

We drifted back toward the ice as the storm shrouded the sky, making it even darker. The cold smell of ice from the belt tickled our noses as it came closer. Jarle's plan was to crash back into the ice – that was beyond our control. Once there, we would safely ensconce ourselves within the pack, maybe even rope ourselves to a big chunk, and ride with it for the night, until morning light gave us enough leeway to try for the wind once again.

Jarle and I took turns climbing the mast, scanning the horizon for chop in the water that signifies wind, but we found nothing but placid water. We were becoming increasingly resigned to an unpleasant evening.

The prospect of spending the night in the ice horrified me. A normal night's watch required constant up-and-down to fight off the ice; tonight would be the same, only without the up-and-down. We would have to stay up through the night to fight for our survival. I had no idea where we would wind up the next morning – but I knew damn well that wherever it was, it would be uncomfortable.

But then something happened. Jarle was down below reading the charts and I sat at the tiller, watching our course, when I felt a slight tickle on the tip of my nose. 'Jarle,' I called out to him, 'I think I smell the wind.'

He poked his head out of the hatch, dubious. The air remained still. 'Do you want me to raise the jib?' he asked.

Jarle was always game to put up or pull down the sails. For him, it was second nature, like tying a shoelace. He was a true blue sailor through and through; he loved sailing, the art of capturing the wind, lassoing it like some kind of wild stallion, and riding it toward destiny. It was his great passion in life, like music to Mozart, and flowed through his veins in place of blood. Without doubt he was a prodigy, gifted in the art of the sea; it did not take a seasoned sailor to see it. What others seemed to question, however, were his methods.

Jarle gladly walked out to the bow and raised the jib. The sail flapped and fluttered, filling just enough to stanch the backward flow and lurch the boat forward. I held the course. Jarle raised his eyebrow, duly impressed.

Riding that thin wisp of wind was like walking a tightrope. All around the tight beam of wind there was nothing, not even a breath, and even the sea beneath it did not curl up like normal. I hung tight on the tiller and kept that delicate little wind in our sails, tacking back and forth, always riding a thin line, just enough wind to keep us sailing.

This was the first time in my life I myself had truly sailed. I had sniffed out the wind, felt it brush up against my cheek like a tingling ghost none other could see. I knew in my heart right where that wind was, the limits to its breadth, an invisible breeze so insignificant it would be lost on a balmy summertime lake, and by instinct I barked commands to ready the jib, time and time again, and Jarle and I hugged a fine course tacking constantly and kept the *Berserk* sailing on a razor's edge all the way to Port Lockroy, first away from the ice and then around the dark brown shadow of an island, one mere step ahead of night the entire way, without the slightest scintilla of room for error, until for the very first time I really felt like a sailor.

We were truly sailing Antarctica the way no other would dare, and for an instant, all those great classic books of the sea came to life and I was elated to be right in the middle of one of them. For the first time I could relate to the feeling pulsing each and every day through Jarle's veins, the feeling that kept him longing for an eternity at sea.

But emotions on the *Berserk* changed as often as the wind. Jarle took over the helm and tried to squeeze into Port Lockroy through a shallow passage that his charts claimed we could clear. He was rushing to get us anchored before the encroaching darkness would make things more difficult, so he sent me to the bow to spot the bottom.

It is always difficult to gauge the depth in the Antarctic waters. The water is always so clear that the bottom can be clearly seen regardless of how far away it is, throwing off perception, creating optical illusions, and making it difficult to judge the distance. Jarle stubbornly tried to force the boat through a set of visible rocks protruding from the shallow harbour – and suddenly we were stuck on the bottom, our keel caught firmly on one of the rocks. Frustrated, he kicked out the spinnaker boom and leaned against it over the water, rocking the boat back and forth until we were free as a lone, red-bearded British sailor rowed out to us in a little dinghy, calling out repeatedly, 'You can't go that way! You have to go around! You have to go around!!' He avoided the rocks and led us the long way around into the harbour, where we dropped our anchor for the night next to another couple of sailing boats. And just like that our day's adventure at sea was done and we were back in 'civilisation'.

'Oil spills are actually good for the environment.' I couldn't believe my ears. The red-bearded Brit was causing jaws to drop all around the table. We were all gathered in the galley of the Pelagic, a sailing vessel that had been chartered as part of 'Mission Antarctica', a British-sponsored expedition that brought a diverse group of students and journalists down south for a couple of weeks to experience Antarctica. Red Beard had sailed alone down to Antarctica in a small 32-foot steel boat and was planning to winter over down there, by himself. He made exorbitant sums of money working as a geologist for oil drilling companies, thus allowing him to set sail for many months at a time, and was regaling the gathering with his bizarre philosophy of the world.

ANTARCTICA II: SNIFFING OUT THE WIND

'You see, the oil that spills is actually eaten by microscopic bacteria that live in the water and feed on it,' he explained to all of us. 'Other forms of sea life then feed on the bacteria, and the entire ecosystem thrives.' I didn't know whether to laugh or cry. He actually believed himself. I seriously doubted his sanity and could only imagine the conversations he was going to have with himself throughout the long Antarctic winter.

We were joined in the galley by Dave, the curmudgeonly, sour-faced, gaunt, British base commander in his fifties who never smiled beneath his salty beard, but nevertheless always welcomed us for tea; his lone cohort on the base, a pleasant, dark-haired, quiet, studious bird-watcher who never lifted his nose from his ornithology books, but nevertheless always welcomed us for tea; and two cool, young Australian mountain climbers in their twenties who had cut short their successful expedition and were waiting another few weeks for their ride home on a passing cruise ship from New Zealand. They spent most of their time at the British base, drinking tea.

Of course, the entire Mission Antarctica team hosted the event: a garrulous group of young students and journalists from throughout Europe and the UK; their leader, a former MI5 commando who took an immediate liking to us; and the charter ship's captain for the run, Hamish, a bitter Irishman with a thick head of red-blond curly hair and a twinkle in his eye who for some odd reason did not seem to care for us at all. My guess was that he did not care for my captain's style of sailing. The *Pelagic*, named for a wandering seabird, was a legendary boat in these waters, and though Hamish was merely the captain and not the owner, it seemed as though he felt the sailor's rivalry with Jarle.

But the MI5 guy loved us. He kept imploring us to tell the youngsters about our trip, what it was like to really feel the Antarctic in our hands, on our faces and beneath our feet.

That was the purpose of Mission Antarctica, the reason the great millionaire philanthropist Robert Swan had endowed the program. MI5 felt that his group was only getting a broad impression in their quick cruise, whereas Jarle and I were truly a part of it, and it was he who had invited us on board for the party.

At the end of the evening, during which the red wine flowed freely, he pulled me aside and looked me in the eye. 'Your captain is young, and somewhere along the way, he's going to make a mistake,' he said to me. 'And when he does, it is going to be your responsibility to make sure he does the right thing. Your lives may depend on it.' I was a bit taken aback, honoured that this veteran military commando felt me worthy of such a statement. But I also respected him enough to know that he must have said it for a reason.

The next night, our last at Port Lockroy, we were invited for dinner at the British base by curmudgeonly Dave, the Grinch of the Antarctic. It was becoming ludicrous. We were going to more dinner parties in the Antarctic than I did at home!

The old British base had been constructed in the middle of the last century as part of the old whaling station. The dank wood smelled like wet roasted chestnuts and mulch from a forest floor, but was warmed by a pot-bellied wood stove that made the place feel like you were sitting in the living room of a country cabin with family.

Years ago, it had undoubtedly supported the family of British whalers who had left large bones scattered intact on all the beaches. The whalers, a notorious bunch akin to pirates, would have had no idea – nor would they have cared – that the debris from the carcasses, as well as the large metal vats used to distil oil from the blubber, would outlive their legacy to remain behind as relics to be pored over and pondered by tenderfoot tourists in pink down coats who pranced on shore between each rendezvous with a prawn cocktail.

These days, Port Lockroy remains as a living museum that caters to cruise ships and the occasional sailing boat. Inside the old wood base, tourists can get a little stamp in their passports to show the world they've been to Antarctica. But ironically, even though Port Lockroy is a definite stop on most cruise forays, extreme weather conditions often make it difficult for the rubber Zodiac dinghies to land or even for the large ships to anchor outside the bay. Luckily, during our stay the wickedly windy conditions kept the only cruise visitor literally at bay, leaving the giant whalebone playground for us.

By now, my toes were completely numb most of the time – even after hours spent drying out. I began to worry that perhaps feeling would never properly return to them, but realistically knew that my options were limited. Still, upon arriving for dinner I felt compelled to ask sour Dave if he knew any remedy.

When knocked with a knuckle, my toes sounded and felt like hard wood, and had begun to turn chalky white at the tips, especially the big toes. Also, the wound on the second toe on my left foot – the opened blister remaining from the hike in Torres del Paine in December – had still not healed under the constant icy moisture; I had begun to doubt it would ever heal. The toe itself began to shrivel a bit and certainly would be the first one to go. I suspected that perhaps my entire set of toes had been infected with the incipient stages of frostbite.

'You don't have frostbite, trust me,' Dave scowled, almost annoyed that anyone would dare ask the question. 'If you had frostbite, your toes would be black.' He was right – and he was wrong at the same time. Indeed, I had the initial stages of frostbite, but it was not bad yet. Still, I wanted to keep it from getting any worse. I asked him if he had any ideas about how I could heal them.

'Keep them warm,' he frowned. I wanted to toss him into one of the whale vats and leave him there.

We were delighted to learn that two old friends would be joining us for the festive dinner planned for that evening: Wolf and Reiner, the Laurel and Hardy of the Antarctic. I loved those guys. I loved the way Wolf worked Reiner to the bone. The poor little guy never hauled less than 50 per cent of his body weight, always loaded to the gills like a pack mule walking uphill. Somehow, watching him struggle to maintain his balance made me feel like my job was easier. They had dropped off a team of elite German rock climbers at the base of a nearby mountain, and had a few days to kick back while the team attempted a virgin conquest of the peak. Until then, they had nothing to do – so they joined the little party growing over at Port Lockroy.

Wolf, German by birth, had settled down in Puerto Williams with his attractive Chilean wife and their two young children, chartering out his boat all summer long to get them through the long winters. He was tall, blond, intellectual, quiet, and completely unflappable. Reiner, a fellow countryman, was his first mate, his second mate, and his rodeo clown all wrapped up in one small package, like a miniature wrestler. I loved the fact that Reiner and I could step aside and swap sailors' stories of working for the man, since we were both left at the mercy of the whims of our captains. From Puerto Williams on, we would run into these guys again and again, and each time Wolf always generously opened the hospitality of his galley, serving up delicious pickled German meats and an excellent spread, including wine. At Port Lockroy Wolf was also gracious enough to pick us up in his motorised dinghy, saving us the long row to shore.

ANTARCTICA II: SNIFFING OUT THE WIND

That night Wolf warned us that our planned route to the south was especially thick with ice that year. He had been unable to penetrate much further than 65 degrees before the ice simply became too thick to go on. Calm and even-keeled as ever, he suggested we watch out.

At the end of the night, we all stood in the back room, gearing up in the dark. When we emerged into the light of the foyer, Reiner had his clothes on backwards. For the first time, grumpy Dave cracked a smile.

'Ucchhhh, Reiner,' Wolf hissed, frustrated. 'We're going to have to start making drills again.'

We all laughed out loud. Jarle and I continued to laugh about that line for the rest of the trip. Whenever things got tough on us, we would bust it out. With Manuel, half-wool Hank, and now Reiner, we were beginning to build up a common frame of reference.

The LeMaire Channel is a small, narrow strait that leads between two rows of steep mountain cliffs. The route is the most-direct inland waterway leading to the south and as such acts as a funnel for both strong currents and the large chunks of ice they carry with them.

A couple of days later we were in no-man's land, heading straight for the LeMaire Channel. As we headed toward the thin strait through a series of mountains, the collecting ice grew thicker and thicker and as the evening wore on it became apparent that we would not make it through the strait that night. Though we could see the mouth of the opening to the channel from a distance, we knew that we did not have enough strong light remaining to challenge it that evening.

Then, as Jarle studied the charts searching for the nearest anchorage, the wind died completely – while we were still caught squarely in the current of ice. We spotted a small bay, a possible emergency harbour, beneath a mountain far off to our left and turned to make our way toward it when everything came to a standstill.

Jarle attempted to start the engine, to no avail in the cool, misty proximity of the ice. He became concerned. The slow current had already taken hold of the little boat and was drawing us closer to the mouth of the thick ice – ice that we preferred to challenge on our terms in the brighter light of day. We were slowly being sucked down the drain.

Jarle readied the dinghy. He attached the iron chain of our spare anchor to a rope, fixing one end to a cleat on the bow of the *Berserk* and the other to the stern of the dinghy. Then, leaving me at the helm, he climbed over the rail and dropped into it.

I took the tiller and steered the boat toward our uncharted harbour in unknown waters, a far cry from Columbus discovering America but relatively speaking in the same spirit. Jarle grabbed hold of the wooden dinghy oars and dug them deep into the icy water, forcefully moving it out of the way with his callused hands and muscles and using the dinghy to drag the *Berserk* along behind it, much in the same way that a locomotive pulls a trainful of coal cars up the side of a rocky mountain.

I guided the boat to follow behind the little dinghy, using the tiller and the rudder to cut down the drag of our fishtailing. Suddenly, my ears perked up: something had dropped into the water. We were near enormous, tall glaciers that calved in half regularly without warning, dropping their mountainsides into the water constantly, creating great danger with the potential to capsize the boat. But this time, the sound was not the dropping of avalanche ice. There it was again, quite unexpectedly – yes! WHALES!

Jarle continued to row, becoming more and more excited. He heard them too, looking back over his shoulder to see where it was coming from. We saw them at the same time: a pod of three small, black Minke whales, barely larger than overgrown dolphins, surfacing through the ice and swimming around the small dinghy, accompanying us until Jarle's rowing had managed to drag us out of the pull of the current and into the backwater eddy of a large bay surrounded by steep mountains of ice.

Jarle guided us closer and closer to shore looking for a place to park. We had to find a happy medium – we had to be in water shallow enough to be able to drop our anchor and have it take hold, yet at the same time, we could not park too close to the mountains of ice. At this time of year, late summer in Antarctica, the ice had sufficient time to melt. The loose chunks, which vary in size from a marble to the state of Rhode Island, break loose and drop without warning. Even if they did not crush the *Berserk* with a direct hit, the resulting tsunami of water and ice from a significant chunk's impact could broadside and capsize the boat with a sudden final fury.

I grabbed the video camera, panning it to show the silvery gloom into which we were heading, and as the lens captured the entire scene, I spontaneously gave the little harbour a name, calling it 'Skull Harbour', almost as a joke. Only later would I realise that indeed the harbour had no name until I named it thus, and as such, I had become, quite unintentionally, an explorer.

We attempted to drop the anchor, but found the water too deep, and it did not hold. Again and again it went in and out of the water before it finally seemed to take hold on the fifth try. I breathed a sigh of relief; my forearms throbbed, swollen like Popeye's. But I had nothing to complain about: Jarle had rowed us into shore for nearly an hour, a task much more gruelling than dropping a paltry anchor a few measly times.

At least we were finally settled, for the time being. We were both exhausted and desperately needed a hot meal and good night's sleep. Jarle cooked us up a pasta and onion meal – he did all the cooking, ever since Manuel had flooded the kerosene stove and it had taken him over an hour to clean it out and get it going again – and we polished off the evening with a warm cup of coffee, sugar and powdered milk for me and hot chocolate for the boy captain.

Drinking three cups of coffee before bedtime always had an undesired side effect. Although I was always so thoroughly exhausted that I could fall asleep immediately, caffeine or not, I nevertheless would find myself with a full bladder that required a trip up through my private bow hatch to relieve myself of mounting pressure. In the meantime, Jarle and I would warm up in our sleeping bags and joke about the day's events, laughing and telling stories like two prospectors without a campfire. These indeed made up the special moments, the private moments that can never be properly captured or recreated – where the hopes of the future intermingled with our recently-shared experiences of the past, with laughter the suture to bind them, and we were happy, genuinely happy. All of Life's possibilities were before us, the world of pain forgotten, and eventually we would fall asleep, exhausted, with smiles on our faces, to live in our dreams – until the first crack of ice awakened us.

In Skull Harbour, chunks of ice bombarded the boat all night long. Wind ricocheting down the canyon walls that encircled us kept us feeling downright icy, resulting in our coldest night yet. Neither one of us wanted to get out of his sleeping bag for any reason.

On this most frigid of nights, south of cold, the captain blessedly decided that no watch would be necessary. 'If you or I get up to go to the bathroom, make sure the anchor is holding,' he called out from the warm depths of his bag. We found ourselves in agreement; we were completely uncertain whether it would hold or not. The water in our little harbour was deep and filled with moving chunks of ice.

ANTARCTICA II: SNIFFING OUT THE WIND

For my part, I simply hoped that I would not be a human ping-pong ball, bouncing up and down through the hatch every five minutes to fight off the ice. Our hold was precarious at best. The wind buffeted off the icy cavern walls like a pool ball caught on the table, whipping around in circles until it hit the bow of the boat and stretched the green anchor line taut, pushing us to the south end of the cavern.

I hoped beyond hope that it would hold but had my most sincere doubts. Periodic forays to the deck would be by necessity quick, leaving no time to yank on boots; within minutes, my fragile toes would be refrozen. Jarle had true Viking's foot; he would walk out to the deck barefoot in a snowstorm, through flurries sticking to the fibreglass, and spend half an hour cursing in Norwegian and fending off marauding ice attackers like a jousting jester, the pounding of his feet reverberating basslike through the bow, each reverberation eventually wending its way through my sleeping bag until he finally pushed the cumbersome intruder under our anchor rope and away from the rap-rap-rapping on the side of the boat.

Naturally, he expected the same of me, and often I would find myself fending off my own newest sworn enemy, yet another block of ice seemingly attracted to the side of the *Berserk* like a steel ball bearing to a magnet. One never knew whether a battle would be over with one quick shove of the stick, or whether it would require massive, time-consuming manoeuvres. The worst possible case scenario required the waking of the other; regardless, the other would be surly, aggravated beyond belief at having been rousted. Even worse, sometimes we would get such a monster berg that we would have to haul up anchor and move the boat itself to extricate the rope from its hold.

Tonight, of all nights, I hoped to avoid night manoeuvres. Both Jarle and I were exhausted. The difficult sailing conditions wore us out and we both needed sleep. On this night, in our most remote and difficult anchorage, we threw caution to the wind – and the wind tossed it right back in our faces.

Toasty inside my bag, I opened my ears and listened, trying to set the alarm in my mind to wake me in the event of an avalanche. We may not have time to move the boat, but at least we could hang on and hopefully ride out the ensuing crushing wave of debris.

Early in the evening, small cubes of ice knocked into the boat. At first, one or the other of us would go out to check on it, using the stick to push them out of the way. We were accustomed to the constant up and down and had become able to ascertain the severity of the situation, even the shape and size of the ice, by the booming kettle-drum sound it made when hitting the side of the *Berserk*. But as the night wore on, the thudding drumming on the side of the boat became a tinking sound, much like a thundering anvil becoming a tiny hammer or a booming bass drum becoming a toy snare, until eventually it seemed as though the drumming had stopped completely, the wind had stopped whistling off the side of the mountain, the anchor was holding, and the boat was secure. In such conditions, we both fell into a deep, blissful, warm sleep in a place beyond care and got the rest we so desperately needed.

I awoke early the next morning feeling refreshed and astounded to feel a bit of warm sunlight peeking through the hazy frosted window above my bunk. I popped out of the hatch and immediately changed my mind.

Blocks of ice stretched endlessly before the *Berserk* in every direction. During the night, the course of the wind had changed, and every chunk, cube or growler that had been funnelling toward the strait had turned and headed straight for us. The mouth of the channel had emptied her motherlode, dumping it in our lap. The unceasing cacophony of the barrage had stopped only because we had become but another cube in the drink.

I squinted and looked toward the faraway, majestic mountains near the LeMaire Channel, shining brown, illuminated by sunlight. The blanket of ice covered the water all the way to the base. I looked behind me: the nearby blue walls of ice blocked our escape backward. There was no wind. Our engine did not work. Jarle's greatest nightmare had come to fruition.

We were completely trapped.

Legend describes the infamy of many a boat crushed between colliding walls of ice. Many a night early on, when Manuel's paranoia held sway, we lay awake in our bunks like kids on a camping trip telling ghost stories, giddy, excited, frightening ourselves with such possibilities but laughing them all off like a corny knock-knock joke. Almost as if to emphasise the potential of the threat, Jarle told us about his greatest hero, Shackleton.

'Who?' I asked. I had never heard of him.

'Sir Ernest Shackleton,' he replied, reverence in his voice. And he told us the British explorer's by-now familiar story: in 1914 Shackleton had set off in his boat the *Endurance* with a crew of 28 in an attempt to be the first person to cross the Antarctic continent. But early in the season his boat had been caught and frozen in the ice. Eventually the mighty forces of nature became too much – the walls of ice met and crushed the hearty wood of the *Endurance* to splinters – but not before Shackleton evacuated his entire crew onto the ice. With no recourse and dwindling supplies, they set out in their small fleet of lifeboats, eventually reaching nearby Elephant Island. Realising help would never arrive in such a remote spot, Shackleton fashioned a mini-sailing boat out of one of the lifeboats, hopped on board with three of his crew, and set sail for a British military whaling station on

South Georgia Island, some 650 nautical miles away across the roughest seas in the world.

In perhaps the single greatest nautical feat in history, Shackleton reached South Georgia – but landed on the wrong side, the south. Starving and weary, he and his crew hiked over the peak of a never-before-scaled 11,000-foot mountain to reach the base on the other side, eventually returning with a ship to rescue alive each and every man that had originally set off with him.

Jarle boasted often of Shackleton's tremendous accomplishment. To him, Shackleton was more than just a hero – he was a way of life, a father figure in the family of sailors that spanned history. In a way, Jarle appeared to be a direct descendent of the very spirit which had taken hold of Shackleton. One of the very reasons Jarle wanted to visit South Georgia Island was to visit Shackleton's grave. Like all great explorers, Shackleton simply could not stay away from the sea and the ice, could not deal with the reality of civilisation to which he had returned and found so unwelcoming, colder than any polar region could ever be. He had returned to the great, frigid South Seas and had succumbed, falling into his grave on South Georgia and remaining there for all eternity.

Now the ice had extended its invitation for us to join him. If the sturdy *Endurance* could get caught and buckle, certainly so could we. We only had to hear it so many times to realise the potential existed – and that morning, we felt the threat keenly.

I climbed the mast, looking for a way out. Down below, Jarle steeled for battle, hoisting the jib. Any slight bit of wind would propel us through any lead we could find. We had to get out before the ice fused together.

We crept along at snail-like speed as Jarle jockeyed between bow and stern, a one-man-band. He used the stick to push off the ice when the bow rode up high, threatening to get stuck land-borne, then ran back to the cockpit to grab the ropes hanging from the boom for the main sail with one hand and the tiller with the other. Slowly, as the breeze picked up, he began to work our way out.

I scurried down from the mast to take over the jousting and walked out to the bow, pushing away large chunks of ice with the stick. Already, the thick chunks had started to piggyback over each other in their haste to enclose us. I reached out with the stick, pushing an ice boulder with all my might, trying desperately to force the ice away – and the stick dropped, disappearing beneath the ice, gone forever.

I climbed the mast again to spot for an opening. In an incredible feat of sailing bravado, Jarle grabbed the wind by the throat and held fast. He raised sails, yanked ropes, steered with his boots. We picked up steam, forcing our way through expanding leads in the ice.

We broke free. I looked down from the mast. We had taken some pretty severe hits, right on the nose, but she seemed to be holding up all right. Jarle beamed, giddy with delight. He unfurled the small Norwegian flag in the wind as we left the coagulating ice in our wake and shouted with glee: 'Sailing in Antarctica!'

Sailing in Antarctica. Many had arrived with such an intention before us, but most had engines. Without knowing it, our weakness had become our strength, we were actually forced to sail, most of the time, in the most challenging region in the world, a boy sailor and a novice first mate.

Icebergs breathe with a life of their own. On the water, they rise up and swallow the sea by the gulpful, then crash back down with a white splash, creaking and moaning their ugly roar, as if they are alive, like a breaching whale. Every so often, they somersault in place, like a dolphin, taking anything in their path with them. And most of all, like Man himself, they will kill without remorse. Anyone who says that ice is not alive has not seen it dance nor heard it speak. It acts with a will of its own, completely of its own accord, and answers to no one until the time when it passes drop by drop into eternity.

The wind died completely. Once again, Jarle dropped the dinghy over the side and rigged up the anchor-chain towline. Unfortunately, since he had rowed yesterday, now it was my turn.

I was not happy about it. Unlike last night, we were no longer in the confines of a protected cove. Instead, we were bobbing randomly through a field of enormous blue icebergs scattered throughout the low, flat rock islands and mountains.

I climbed into the dinghy reluctantly and grabbed hold of the oars. I cast out onto the choppy water, hoping the small waves wouldn't crash over the side and swamp me, and rowed until the bowline stretched taut.

My arms ached after the first tug. I dug the oars into the water and heaved with all my might, feeling the *Berserk* tug after me. I rowed and rowed and rowed, feeling the irritation well inside me with every stroke, pulling the heavy boat after me.

Piercing cold emanated from a huge, flat, roiling blue iceberg off to our starboard side. Every time it bounced up and down, icy air gushed out from underneath it, forced out like a cold, wet, bad breath blown specifically in my direction. The iceberg stretched for over 300 feet. I tugged the oars, shut my eyes, gritted my teeth, cursed and muttered in my own mind, until my shoulders burned, my biceps spasmed and my back flat-out hurt. I couldn't pull another stroke. I looked at my watch. Barely five minutes of rowing had passed. Last night, Jarle had gone for nearly an hour. I was in Hell.

I shut my eyes and kept going. I had no choice. If the boat stopped moving now, the recoil from the bouncing iceberg, only a few feet away, would suck us into its vortex, beneath its heaving mass, and swallow us down into its belly like Jonah's whale. My eyes raged with fury. I rowed. We were barely beating back the current.

After thirty gruelling, miserable minutes, we were barely at the midway point. No end in sight. No wind. Little headway. I did not know how much longer I could endure.

Jarle stood on the stern, puttering around. He never stood still for an instant. Like all boaters, he knew there is always something more to do, another rope to roll, a stay to wax, a sail to sew. This time, as usual, he worked on the engine.

'Jarle!' I screamed back at him. 'Can you try the engine? I don't know how much longer I can do this.'

'Keep rowing now!' He understood our predicament.

Early day had been warmed by sun. Jarle lit the stove and popped in the spark plugs. Nothing. From the bouncing dinghy off the bow, I watched him try and fail repeatedly. Frustration mounted.

Suddenly, the engine caught. Immediately Jarle kicked the throttle into gear and the *Berserk* lunged forward, passing me in the dinghy. The rope swung around until it stretched off to the side, where I bounced along on top of the pounding waves, holding onto the sides of the dinghy for dear life.

Jarle called out to me from the cockpit. 'Come on now!' he shouted. 'Pull yourself over with the rope!'

Hand over hand, I drew myself in the bouncing dinghy toward the back of the *Berserk* until I reached the rope's limit. Still, the bow of the dinghy was more than three feet from the back of the boat.

'Climb on board!' Jarle shouted, afraid to slow the boat down for fear it would stall. He reached out toward me. From the dinghy I held forth my hand.

'I can't make it!' I shouted back.

'Yes, you can!' He turned around to steer.

'No, I can't!'

'Just do it!'

Frustrated, I tiptoed forward in the dinghy as it bounced hard on the waves. The bow of the little yellow corncob boat began to dip. I continued. The bow dipped further, this time taking on water. In a flash the dinghy filled with cold water, starting at the bow and working its way astern. In three seconds the entire dinghy filled – with me still standing in it. The oars and the bailing bucket floated away immediately.

I leaned forward and grabbed the rope holding the dinghy fast to the boat just as I went under for the first time. 'Four minutes' rang through my head as the icy waters took their first stabs at my heart. The *Berserk* plowed onward at high speed, Jarle oblivious to my plight as my body surfed underwater in front of the submerged dinghy. I craned my head up and out of the water to see Jarle turn around panic-stricken, his eyes opening wide. He dropped the tiller and leaned back down over the rail.

'Grab my hand!' he shouted, reaching out toward me.

I held the rope fast with my left hand and reached up toward Jarle with my right, envisioning Michelangelo's ceiling of the Sistine Chapel as my hand reached closer and closer toward my salvation. But the friction of the speeding *Berserk* proved too much. Just as my hand was near enough to grab hold, a wave of cascading water crashed smash into my face, immediately dragging me completely under once again. Jarle's shouting became blurred, drowned by the water. I would be next. I flailed but luckily caught my free arm on the rope, spinning sideways then back again.

Dawning realisation set in: I had to do something myself or I would join a long list of visitors felled by mishap. I shut my eyes, bracing my face against the cold rush, holding onto the rope for dear life. Ignoring the stabbing spears of hypothermia, I reached forward with all my might and took hold of the rope further up. Hand over hand I worked my way against the current, completely submerged. I opened my eyes underwater and saw the steel tail of the wind pilot sticking out from the back of the boat. Reaching out as my limbs slowed down, I took hold of the tail and held fast, eventually scurrying back above the surface where Jarle took hold of my arm and hoisted me fully back on board.

By now he had reluctantly stopped the engine, jeopardising our forward progress. I stood in the cockpit, soaking from head to toe like a frozen scarecrow dripping with icicles, shivering uncontrollably.

'Go change your clothes,' he told me.

'What about the dinghy?' I asked.

'I'll take care of it.' Jarle grabbed hold of the rope and toted the waterlogged boat toward the *Berserk*. Full of water, it must have weighed a hundred and fifty pounds. I needed help to hoist it on board, but Jarle, tough as nails, had no problem doing it alone. He had learned the hard way. I looked back and saw our two oars floating away toward the iceberg, way back behind the boat.

I could feel the chill entering my bones and begrudgingly obliged, crawling down below and slowly peeling the dripping wetgear and soaked wool from my body. By the time I changed and climbed back up into the cockpit, Jarle was miraculously rowing the dinghy back to the boat, using both of the recovered oars.

'How did you do it?' I asked, astonished.

'I just did it,' he answered.

I sat next to him waiting for the blue inside me to go away and the red to re-enter my arteries as he tried unsuccessfully to start the engine again. Eventually, he got it started and we continued our long cruise toward our destination, the old Vernadsky Station. But the chill remained lodged in my bones for the rest of the afternoon and for days after that. That afternoon, I sat glumly at his side, saying nothing and shivering, feeling the cold leave my body much slower than it had entered, watching the island and iceberg world pass me by, contemplating how close I had come to losing my existence, unable to shake the thought, not afraid, not tamed, but with a profound understanding and kinship with those who had come before me but had not been so lucky.

CHAPTER NINE
MAD RUSSIANS AND UNCLE SAM

My birthday celebration was in full swing at Vernadsky Station when the boatful of mad Russians arrived. They rode a rusty steel Soviet-era naval sailing vessel that had been decommissioned by the government and were attempting to become the first Russian sailing crew to circumnavigate the globe, and had chosen the route around Antarctica through the great Southern Ocean. Of course, they chose to stop at the home of their Ukrainian brothers to drink some vodka before continuing on their way.

Their captain, who bore a spitting resemblance to film director Martin Scorsese, guided a crew of five; three crewmen, the ship's curly-haired doctor, and a journalist, who tagged along to document the trip. The bald, heavyset journalist, extremely proud of Mother Russia, carried with him photographs of his beloved countryside, his beloved wife, and his beloved Kalashnikov assault rifle. The three crewmen wore striped blue shirts and looked like they had stepped in lock-step unison straight out of a 1950s' propaganda postcard, ready to burst into song.

BERSERK IN THE ANTARCTIC

The ship's doctor had a look in his eyes like I had never seen, a deep, glazed, faraway gaze of clairvoyance. He seemed to be on our plane of existence but seemed to be watching another at the same time; his gaze was discomforting and reassuring all at once. He looked at me like a caring family member. In fact, every member of the Russian crew was extraordinarily friendly, open and gracious – though only the first mate spoke even limited English, making communication between all of us extremely difficult. But kindness transcends language barriers.

The old Soviet era rustbucket was a sailing vessel through and through, without many of the amenities one finds on the more modern western ships – including a motorised anchor winch. The anchor on the *Urania 2* weighed two thousand pounds. In order to drop it or lift it, all six crewmembers had to stand by at the ready. Lifting it back up to the side of their ship proved to be a miserable, gruelling, bone-jarring experience, one that no crewmember ever wanted. So instead of dropping anchor, the Russians simply crashed their ship into the ice outside of Vernadsky, plowing through the bergs until their giant beast eventually ground to a halt outside the station. Then, confident the great beast wouldn't budge an inch, every single one of them jumped over to land and joined us in drink, completely unconcerned with how they would bother to get it out of there.

The captain came across as a gleaming, brilliant madman with a sharp-cut black beard and beady, knowing eyes. He could not speak a word of English but immediately found instant kinship with me, describing in great pantomimic detail his grand adventures on the high seas battling fierce waves. When he looked up from his glass of vodka toward the ceiling, I could see reflected in his eyes the waves crashing down on him and the permanent, pressing impact they had made. He guided the ship toward her destination, confident he would return to Russia a hero.

The Ukrainians were delightful, top to bottom. They welcomed us with open arms like true comrades – almost like distant relatives they didn't know they had who had decided to pop in for a visit unexpectedly and stayed for a few days. They didn't even bother to question our credentials; the fact that we were there was enough.

Immediately I struck up a friendship with a middle-aged, soft-spoken Ukrainian from Odessa named Slavik. When I discovered his hometown I was delighted – the grand set of steps leading down to the harbour had been used by pioneering filmmaker Sergei Eisenstein for the scene of a revolt that became known as 'the Odessa Steps' sequence from his classic *Battleship Potemkin*. Slavik proudly grabbed a series of postcards that he kept stashed underneath his bunk and sitting down on it next to me showed off his hometown card by card, graciously giving me the Odessa Steps card as a gift.

As soon as we arrived, the base's steely commander ordered his youngest subordinate, a youth who appeared to be his teenage son, to take us down to the shack. 'Come with me,' the youngster said. I figured he must be some kind of student. 'No, I'm a scientist,' he told me. The Ukrainians held a long-term lease on Vernadsky Station from the British, who had rented them the base as well as a bizarre planetarium device used for measuring the gap in the ozone layer. This little kid spent hours a day making detailed measurements.

He took us for a sauna in a little shack on a rock near the water's edge. We stripped, rappelled nude down a rope into the icy water, then ran back inside repeatedly, in succession freezing then boiling, before heading off to dinner. The food tasted incredible: cold spiced meats, pickled cabbage, potatoes. They had more kinds of chili sauce on their tables than we had types of food on the *Berserk*. The cook was a short, squat, friendly man who delighted in watching us relish the meals his comrades had grown sick of over the last eight months, and before we left he gave me a home-made business card, advertising his 'Antarctic Cook' services. In his picture on the card, his head was shaven except for a lone knot of hair at the top. I asked him why.

They popped in their home videos, the ones they took when they sailed on their mothership south of the equator for the first time and all shaved their heads save for a little Hare Krishna-esque ponytail on the top, and then did a funky limbo dance under a stick like Caribbean voodoo. They explained in broken English that this was the haircut of the Kazakhs. 'Cossacks?' I asked. No, Kazakhs. 'Oh, you mean like Kazakhstan,' I explained. No, that's Kazakh. Kazakhs. Kazakhs. They became irate. Kazakhs. I had no idea what they were talking about. I felt I was right. They must mean Kazakhstan. They turned off the video.

The big, doughy radio operator popped in some vintage Soviet comedy films from the late 1960s. He explained that his countrymen considered the lead character to be the Charlie Chaplin of the Soviet Union. Together we watched the exploits of this young character, a blond, fair youth who found himself mired in situations in a bustling, modern Communist Moscow. I was completely fascinated: never before had I seen an image of the country in this way, colourful, bright, modern, happy; I had always imagined it in black and white, filled with soot and filthy factory chimneys belching black smoke into the clouds. And, with the others, I laughed, though they had certainly seen these classics many times. I wondered why I had never seen them before; the comedy in the situations, a man trying to find work, dealing with women, criminals and bullies, had universal themes.

After the movies, we retired to the southernmost bar in the world, where the Ukrainians brought out pitcher after pitcher of their special chilled vodka. By the time midnight brought the arrival of my birthday, I was already lit. When Jarle, more trashed than anybody in the bar, announced that it was my birthday, the Ukrainians began pouring the drinks even stronger.

Eventually they formed an ad hoc birthday committee and we gathered around in a circle for a formal pronouncement and gift-giving ceremony. One by one, the commander and officers of the base stepped forward, next to the translator, and orated in fine fashion, eventually raising their glass high awaiting the imminent toast, and then we would all drink our shots of vodka together, in the unison of Antarctic brotherhood. Too bad the Chileans weren't around.

They called me forward. I could barely stand up. The base's doctor, a frail, thin man straight out of *Doctor Zhivago*, began to speak: 'Let it be known that in Russia and the Ukraine, we welcome people of all races and religions to our land.' He beckoned me forward and handed me a small gift, a framed picture of the station. I did not know what to say; I was speechless. Jarle poked me in the back.

'Shake his hand, man,' he whispered. I held out my hand obliviously and we shook. One by one, the Ukrainians called me forth, made bold pronouncements and handed me gifts, seashells, sweaters, each accompanied by a large swig of prime vodka, worth its weight in gold in the Antarctic. To this day I wonder what I have ever done to elicit such good fortune.

Then, soon thereafter, the Russians arrived with great aplomb, kick-starting the party back into high gear, with handshakes for their brothers and backslaps for their comrades, and sailors' stories of mountainous waves and terrible storms and lonely, solitary battles against the elements all across the Seven Seas.

Around dawn Jarle, completely drunk, gave the command to head back to the boat. 'Are you going to sleep?' he asked the base's radio operator as we hastily threw on our jackets.

'No,' the doughboy answered indignantly. 'Now we are going to start drinking.'

The next day, my birthday, I did not leave my bunk. Dark weather moved in and both Jarle and I were a bit hungover. Upon returning to the boat, we had discovered an enormous iceberg encroaching on our anchor chain. Jarle, drunk and slurring, demanded that we move it. I had no idea how. 'I'll show you how!' he screamed, leaping from the bow of the boat onto the giant ice mass and digging his fingernails into the ice to hold on, like a rider taking hold of the mane of a wild thoroughbred. He slipped and slid and rode the berg, always inches from dropping down into the black water below, before eventually calling it quits in disgust. Now, the day after, we both mellowed on the boat.

Perhaps the most interesting fellow we met the night before was the Mad Scientist. A tall oak of a man with a full shock of wavy hair, he was in the processing of undertaking a secret mission of his own devising: an attempt to breed giant guppies. The genius of it, I thought to myself. Did he really think he could do it? The rest of the crew on the base dismissed him as a wacko, but I could relate. If he could succeed, at the rate guppies bred he could conceivably solve the world's food shortage. Brilliant! I hung on this man's every word – until he pulled out his favourite dog-eared copy of *Playboy* and offered to let me have a look. Then I ran.

We only saw the mad Russians once more. Two days later they invited us to visit their ship before they cast off. We arrived promptly as scheduled at 7 a.m. and already they were pouring vodka. On the *Berserk*, we NEVER drank under sail, a sacrosanct rule with a violation punishable by death. But here on the *Urania 2*, the applicable laws seemed to be the opposite.

The ship was an old war horse. Not only did it look to be a relic of the old, crumbled Soviet empire, by all appearances it could have been a relic of the War of 1812. But the lesson to never judge a book by its cover became more than apparent when we walked down below deck to find spacious, wood-panelled cabins and a large open galley. The air below was cold and damp, but we were used to such conditions on the *Berserk* and found a strange camaraderie with these Russian shipmates. I began to understand the Law of the Sea and the unspoken bond between sailors regardless of nation or flag. But more than that, seeping through my stubborn skin, borne of a lifetime of travel and experience, I began to experience a strange sensation: all fear of the evils of men unknowingly began to dissipate. Constant bombardment through television and the media and formal education had led me to believe that the history of the planet was paved with the blood of man by ruthless hordes and tyrants. While that may indeed be true, I learned that the opposite is the truer case: man is essentially good, the good far outnumber the wicked, and here, in what by all appearances had historically been the most remote, blighted place on the globe, the gathering of men that takes place revels in the shared joys of life and the mutual hardships overcome, relegating the fear, the misery and the tyranny to a second-tier citizen somewhere back in the far-off struggles of the world.

While mad Martin Scorsese showed the Ukrainians and my captain around his ship, one of the musical crewmembers called me over. Standing next to him stood the bug-eyed doctor. His eyes were piercing blue lasers. The crewman told me that the doctor had something for me. He reached out and handed me a vial of Russian ointment. I looked up at the doctor. Why was he giving me this? He had an eerie, almost spooky look in his gaze, like a clairvoyant. He didn't say a word. He just curled his lips into a grim smile, a curt upward sneer, and nodded. In broken English the Russian crewman, who had spent the summer in Alaska, told me: 'He says you will need this.' I will need this? I thought to myself. How does he know I will need this? What does he see in his faraway plane of existence? I tried to reason to myself, as I humbly accepted the offering, that he, as a man of medicine and science, understood profoundly the bumps and bruises of outrageous fortune that would certainly befall me as the first mate, second mate and only crewman on the *Berserk*. But I could not shake the irrefutable feeling that he saw something much more, deep beyond. I instantly became convinced that he handed me the medicine because he had gazed into the future and he saw that I would need it. The Russian continued: 'You rub this on your body, and it makes the pain go away.' Hmmm, I thought, sort of like Deep Heat, good to relieve severely sore muscles. What did he see?? He was not smiling. He was not taking this lightly. Neither would I. He saw something, something that was going to happen, a cloud looming on the horizon, and now all I could do was wait for the storm to arrive.

But before I could probe any further, it was time to say goodbye.

And we lifted our glasses and Captain Scorsese toasted to a safe journey and the unequalled hospitality of our Ukrainian brothers, and we all downed our shots of pristine Russian vodka and hugged our goodbyes, and Jarle, the mad guppie scientist, the base commander and I watched from the shore while the heavyset Kalashnikov journalist scrambled up the icy, slippery rock shore to snap a picture and somehow the six mad Russian sailors rocked and kicked and pushed their dinosaur off the ice and started the engine and took off to be the first Russian sailing ship to circumnavigate the globe. Years later, I heard that they didn't make it, because somewhere in the great southern sea on their way to New Zealand their mad captain led them into a furious storm that won the day. And when I heard the tale, details scant and curious, my heart sank deeply for them, for I truly consider them my friends. But by then, they were somewhere on the other side of the globe, the journalist back in the fields of the great Siberian steppes with his blushing bride in one hand and his Kalashnikov in the other, the crewmen back in the lockstepped musical of their happy lives, the doctor mysteriously catering to the needs of the needy, and mad Martin back at the helm, furiously fighting his way back out to the equally mad ocean through a sea of bureaucracy that neither he nor his great nation would allow to defeat them, to the place he belongs, out on the sea once again. Or so I hoped.

Everywhere we went, Jarle asked the chief engineer to look over his little engine. He was so proud of the little engine. It had been given to him by his grandfather, whom he had loved more than anyone in the world. His grandfather had died and now all that Jarle had left as a shard of a memory was the little blue 7.5 HP Suzuki lawnmower engine that he had solidly painstakingly secured beneath the back hatch. Jarle had spent most of the trip pulling apart the little bastard, yanking out the starting coil, blowing on it to evaporate the salty residue, pulling out the spark plugs, swearing they were brand new when I suggested repeatedly they may be the problem, changing the gas, drying it out, everything. Now, here at the Ukrainian base, he once again brought on board the base's chief engineer, the man responsible for keeping the entire base operational.

The engineer looked a bit like a big teddy bear, with a full black beard and bushy, black Ukrainian eyebrows. He didn't speak a single word of English. So, he brought along with him not one but two scientists from the base to translate. I stood in the shadow of the doorway, looking out through the hatch and watching the from-me-to-him-to-you conversation unfurl like a ridiculous child's game of telephone, the message becoming more and more obscured with each passing breath. The burly engineer shook his head, gesticulated, threw his arms up in the air like a maniac, and his minions translated to Jarle, who gestured back in kind.

Eventually, the engineer determined he knew the problem and he handed Jarle two brand new, in-the-box Russian sparkplugs. Jarle refused them. The engineer threw his arms up in the air, gestured again, demanded that Jarle try them on for size. So he slid the new sparkplugs into the engine and, lo and behold, with a tug of the cord it started immediately. Beaming, the triumphant bear-man nodded emphatically before stepping off the boat with his comrades.

But Jarle was not yet to be bested. He quickly switched out the new sparkplugs and put back in the old ones. It wouldn't start. So, he took out one of the old ones and put in one of the new ones, saving the other for later. He tried again, the engine started, and there were smiles all around.

Then came the day we were to leave. We said our farewells, thanking them for their unequalled hospitality, and we hoisted our sails, working our way out of our little inlet with the wind. We passed by the wooden gas dock on our way out to the bay, the men of the base waved goodbye, and went back inside. It was a sunny day, the Antarctic sky a blue between powder and cobalt, hardly a cloud to be seen. Jarle bent down and gave the engine cord a yank; it sputtered, didn't even bother to kick, and died out. He tried again, and again, and again, to no avail, his frustration mounting with each yank until suddenly it cracked and he was momentarily defeated. As the *Berserk* lingered in its windless way, Jarle sank down on his haunches and began to cry, the tears streaming down his face.

I stared at him dumbfounded. I didn't know what to say. My jaw dropped slightly. I decided to say nothing. I just stood at the tiller and watched him release his frustration.

After a couple of minutes, Jarle rubbed the water and snot from his face with his hand, sniffled and spoke. 'I'm sorry,' he said. 'It's just that I came down here to explore Antarctica and have an adventure, and all I've been doing is fucking around with this damn engine.'

I didn't say anything. What could I say? He was human after all. With the responsibility he shouldered, I would have cracked long ago. At that moment, I respected him more than ever.

He took the tiller, turned the boat around and guided us back toward the gas dock, where we tied up again. He ran back inside and came out dragging the burly, bearded engineer. Once again, arms flew into the air wildly as Jarle explained that the engine still didn't work. The engineer leaned down into the back hatch to look at the engine. He shook his head and shouted something in Ukrainian. He took off the cover, leaned down and yanked out Jarle's old spark plug. He turned and held it up in the air, under Jarle's nose, muttered something in Ukrainian, and nonchalantly tossed it overboard, where it fell to the bottom of the beautiful blue bay. He stood and walked off the boat and that was the last we ever saw of him.

With two new sparkplugs, the engine worked for the rest of that day, most likely because of the sunshine. But we were drained emotionally and did not have it in us to travel very far. We followed the shoreline until we found a big, dripping cave and decided to anchor and explore. We needed a rest. We took turns taking the dinghy out under the overhang, where there was a little cool, damp beach hidden from the light. On the way in, I looked down through the transparent water and could count the rocks on the bottom, the water so clear and bright in the sunshine it became impossible to discern the depth. It could have been ten feet deep or a hundred; it was impossible to tell. The veil of water was no veil at all, like looking through fresh clean air, like a wisp of magic, a disappearing act.

I saw something pink in the water, something moving, and I realised it was a starfish, crawling along near a florid sea anemone. All this life going on, right underwater, right before our very own eyes, and we didn't even know it. We were aware that life existed, certainly, but we didn't truly understand that here indeed thrived a vibrant, living ecosystem, not a half-dead world that awakened for a few sordid months each year like a quick dawn but rather an entire world, colourful, imaginative, beyond our ability to comprehend, just as wonderful as any other ecosystem to be found worldwide, whose colours vibrantly existed year-round lacking only the bright warmth of sunlight to illuminate them, to awaken them again each summer from their slumbers. And here we were, catching them in the act on a sunny day, and in a little damp cave on the other side of nowhere these creatures, this Life, was indeed wide, wide awake. There we were, in the right place at the right time, lucky enough to experience it, only a few short hours removed from one of the emotional low-points of the expedition.

And, unbeknownst to us, one by one, these moments were accruing, like pixels in a Seurat painting, latching on to our souls one after the other, a picture vaguely forming. Without even knowing it, Antarctica was seeping into our blood.

I had never experienced anything like it in my life: everywhere we went, we were treated like royalty. I could not quite comprehend just why it was that we deserved such treatment; after a while, I chalked it up to everyone thinking we were going to die. Still, they were leaving us with one beggars' banquet after another. Sure, we could fiddle while Rome burned – but you can be damn sure we were determined to belt out one hell of a tune.

So it was with such high expectations that we approached the American base, US Palmer Station, on Anvers Island. Since everyone else had treated us like royalty, surely my fellow Americans would top them all. I had argued with Jarle, begged, cajoled, whined – I all but demanded a stop at Palmer, and wanted to stop there last of all. In life, I had come to eat my meals one item at a time, to savour each taste individually, almost methodically, before moving on, prioritising them worst to best, first the asparagus, then the potatoes, and last and best of all, the meat. For me, here and now, Anvers Island was to be the meat of all Antarctic bases, and I was looking forward to it most of all.

I could hardly contain my smile as we sailed our way north reciting the mantra of 'US Palmer Station' like it was some sort of Valhalla, Shangri-La and Kingdom Come all wrapped up in one. 'I wonder if we'll see the *Lawrence M. Gould*,' I said aloud, regaling Jarle with my earlier encounter with the ship's overzealous third mate and engineer, almost like we were heading for Disneyland hoping to see Mickey Mouse greeting us in front of Cinderella's castle.

This was to be our last stop in civilisation before heading out to sea for two months. Jarle wanted to get as much kerosene and petrol on board as we could handle; we were running low, even without a fully functioning engine, and we were not sure when we would get another opportunity to replenish our supplies.

Personally, I was excited at the prospect of getting some news from the world. Whenever you head out of civilisation for long stretches, there are always exciting things that happen in the real world that you don't find out about until much later. Most are completely insignificant, allowing a person to catch up quickly, whether it's a hit movie or a popular song; others, like deaths of known people, hit harder. Imagine how difficult it is to keep up with the world from the front row seat of your very own desk, then imagine you don't read or hear anything for a few months and you begin to get the picture.

For my part, I desperately wanted to know who won the Super Bowl. We had been out of communication for nearly three months. At home, I would watch every available football game, week in week out. It had been years since I had missed a Redskins game, much less an entire season's worth. For the first time in my life I had not watched the Big Game, the greatest American sporting spectacle, and had only snippets of the season to go on. Surely my fellow Americans would enlighten me.

And then there was the matter of the Academy Awards. Back then I actually cared who won. Back then, I was a budding filmmaker with visions of grandeur: someday that would be me standing at the podium. Since boarding that plane for Machu Picchu, a half-year's worth of releases had piqued the public's curiosity. Scores of films, modern masterpieces all, surely must have been released and nominated in my absence. The possibility of one all-encompassing burst of information overload was almost too much to bear.

Jarle could not have cared less about any of that nonsense. He probably could not have even named a single team in the American football league or a single film that had been released since he left home two years ago. He only cared about one thing: fuel, plain and simple. But for my part, I was proudly going to show him the American way and I was convinced of it. Call it hubris. It backfired.

Far in the distance I could make out the odd geometric shapes and colours of the base, the biggest we had seen yet. My heart began to thump loudly and uncontrollably under my wet suit. Jarle clicked on the VHF radio and called out to the base. They answered, and Jarle, after identifying us, asked for permission to tie up to their dock.

'Permission denied,' came the response. Jarle looked over at me angrily. The disembodied radio voice went on to explain that they were expecting a large delivery – including new base crewmembers as well as supply materials – sometime within the next 12 hours. The entire process would be hectic and rushed, and the National Science Foundation would be upset if they found a small sailing boat in their way. The base manager, a punctilious, by-the-books bureaucrat who identified himself as Ron, went on to tell us that it was base policy that any boats arriving without arranging prior permission were never allowed ashore, American on board or not. He suggested that we dock where he sent all other unexpected visitors – in a small bay about half a mile south of the base.

Jarle was furious. We turned around and headed to the bay, where we dropped anchor. The early afternoon sky was overcast, grey and cloudy and damp. 'We are receiving a fine welcome from your fucking Americans,' he shouted, and the tirade didn't stop there. It went on and on and on until my ears began to ring and I felt like I was in a bowling alley with pins crashing all around me. I had told him about my previous meeting with John, the third mate from the *Lawrence M. Gould*, and when he inquired as to the identity of the supply ship, I was happy to discover that indeed my friends were making the drop-off. Throughout that afternoon, as Jarle's cursing rang through my ears repeatedly and I began to feel a bit like cartoon character Fred Flintstone shrinking in the big chair of the office as his boss Mr Slate reamed him a new backside, I found myself hoping that my contact with John would pay off and that he would have enough clout to get us ashore.

As afternoon became evening, we were left with nothing to do aboard the *Berserk* but wait. I stuck my nose into a soaked and dog-eared, trashy mystery novel that Jarle had lying around and tried to escape. I would have read a toothpaste carton at that point. Again and again and again Jarle berated me about the Americans and about how we needed to contact the *Lawrence M. Gould*, and about how we needed that damn gasoline and about what a fine, freaking, half-wool welcome we had received. My nose plunged deeper into the book.

Finally around 11 p.m. Jarle turned on the radio and heard chatter. The *Lawrence M. Gould* had arrived, and the load-out process was in full-swing. Jarle picked up the handset, identified himself and asked if John was on board. The radio operator replied that he was involved in the load-out process, but that he would try to locate him and let him know we wanted to speak to him.

About half an hour later the radio crackled and John's voice came over the loudspeaker. Jarle handed me the handset and I said hello. I told John how we had sailed down on the 27-foot *Berserk*. 'Yeah, congratulations on making it down to Antarctica,' he said sincerely. 'I knew you were dead-set on it. I knew it was your dream. I thought you'd make it.' He sounded harried. He explained they were still in the middle of the loading process.

Jarle prompted me constantly. Finally, I mustered the courage to ask him if we could come aboard his ship for a visit. 'I'm afraid that's not going to be possible,' he replied instantly. 'The NSF guy is on board supervising the supply drop-off, and we're not allowed to have any visitors.' Bureaucracy and regulations – getting hit squarely in the face was worse than taking on a monster wave. 'We're only going to be here a couple of hours, long enough to load off the cargo, and then we're moving on.' The excited lilt of the sailor on shore leave, the guy who bought a case of beer and gave it all away to the backpackers, was gone – replaced by the unemotional, computerised tolling of a mid-level clerk. I might as well have been talking to the computer HAL from *2001: A Space Odyssey*.

'Good luck with the rest of your trip,' he said, signing off. That was the last time I ever spoke to him.

Jarle stared at me for a long instant before launching the next salvo of abuse. It would continue throughout the night. I had no recourse but to suck it up and take it like a man, because he was right. I could not have imagined a more hostile welcome. The long-promised Valhalla of both the American base and my good friend John on the

Lawrence M. Gould had proved to be as much of an illusion as a mirage in the desert, in this case suitable for the biggest desert in the world.

A couple of hours later, in the middle of the night, after successfully dropping off their load and picking up the scientists they were to take back with them, the *Lawrence M. Gould* pulled away from the dock and set off into the ice once again, taking my memories of the friendly sailor along with it and leaving me alone to suffer the indignity of Jarle's constant harping of how poorly I had been treated. Personally, I felt I was owed nothing – which made it all the worse, since I had to hear about it anyway.

That night, after cooking up some pasta and onions, the wind began to howl outside as we drifted off in our sleeping bags. The boat bounced and rocked up and down, nothing out of the ordinary. I was more glad than usual for the rest because for the first time in hours I was not on the receiving end of verbal abuse.

I peered out the foggy window over my bunk early in the morning and bolted upright. 'Jarle!' I screamed. 'We're drifting into the rocks!'

The rocks were close and getting closer. Looking through the window was like peering at them through a magnifying glass. We had crossed the safety margin long ago. We had to act immediately.

The wind direction had changed and now came straight from the west, strong, pushing the boat closer and closer to the protruding black rocks that littered the shallows near the shore. Barely dressed, I yanked up the anchor as Jarle raised the sails and began to steer us away from doom. It was a close call, the closest we'd had yet to running aground, and the wind still blew fiercely in our faces.

Jarle steered us out of the bay and made way straight for Palmer Station. It was the proverbial last straw. He knew that the anchor wouldn't hold and that our moorage was no good anymore. 'What are we going to do?' I asked. I felt racked with indigestion, because deep inside I already knew the answer.

'We're going into Palmer Station,' he shouted to be heard over the roaring wind.

'But we don't have permission.'

'Fuck 'em,' he shouted. 'It's an emergency situation.'

True enough, we had no anchorage in which we could safely secure ourselves. But I was not happy at the prospect of dropping in unannounced on my fellow countrymen. Jarle was using this as a pretext for getting us ashore but his inscrutable reasons were more than valid.

'Get the dinghy ready!' Jarle commanded as the base came into view. I dropped it over the side, noticing the significant whitecaps rearing all around us. Rowing would not be easy. 'Get ready!'

'What do you want me to do?' I asked. We were just outside the base's sheltered bay. The red barn-like buildings loomed large.

'Take the rope to shore and tie us up,' Jarle shouted. 'But you must do it quickly. If you don't do it before the boat blows out, you'll have to row back and we'll have to start all over again.'

I climbed into the dinghy and got ready. The wind kicked the sails full and we plowed quickly forward, the cresting whitecaps swirling around my little corncob bathtub as I readied the oars.

'Now!' The *Berserk* cut to the right and the dinghy ricocheted off to the left, toward shore where a small crowd had begun to gather. I rowed as fast as I could, but the wind and the waves were strong, conspiring against me. I didn't make it. The rope ran out and I let it go as the *Berserk* circled around to the right, readying for a second try.

I drowned out the sights and sounds from the nearby shore. I didn't have time to be distracted. The gathered Americans were close enough to see the shapes of their heads under their parka hoods but still far enough off so that their individual faces remained indiscernible.

I furiously rowed back out to the boat and held on behind it as Jarle circled us around for another try. Again, at just the precise moment, he screamed 'Now!' and I let go, rowing against the wind toward shore. I rowed as mightily as I could, but it still wasn't enough. Again, the rope ran out long before the dinghy was anywhere near shore, and once again I had to row back out to the circling boat.

By now my swollen arms were tired. Though I may have looked somewhat macho making my way to shore in a corncob dinghy in rough seas wearing tattered wetgear, I felt merely incompetent and simply wanted the emergency manoeuvres to end. Maybe I was getting lazy in my old age.

This time Jarle vowed to get me in even closer. We would not get many more tries at this – I was becoming exhausted. This time, he swung me in closer than before; the little boat skipped over the waves like a stone on a pond, and I landed on the rocks, quickly dragging the boat ashore.

I looked valiant, I looked heroic, I looked like an idiot – but I certainly made quite an impression on my fellow countrymen, who were accustomed to seeing their visitors arrive in fancy Zodiac dinghies replete with shiny new outboard engines. I turned my head for an instant to take in my surroundings and noticed a cute girl, her round, red face and blowing blonde hair covered by her parka hood from the blistering wind. She smiled demurely. Lord, I missed seeing that in a stranger.

I stepped into the water and dragged the dinghy up onto the rocky shore, ignoring the low murmuring of the nearby crowd. I looked up and noticed a heavyset doughboy ambling toward me. He was wearing shorts. It was in below zero. It was Ron – the base's general manager, the guy on the power trip and Jarle's instant bureaucratic nemesis. I tried to ignore him as he closed in on me.

Finally Ron stood over me, frowning a dopey grin, and I could no longer ignore him. 'What are you doing?' he asked.

'Tying the rope to a rock,' I explained matter-of-factly. I didn't know what else to say.

Jarle and Ron went at each other from the start, toe-to-toe like two bantamweight boxers throwing a flurry of haymakers that landed consistently but never carried the requisite force to knock the other out. They danced a bureaucratic dance together, much like the playful fur seal pups we would see wrestling on a rock.

After firmly securing the *Berserk*, Jarle ventured ashore for the first time. 'What are you doing here?' Ron asked him, though he knew damn well the answer. And Jarle told him what he wanted to hear, but not quite the way he wanted to hear it: 'We had an emergency situation. The wind pushed our boat into the rocks and we could not hold our anchorage there anymore.' There was nothing Ron could say. He had no countermove. Checkmate. He exuded all of the characteristics of the feckless bureaucrat, the guy everyone on the base had a complaint about who had the overwhelming responsibility of holding the fort together, the quartermaster, not the drill sergeant, the kind of guy everyone laughs at behind their back – but the kind of guy who has the slippery skills to not only get it done, but get it done right, and if you don't watch it, it's you who finds yourself in checkmate, though without the requisite time to tilt your king. The kind of guy who didn't like wrinkles in his plans or in his shirts. The kind of guy who wears shorts in the Antarctic.

Later, he called on the radio and invited us to come ashore that afternoon for a look around the base and to join them for dinner. The meal was exquisite. It was like one of those all-you-can-eat buffets with just about every type of food group imaginable, and a complete dessert table. We might as well have been in Las Vegas. I hit the jackpot and ate like a pig. We had caught them on a good day; because new crewmembers had arrived with the recent delivery, the dessert selection was extra-special.

I was feeling a little shy, for a number of reasons, including the fact that we had literally barged in uninvited, forcing their hand. But the base had a large complement of crew and scientists, over fifty, and a high turnover ratio, so they were used to visitors and were for the most part nonchalant. No one seemed to really care that we were there at all; to them, it was no big deal. The Ukrainians practically threw us a parade.

Also, being back amongst my fellow Americans was a weird feeling. Though normally talkative, friendly and open, in my heart I feel shy, and prefer to remain quiet. As I grow older, I find myself preferring to say nothing.

But most of all I stank. I had been wearing the same musty, damp clothes for most of the trip and by now we on the *Berserk* had become inured to the aroma that invariably followed us wherever we went. We had spent months in the open salty air, which now clung to our cheeks and our necks and our hair like a little baby. We smelled like sailors mixed with puppies without the Old Spice to cover it up. The constant wetness had cleansed us of the worst of all possibilities but left us with something equally discernible and decidedly unpleasant. For my part, I knew we had completely lost perspective. I was acutely aware it was there, hanging in close proximity to the air around us like a Kirlian aura, the strange salty, musky, dank patina of the sea, like we were cattle in its fields grazing on its crops and now we had just entered the barn. I was mortified, and refused to take off the green jumpsuit that I was wearing, the one Manuel had left behind, because the undergarments were even worse. And then I became paranoid, certain that it would be noticed.

So I sat there at the Vegas buffet and gorged on chocolate cake and potatoes au gratin and fresh vegetables in the middle of Antarctica while clammy sweat pored out of me for any number of reasons, and I sat there quietly and self-consciously trying to remain as inconspicuous as possible, but it simply was not possible.

After dinner, most of the base relaxed. There was a pool table in the room next to the kitchen, and the walls were covered with videos. What a great gig. A person could have spent years there just watching the movies. The shelves were filled to the brim and the wallpaper seemed to be video covers. I thought that I should send them a copy of my first film, but then I figured no one really cares anyway.

But then one of the American guys walked up and handed me a complete list of all the Academy Award nominations. He had found it on the Internet and printed it up for me, having heard my inquiry on the VHF radio. I pored over the list, commenting to myself on the expected (*Saving Private Ryan*), the unexpected (what is this *Shakespeare in Love* crap?) and the long-awaited mysterious (*The Thin Red Line*). My jaw dropped with excitement. Nobody else gave a damn.

As we walked through a tour of the base, Ron introduced me to the base's doctor, a tall, thin, bald fellow in his late forties with a thin, black beard. I was growing increasingly concerned with the numbness in my toes. The feeling returned with less and less frequency, and it was becoming more and more difficult to get any feeling to return to them at all. My wound had still not healed, and was open and oozing. By now, the tips of my toes never regained feeling at all and had turned bone white. The numbness was spreading.

I could knock on the tips of my toes with my knuckles; it sounded like wood. My toenails, frozen for months on end, had begun to splinter like warped wood; soon they would begin to fall off completely.

Immediately upon meeting the American doctor I explained my situation. I told him about the encroaching numbness, about my anxiety regarding frostbite, about how I could knock on my toes like they were the doors to a mansion. I asked him what I should do to prevent it.

'Keep them warm,' he answered, and smiled, walking away. It was the last time I ever asked the question.

A little later we headed over to the small bar in the building next door. The party began and so did the drinking. It was just like being at someone's living room party back home. People shed their outergear and wore regular clothes, not Antarctic clothes. The room was heated, unlike the *Berserk*. There was warmth and merriment and rock music, which Jarle took great delight in turning to such loud volumes that it elicited angry glances of protest from the annoyed older patrons hugging the bar with their elbows.

While Jarle fiddled with the music and the crowd, I sat at the bar sweating in my green jumpsuit. I was in the middle of a drink and a story when the cute blonde girl from the beach plopped herself right down on the stool next to me and smiled. She introduced herself, Tracy, and told me that she had watched our landing that morning and had never seen anything like it. She had been worried that the little dinghy would sink under the pressure of the whitecaps in the bay and the wind. I beamed, smug and proud. She sat next to me and we chatted for hours. She was friendly and flirty and her attentions were more than welcome. I couldn't believe my luck: what were the odds that I would travel down to Antarctica and meet a hot woman? The girl announced that she was a krill scientist studying the migration patterns of the small, protein-rich food source that seemed to provide the staple support for most wildlife found in the region. As the evening wore on, I thought I had a shot and became certain we would stay in touch and rendezvous when she returned to the States, because fate had brought us together.

'I can't believe you guys made it in that little bobber.' It was one of the new support crew, a blond guy from Minnesota who had signed on for a year and was fresh off the boat. The base housed not only scientists but support crew consisting of cooks, engineers and maintenance staff. The husky Minnesota blond and I struck up an instant camaraderie; he instinctively seemed to understand what compelled my voyage, and for the first time, while speaking with him, I felt at home. He talked about how he had made the voyage in the *Lawrence M. Gould* and felt excited to begin his yearlong sojourn, uncertain what to expect. For him, making it there had been the accomplishment of a dream, and he understood how strong my desire must have been to ride 'that little bobber' to see the great southern ice.

He called out for shots, and we filled our cups and raised them high. Though normally shy and hesitant in such instances, with liquor flowing through my veins I had relaxed. Raising my glass, I called out the toast.

'God bless America,' I said, lifting it a bit higher. I was at a loss for words and did not know what else to say. I love my country and was glad to be home. It was the first thing that came to mind.

The blond guy smiled but Jarle shook his head in obvious dismay. 'That's so half wool,' he chuckled. I cannot imagine what he would have had me say.

We downed our shots, adding another warm sting to our buzz. Jarle may not have understood, but the meaning was not lost on the guy from Minnesota, who understood that the paucity of words somehow captured the sense of longing one inevitably feels for home, wherever or whatever that may be.

The next day Jarle invited Ron and his girlfriend to join us on the *Berserk* for dinner. He spent the late afternoon whipping up a lavish meal of pasta and onions, and cracked open the fancy plastic and our best carton of cheap wine for the occasion. When Ron zoomed up in a motorised Zodiac and stepped aboard with his girlfriend, he was ready to show them a good time, *Berserk*-style.

Ron's auburn-haired girlfriend, from the hills of Tennessee, was hot and sexy in a way that defied her allegiance to a buffoon, as if the circus trapeze artist was somehow dating the clown. She was friendly and funny and downright nice; how she had graduated from the corn hollows of Appalachia to Ron's bed baffled me completely. I had travelled to Antarctica in the hope of unravelling some of Life's mysteries, not adding to them.

Ron and his girl settled into our little stern galley. We sat around and poured wine into plastic cups and laughed and chatted with his girl – while Ron's countenance slowly started to turn green. It was a pleasant night; the water in the bay was calm and tranquil, the wind momentarily at ease. By the time Jarle dished out the spaghetti, Ron looked like he had just stepped off the Waltzer at the local carnival. He excused himself and stepped out into the night air, where he remained for a minute or two before announcing he would have to return to shore. Once again, Ron had defied all expectation: against any and all odds, he had become instantaneously seasick.

Ron's amused girlfriend shrugged, wolfed down the remains of her spaghetti like a trooper, and then excused herself to join her shivering boyfriend for the short ride back to shore, where she would attempt throughout the long Antarctic night to nurse her man back to health. Just like that, the party ended – and with it, our visit to the American base, where the man in charge, the man responsible for running the whole show, the tough guy who ruled his island empire in Bermuda shorts and with an iron unyielding fist swathed in thick red tape, had become seriously ill after spending only a few short minutes below deck with us on the *Berserk*, docked at port in the calmest of seas.

The next morning we were ready to leave.

'Do you like chocolate?' My lithe, blonde krill scientist stood before me on the beach, beaming and lovely beneath her parka in the muted morning light. She reached out and handed me her monthly allotment, a huge, thick Cadbury brick worth its weight in gold. I accepted it humbly, feeling the slight flush of embarrassment fill my cheeks, because I had nothing to give her in return, no flowers, no chocolate, no kiss. I felt like I was in school again, the same feeling inside as when I picked out a locket in the five-and-dime for my first girlfriend, proud and scared at the same time, uncertain what the future would bring. She stood nearby on the shore while Jarle fiddled with the ropes, packed away the gas he had miraculously scored from Ron, and called for me to go.

I said thank you again and looked away shyly. Everyone wants Love; no one is quite sure where if ever they will find it; many spin its illusion from cobwebs plucked out of the air right in front of them. I took the gift at face value, for what it was – but the act of giving it was not lost on me, and I was not sure what it meant.

We pulled up the ropes and cast off, and I waved, watching my Americans and the base and my krill scientist fade into distant memory behind us. Below deck on the bunk cushion I twirled the chocolate brick around in my hands again and again, wondering what it all meant, before finally tucking my treasure away safely for a future time when I would savour its delight and feel the flush resuscitation of memory fill my soul once again. I did not know when I would crack the seal, but I knew I would save it for a truly special occasion.

CHAPTER TEN
THE LAST ANCHORAGE

We left the American base on a sunny, warm Antarctic day, deciding to stop and explore a nearby ice cave, which some of the Americans highly recommended.

We pulled ashore on the dinghy ready for a day out on the 'town'. Jarle and I both liked exploring best and days like these were few and far between: sunny, warm, blue. We followed directions to the ice cave and parked our dinghy.

After strolling through the big blue cavern, we found ourselves amongst a colony of seals. They were basking in the glory of the summer sunshine and wrestling with their noses on the rocks. The beachhead in the heart of the Antarctic summer was clear of snow, a prime location for the afternoon soirée they seemed to be having.

By now, I had already touched just about everything that moved down there. But I really wanted to get close to a seal. Legend had it that the fur seals were notoriously vicious and ill-tempered. And I wanted to prove the legend wrong.

By now, we had our act down to a science. Jarle had brought along the video camera to capture the walk through the ice cave. We always lugged the whole kit with us: camera equipment, Norwegian flag, and, of course, the little plastic

Viking helmet. How could we go anywhere without that? I wore it most of the time simply because it was easier than carrying it.

With Jarle watching, I walked down the little hill toward the seals. Immediately one of the seals began to bark and growl viciously. I hesitated and waited to see what it would do. When I took another step forward, it growled again – only this time it took a step toward me, protecting its turf, ready to bite.

I wanted to calm it down, to let it know I meant it no harm. Unconsciously I started singing, in a low voice. I started out with a sailor's song, an old Irish shanty sung by a group called the Dubliners, a favourite that Jarle played constantly on the boom box. I sang the song again and again, louder and louder – reminding myself of the time I sang the German drinking song '*Au du Lieber Augustine*' with a drunk Italian on the rim of Ngorongoro Crater in Tanzania at such a loud volume that the lions roared at night and the local tour guides complained.

The little aggressive seal seemed curious – but I soon ran out of patience in singing the same verse over and over again (it was the only verse of the sailing song I knew). So I decided to sing one of the few songs I know in its entirety: Kris Kristofferson's 'Me and Bobby McGee'. My all-time favourite, I relate to its winsome tone of longing to re-experience the road past. I sang low, so that only the seal could hear me, but I put my soul into it, like I was singing alone while walking through Glacier Park in Montana.

As I sang, I stepped slowly toward the seal. To my pleasant surprise, it soon stopped its guttural barking and began to creep toward me as well. I continued singing, stopped moving and kneeled down. The curious little cutie came closer, tilting its head. Sensing a bond of trust had grown between us, I lay down on the ground, stretching out and relaxing.

The little seal came closer and stuck its nose toward me. I reached out my hand, held it out, and he touched me with his nose. Then, a most curious and remarkable thing happened: he rolled over on his back and reached his nose out toward me again, literally placing his head in my lap. I could not help but smile. We had crossed a bridge of friendship together that transcended our species; we had overcome prejudice and fear and were now friends. By singing, I had comforted the seal and communicated my benign intent. I was becoming increasingly sure of my ability to communicate with animals.

I could have played with that seal all afternoon, but after a few minutes more, Jarle called out and the seal ran off to play once again with his pals.

Jarle wanted to either do some more filming or head back to the boat for some work. If I'd learned anything by now, it's that there's always more work to do on a boat, and since crap rolls downhill, the further down you are on the totem pole, the more of the grunt work you're expected to do. I was feeling lazy and wanted to enjoy the rest of a pleasant afternoon outdoors. I was sick and tired of filming or working. I simply wanted nothing more than to lay back and relax – just like a seal.

Three huge elephant seals were sleeping on the beach, while the *Berserk* bobbed in the little harbour off shore behind them. As we walked back to the dinghy, I boldly announced: 'I want to touch one. I want to lie down on it.' Jarle chuckled. He didn't believe me.

He readied the camera. 'Go ahead,' he announced. Slowly I walked toward the slumbering beasts, the largest of which must have weighed a ton and a half. The big one, in the middle, was facing the water, but the other two faced inland. I approached from the right, not even bothering to sing. The one closest to me seemed to be a female; she had a broad, round, smiling face and was a light tan colour, like coffee with extra cream.

The smile on her face set me at ease as I kneeled down to the ground and began crawling over toward them. Without much ado, after a bit of informal jousting, I made my way over to her side and put my hand on her shoulder, looking up at Jarle and smiling, posing for a snapshot with an old buddy.

I slowly crept closer to the big elephant seal in the middle until, confident that they were my buddies, I was sure they would not bother me at all, any more than I was bothering them. I turned around and leaned my back slowly against the big guy; he did not stir. I made myself comfortable, forgetting the helmet was still on my head as I shut my eyes, enjoying the serenity of the moment. My left hand hung within inches of the smiling mouth of Big Momma, and I could have been a bit concerned that she might decide to take a little unexpected chomp, just to see how I tasted. But right then I didn't have a worry in the world. I shut my eyes and forgot where I was, living in the moment and taking an afternoon nap with the others. There was no boat, no *Berserk*, no sailing – just a bunch of us animals chilling in the afternoon sun. I felt completely safe in the company of my animal friends.

Jarle grew tired of filming the entire escapade – after a while, he too decided he wanted to lie down with the elephant seals. He set the camera on the tripod and turned it on, leaving the tape rolling as he lay down a few feet away and slowly crabbed his way toward us, inch by inch, nervously looking over his shoulder and holding his little Viking helmet on his head with one hand as he crawled closer and closer. Suddenly, when he was only inches away, the third elephant seal – a young male on the far side of the big guy – raised his head and lunged toward us with a load roar, poised to strike.

Jarle bolted upright, and I leaned forward to a sitting position. 'This is so half-wool,' he chuckled as he walked away, back to the camera. The young male, irritated by Jarle's approach, put his head back on the ground, an act of détente. I shrugged my shoulders and leaned back down, instantly relaxing and shutting my eyes again.

'David, watch out!' Jarle screamed. My eyes opened too late. The young male reared his head again – only this time, he didn't stop with a roar. With a monstrous bellow he lunged his gaping jaws across the big guy and tried to bite the horns off the plastic Viking helmet resting on top of my head. I felt the elephant seal's hot, sour-milk breath hitting the back of my neck and instinct took over. I shot upright to a sitting position just in time, just as he knocked the helmet off my head with his mouth, as if to teach me a lesson. He missed taking off my entire head by inches.

I looked back at him in disgust as the young male cockily returned to his previous position. I looked over at Jarle. 'Now look what you've done,' I joked without a smile. 'You've gone and ruined the party.' With an emphatic quick flick of the wrist, I leaned over and quickly snatched back the helmet, putting it on my head again and looking over at the coffee-cream creature at my side as she smiled reassuringly while the big guy snoozed on.

I didn't know it at the time, but the day's events would prove to be a turning point in my life.

It was time to head home. The autumn Antarctic storms were due to kick in at any time, marking the beginning of the ice's march north. The autumn storms were notorious for arriving with ferocity and remaining for a week at a time, blowing so harshly a boat could not leave its anchorage safely. Jarle had explained to me their severity and warned about their significance: once the autumn storm season began in earnest, it was unlikely to let up. The Drake to South Georgia, some of the most dangerous waters in the world, would boil over, a tempest in a teapot, and we would be caught smack dab in the middle. We had no choice. We had to leave before they began. And they were about to begin, at any time.

We were making our way back up toward Melchior, where we were planning to set off from again, when the first of the real autumn storms hit. For three days we were stuck lashed to the side of an enormous rock at the edge of an island just off the strait. The wind blew fiercely from the north, strong enough to knock hats off our heads. Most of the time, snow and rain fell miserably on the uninviting grey land. The sky was grey, the rock was grey, the water and the land turned grey, as if all life was in the process of evacuating, all blood draining from the body, the living organism of Antarctica turning to ash. For days we were stuck in our bunks, reduced to staying in our bags for warmth, reading to pass the time and only occasionally setting foot on shore long enough to be attacked by skuas before scampering back to the safety of our beds.

On the fourth day, we grew tired of the rock. The weather loosened a bit and Jarle felt we should make a break for it. We cast off from the secure anchorage and turned, heading out into the choppy waters of the strait.

By the time we cleared the island, the passage roiled with whitecaps that kicked cascades roughly over the bow. Jarle sent me up front to deal with the sails as the boat bounced up and down hard. The wind had changed directions and was coming from behind the port side, but blew so strongly we had to switch to a smaller sail. I barely hung on as the front of the boat plunged down into the water like a diving submarine, submerging and bringing most of the small choppy wave up with it like a shovel lifting wet dirt, over my head, into my face and down my neck to my torso. The wind screamed and blew in our faces as we fought our way along.

Jarle knew we had made a mistake by setting off. Immediately he began to consult his charts, searching for a safe haven. He located a small narrow inlet on the next island and we headed straight for it.

When we arrived, we discovered another boat moored in the inlet, held taut against the fierce wind by two ropes like a fly in a spider's web. It was the Italian guy who gave us apples, the guy who thought Jarle to be an irresponsible sailor – in his mind, we proved the point again by arriving under such dreadfully hostile conditions. We tossed him a rope and pulled in behind him for the night.

We were stuck in this inlet for another three days as the wind continued to rage. We left the boat only once, to set up our own anchor lines when the Italian took off the next day; without a functioning motor, we had no choice but to remain behind.

The grey sky darkened. Summer lustre continued to drain from the corpse Antarctica was rapidly becoming; the vampire of Autumn had arrived. It was time for us to go, as soon as possible. The trick would be to make our break without getting caught between the icebergs forever.

Poised to leave Antarctica, Jarle located a small, unnamed island group on the charts, nothing more than tiny black dots on the big map. There were no individual charts, but we knew they were there. We had expected to set off from near Melchior but had unexpectedly come upon the islands and now decided to make them our last refuge before heading into battle against the Drake.

As I rowed to shore in the face of a thick blizzard nearing whiteout conditions, I looked down to see more than a dozen young seals swimming circles beneath the dinghy, playing in the puny wake left by my oars. The surface of the inlet was boiling with these playful pups as they leapfrogged over one another beneath the little corncob boat, skimming both the surface and the dinghy so closely I thought they would knock me over. As I dragged the dinghy up onto the small beach, they joined me and sat up in formation like bowling pins, staring at me and blinking. I looked down at them and called aloud as it dawned on me: 'I don't think they've ever seen a human being before!'

We had found this secluded cove by fluke. Heck, we barely knew there was an island group there, completely expecting to head out to sea before the snowstorm hit. But our last refuge turned out to be the most magnificent spot we found yet, peaceful and serene, the cherry on top of the sundae.

When the blizzard finally broke, we went ashore for one last sojourn. We walked in silence across the soft, moist earth, filled with colourful pink lichens and lime green mosses, feeling it crunch beneath our boots and spring back, drinking it all in. We passed the occasional sleeping seal and climbed up a hill until we stood on the highest point, with a 360-degree vista. Over on the next island a giant wall of baby-blue ice split off with a crack and dropped into the sea. With a delayed puff the air cleared of residual mist and we witnessed our first major avalanche as the chunk fell into the bay and shattered, sending a rippling wave rolling over the scattered blocks of ice.

Back on board, we lit the kerosene stove for only the second time on the entire trip. Jarle wanted to dry out the boat before we were soaked for the next two months. The makeshift tin chimney heated up and unbeknownst to us continued to melt the plastic opening through the bow deck.

We were on the western side of the peninsula. The plan was to cast off into the water and the wind and use them to our advantage, heading straight north to get past the Antarctic convergence zone as quickly as possible, significantly reducing the probabilities of encountering icebergs. Then, we would turn hard to starboard and make our way downwind to South Georgia.

The first storms had already arrived, along with the first taste of autumn. There was a lot to talk about. But we spent our last day out in Antarctica largely in silence, absorbed in the thoughts of what lay behind us – and, more immediately, what lay ahead: the Drake.

CHAPTER ELEVEN
THE SECOND STORM

Snow continued to fall as we shoved off from our final anchorage and slowly drifted out into the swells of the open sea. We spotted a few huge, flat, baby-blue icebergs floating off in the distance, the size of three football fields, and squinted as they faded into the horizon, much as I suspect the earlier ones had arrived.

The first five days flowed smoothly. Early on, the same feeling I had the first time we hit the open sea welled inside me: a slight, rubbery wobbliness that accompanies the regaining of one's sea legs as the ocean rolls in and the swells slowly get bigger, like driving from the countryside into the Wisconsin dells on a curvy road. But soon, the legs came back, the shifts went easily, and, other than a close call with a large fishing ship close to the eleven-mile Antarctic limit, we smoothly sailed through the foggy convergence zone like we were gliding on butter. When we emerged on the other side of the zone, with great confidence we altered our heading and turned right, to the north-east, to South Georgia.

But then, on day five, our first day out of the zone, it began to drizzle. Lightly at first. Then it picked up; the wind began to howl, the mast ropes played their tune against the steel pipe, the seas kicked up, and before we knew it, we had stuck our toe into a storm. Inside, the same feeling generally accompanies the arrival of a storm – a sense of pervasive, uncontrollable dread. It's much like experiencing the beginning of a California earthquake: the shaking starts, there's a burgeoning understanding of what's happening, followed by instinctive fear of mortality and self-preservation, only to be replaced by a momentary sense of false comfort before the fear curve spikes upward in direct correlation to how long the shaking lasts.

With sea storms, first I would watch the clouds loom on the horizon, then change their configuration and gather. I would continue to hope it wouldn't hit right up until the time it did, the pressure mounting within as the pressure dropped precipitously outside. Then, when the first raindrops inevitably did fall, I would think: Please, don't get any bigger – all the way until it was over.

Soon this system began to release its full fury and we were splattered about like a popcorn kernel in hot oil. The seas capped themselves with white foam and the waves grew in size and strength, their irregular rhythm wreaking havoc with our course.

But by now, we had seen plenty of storm action. We were old hands at this, and it did not faze us in the slightest. This was nothing compared to our first storm, where the waves curled over the boat. We were cocksure that we had hit the worst of the worst on our first day out and that nothing else could compare.

'What do you want to do?' Jarle asked me. 'Should we pull down the sails, or should we put on the storm jib and ride it out??'

By now the storm kicked pretty good. The last thing I wanted to do was walk out to the bow and change the sails. The wind whipped wildly; even with the smaller storm sail, it would be difficult to hold the course. Outside it got downright messy. I figured we'd be better off yanking down the sails and battening down the hatches. For once, Jarle agreed – and the sails came down.

Jarle used some rope to tie off the tillers, holding them steady against the constant push of the sea and sky. The boat began to leak a bit through the opening in the bow deck where the tin chimney melted. I reclined in my sleeping bag and watched the water trickle in. The waves began to pound against the fibreglass, stronger and stronger, louder and louder. The boat began to shake and vibrate with each hit, making me feel like I was being pummelled like a piece of pork in a plastic bag shaken in breadcrumbs and softened by a hammer before cooking. But I felt completely relaxed. We'd been through this before.

Suddenly, I heard the loudest crash of all. I did not know what hit us. The boat whirled around and spun, and I bounced off the ceiling like a pinball, then dropped back against the bulkhead as the wood table smacked into my head and every loose object in the boat kicked loose and scattered everywhere. It happened so quickly, so suddenly, without warning. When the boat righted itself, it listed terribly to one side. We were sinking.

I stuck my feet to the ground – and immediately felt ice water crawling up my legs like spiders.

I stood up. Freezing Southern-Ocean water filled the boat up to my chest. I quickly waded out from the bow in my wool underwear and grabbed the red bucket. In the thick water, the underwear fell down to my ankles. I leaned under and grabbed it, pulling it up again.

The starboard window had been completely smashed. Shattered glass lay everywhere, scattered throughout the floating debris. I could see curling waves through the gaping hole, which was being dragged perilously close to the water. The water was closer than I had ever seen it and getting closer. And then it dawned on me: we were going down.

Jarle lunged for the VHF handset and barely grabbed it.

'Mayday, mayday!' he called out, identifying our boat and our last known approximate position.

I stopped dead in my tracks. I knew Jarle by now. He would not call for help even if his own grandmother had fallen overboard; he would simply deal with it himself and maybe, if she was lucky, he would toss her a life jacket. Immediately, at a very profound level, I understood the intense severity of our situation.

I leaned down and dipped the bucket into the water, fighting my way toward the hatch through a miasma of broken glass, spilled oatmeal and coagulating spaghetti. Again the wool underwear dropped to my ankles – only this time I didn't even bother to lean down and pick it up. There simply wasn't any time. Soon they were gone, having disappeared completely, sucked under the bulkhead with the rest of the offal.

I didn't care. We were fighting for our lives. I lifted the heavy bucket of water and debris up through the hatch and started to climb up a bit to toss it out. Suddenly another monster wave rocked the boat, and the entire ship lurched as cold calculating white water took aim and slapped us, crashing through the open window hole. Unprepared for the jolt and barefoot, I slipped on the soaking underwater step, crushing my shinbone until the skin cracked open and bled, dropping the bucket and falling backward into the morass of underwater debris.

Without waiting for an answer from the radio, Jarle – with a look in his eye I had never before seen – pushed past me to get to the cockpit, which was filled to the brim with water. 'Get me a knife!' he screamed at the top of his lungs. 'Hurry!'

I always kept a pocket knife next to my bunk – but I had no idea if it was still there after our spin. Everything was everywhere. I looked over at the only copy of my precious novel, the one I had spent months painstakingly writing in longhand, wrapped in plastic and stuffed into an old backpack placed strategically in the safest, driest spot – right under the broken window. It looked like Niagara Falls spilling over it. I felt queasy. I didn't care. Fuck the novel. I turned and headed back for the bow to try to find the knife. I fought my way back through the sinking boat to find the knife exactly where I had left it. I was shocked.

When I stretched up through the hatch to hand it to Jarle, I saw our immediate problem: the wooden banisters that held the dinghy firmly attached to the top of the bow had been ripped by a monster wave right out of the top of the boat, taking the dinghy with it. Now the upright dinghy was full of water, under the surface of the sea and sinking under its own weight, yet still attached by a tangled mess of ropes to a confused bird's nest of splintered wood, shattered fibreglass, and bent steel. The weight of the dinghy was steadily dragging the entire boat down – right toward the open gaping broken hole that used to house a window. We had minutes at most.

If the window hit the water, we were dead.

I desperately began to heave bucket after bucket of messy water from the inside of the cabin as fast as I could. At first, I tried to fight my way up through the hatch to lift the bucketfuls over the edge, but it soon became apparent that we no longer had that luxury. Our situation worsened and I simply tossed the water out through the open hatch, leaving it to find its way back to sea from there.

Within minutes my legs were blue, the veins even darker as my manhood literally and figuratively shrank before my very eyes. Luckily, I couldn't feel them – or the sharp shards of glass cutting into my bare, numb toes.

As the storm raged, each crashing wave brought another burst of agony as my body heaved uncontrollably into floating, sinking, swimming objects of every conceivable shape, size and sharpness, each with minds of their own seemingly intent on doing me harm. Water continued to pour in through every conceivable opening and we were losing ground. I was bailing for my life.

I had spent the entire trip being careful and considerate concerning litter and debris. But at this moment, we were in a life or death situation. Assorted objects floated, clogged the drains, blocked the way. There was no room for negotiation: if it got in the way, I tossed it overboard, without shame. I was angry. If that's the way you want to play, I thought to myself, this is what you get. The ocean had struck the first blow and all bets were off. Only one thought permeated my every action: Survival.

Out on deck, Jarle leaned out toward the dinghy. Through the bouncing torrent of the storm, he hung on desperately to the mast with one hand while reaching out with the small pocket knife and sawing through the thick green ropes with the other, eventually watching our only safety valve sink away to the bottom of the great south sea.

Inside, I heaved bucket after bucket of water out through the hatch like a machine, ignoring the pain that appeared almost immediately in all of my muscles, swelling and throbbing and aching. I had no time to think of anything else; the slightest deviation of thought could prove fatal. Eventually, however, I did have time and it dawned on me: if Jarle were to be swept overboard, I was in a boatload of trouble. 'What did you do?' I asked when Jarle dropped through the hatch again.

'I cut off the dinghy,' he answered matter-of-factly. 'It was dragging us down.' For the first time I noticed that the listing of the boat had started to ease, though we were still full of water.

How will we get to shore? I thought to myself. He answered before I had the chance to verbalise it. 'We had no choice.'

He waded back over to grab hold of the VHF handset again, and once again he called out for help. 'Mayday, mayday!!' he cried out, even more desperation in his voice this time than the last. I had trusted my life to this boy – and had been willing to follow him all the way to the edge. We were now there, looking squarely over. I didn't like the view.

We heard no answer. We did not expect one. We were hundreds of miles from the nearest shipping route; there would be no logical reason for any ship to be anywhere near the area. Still hopeful, with that unreasonable expectation that accompanies sheer dread, like the ridiculous belief that a basketball player will launch a ball the length of the court with no time remaining on the clock to win the game, we listened – and suddenly, we indeed heard something: the dull fizz of static faded to nothing, and we lost our electricity once and for all.

We had no time to dwell on it – we were still only one well-placed wave away from going under. Soon the blue-black dusk of the great Southern-Ocean night would cover us like a cold blanket for the evening, a velvet funeral shroud. I continued tossing buckets of water and debris out into the cockpit, one after the other, as Jarle scrambled down into the boat and grabbed a long blue cushion used to cover one of the stern bunks. He dragged it, soaking and heavy, up through the hatch and lofted it up toward the broken window. As strong waves continued to crash into the side of the rocking boat, heaving us up and dropping us suddenly down with a bang, he folded it over and stuffed it precariously through the gaping hole, wedging it in as best he could while fighting off the waves but still leaving a wide hole through which the water continued to spill.

He craned his head back down into the cabin, searching for something else to use to fill the remaining gap. He gestured begrudgingly and I reluctantly handed him his own sleeping bag. He dragged it out and stuffed it into the window next to the cushion, rigging a green rope around both objects to hold them in place temporarily.

For the first time since the wave struck, we had stanched the immediate flow of water into the boat. Finally I was able to make progress in bailing and the water level inside the cabin started to slowly go down. Jarle returned to the cockpit and started to haul out the debris clogging the rear drains as he grabbed hold of both tillers, bracing the boat for the long, dreary night battle ahead.

We were still right smack-dab at the beginning of the storm. Even though the hole was jerry-rigged for the moment, Jarle and I were still but one wave from going down. And we both knew it.

This time, the random thoughts became completely unbearable. I no longer thought I was going to die; I knew it. I would never be the same. In an instant everything that everyone had said became true, all the warnings, all the boxes of food – for the first time, I understood it, I got it. I didn't see a hallway with a white light at the end of the tunnel; that would have been imminently preferable to the constant, unedited barrage of memories and feelings that piled themselves upon me simultaneously, one epiphany more painful than the next in great grand succession. Instead of a tunnel, I saw the rapidly approaching ice-cold water of the great Southern Ocean, where I would disappear without a trace, leaving those who cared wondering for all eternity what became of me.

And in that one instant, it became crystal clear who actually did care: my immediate family. I could feel the pain that would reverberate through my father's heart forever, and I couldn't bear it. I could see him staring off into the distance, his eyes watery with eternal agony, as if I had left my body and was looking down. My sister and mother would also care. Other than that, I had no one. A hollow, dawning reality – but an honest assessment nonetheless.

My mind wandered and began to play tricks on me, and I could not control it. Love, of all things, popped into my brain, and I thought of all the women in my life.

I thought of the love of my life; though I had never made love to her, I loved her more than I had ever loved anyone, more than anyone could love. She had been the lead actress in my first and only feature film, *Renaissance*, and I had fallen in love with her the moment I laid eyes on her.

Renaissance dealt with an artist's attempt to reconcile his failure to create works of beauty in a society that seemingly prefers sex, sleaze and violence. I had cast her in the role of Rhonda, a young girl on the cusp of womanhood, who proves to be the inspiration for the lead artist character to continue in the face of the cumulative failures of a lifetime.

On her first audition, held during the day in a vacant nightclub, she had swung around a support pole while reading the lines exactly as I had envisioned them, and I knew on the spot that not only did I want to cast her but that I was madly in love with her, as only a poet can be.

Yet I had to remain professional – so I vowed to myself I would not say a thing until all the work on the film had been completed. The entire process took a gruelling 13 months; I was on the road the whole time in Philadelphia, sleeping in the same room with a 17-foot Burmese python that had no cage, and pining after her. But I was willing to do anything to make the film, much in the same way that I would have done anything to see Antarctica.

During the process, I began to date another woman, my art director. It just happened. One night the relationship simply exploded unexpectedly, eventually blossoming into an equally significant, no-less-profound, different flavour of love. I wound up dating her for eight years – until the spectre of the actress proved to be too much water under the bridge, and forced a wedge into our relationship so deep it would eventually derail it.

Eventually, when the film ended, I called the actress and told her exactly how I felt, that I loved her. Her answer: 'David, you're not in love with me, you're in love with the character.'

Was she right?

Any lingering doubt washed away that day on the water. But there would be no happy ending; a complete acceptance of the unchangeable past became imminent as well, and she floated away on the next wave, suddenly as insignificant as a piece of stale bread.

I thought of my ex-girlfriend. She had been willing to move to Los Angeles to be with me, even though my guilty conscience took over and I called her the night before she was ready to drive across country to tell her the relationship had no future because I was in love with another woman. I was completely honest, an open book. She made me pay for it. She drove out anyway, played 'holier than thou', and tossed it back in my face for the remainder of our fractured relationship until eventually I was forced to make a profound choice: accept her honest, decent love and make it work her way, or acknowledge the reality of a true, profound Love I could never have.

I'll never know if that actress loved me or not. One evening, while I was immersed in a three-hour long argument with my girlfriend, the operator came on the line. 'I have an emergency breakthrough,' she announced.

'Emergency breakthrough?' I asked, astonished. 'From who?'

The operator answered that it was from the actress.

'Go to your whore!' my girlfriend exclaimed, slamming down the phone.

The actress came onto the line.

'What the hell are you doing?' I asked.

'I wanted to talk to you,' she told me. We had a mutual friend in town visiting and she wanted to arrange a get-together.

'Well, I think you just ended my relationship,' I told her, hanging up and promising to call her back.

That night, the night of the phone call, I vowed a pox on both their houses. I knew I couldn't in good faith stay with my girlfriend any longer, but I also knew I wasn't going to pursue the actress either. Like Othello, I blew all my fond love to heaven, vowing never to fall in love again.

One by one, here on the water, all the women I ever loved or desired, large and small, paraded before me; there had been far too few. Instantly all courtships I had left behind ended. My concept of Love itself changed irrevocably, and I felt relieved: rather than live with regret, I was going to die with certainty.

On the other side of the fence fell those indifferent to my plight. Friends and acquaintances from youth, people met in passing, foes and nemeses, would shrug and not miss a beat at my disappearance, if ever they knew. Immediately, these people became completely irrelevant to my life; I would never waste time on them again. They were deleted from my hard drive, sent to the recycle bin and dumped forever into cyberspace.

At the same time, cherished memories became magnified. Little moments of kindness one finds in life, strangers who have extended a helping hand, without ever knowing it instantly became that much more significant.

Years ago, I had been travelling in Africa when rebels took over the main airport in Kinshasa, Zaire and martial law was declared. The military took over the streets and shut the country down, waiting to root out the insurrection.

At the time the insurrection broke out, I was floating on a makeshift canoe down the River Congo. When all foreigners were airlifted out of the country, it immediately became necessary for me to make my way to the border. But there were no paved roads across eastern Zaire at the time, and I got stuck in a crossroads 'town with no name' waiting for the next truck to come along.

A friendly villager offered me a place to stay, in his small backyard. He was alone in the house, taking care of his three young children while his young wife was off in another city, one with a proper makeshift hospital, where she was about to give birth to number four. Without any motive other than kindness, he offered up the complete hospitality of his humble home, even cooking meals for me. I had nothing to do but lie around, read, and walk up to the outdoor corner market several times a day.

Then, after three days, suddenly and without warning, we heard the sound of an approaching truck. Arthur, one of my companions, came running back to tell us that a truck was on its way. We had five minutes to hurriedly arrange our things and jump on the back of the truck – and our friend was nowhere to be found.

I climbed up into the packed back of the idling lorry, scanning the gathering villagers for our friend, but did not see him. Finally, as the truck started to bounce away down the rutted dirt road, I saw our friend emerge from the back of the crowd, holding his hand up to bespeak his goodbye. I smiled and waved back, and he disappeared into the dark. I never saw him again – until that day, out there on the great Southern Ocean.

One after another, in the span of nanoseconds, images and emotions crisscrossed my mind all at once, like single notes on a lone piano, discernible individually but altogether deafening. One after the other, the meaningful people in my life became apparent, under the blanket of one singular thought: I would never see any of them again.

CHAPTER TWELVE
THE RIDE HOME

Hours passed. The storm raged. And Jarle stayed at the helm, keeping the wind at our backs and dodging the monster breakers that curled all around us.

Eventually, I emptied the boat of enough water to see the cluttered floor – and to see my own bare blue bloody legs. I hurled everything I could lay my hands on over the side of the boat, emptying it of shards of broken glass and the soggy cardboard containers and clump after clump of oatmeal and spaghetti that clogged the bilge pump, fighting my way until I could finally see the bottom. Freezing, I looked everywhere, but still could not find my wool underwear. During the fitful bailing, they had disappeared into the bowels of the boat.

I leaned out through the hatch. Jarle smiled. 'I have never been more proud,' he said to me, 'than when I saw you bailing with your dick in one hand and a bucket in the other.' He reminded me that there is no better pump in the world than a desperate sailor with a bucket. I smiled back, glad to oblige. ' Do I have time to put on some clothes now?'

Darkness descended on the great Southern Ocean and we were caught in the midst of a dark spider's nest, a teapot in a tempest. We were not concerned with control or direction, simply with staying afloat. Water and waves continued to pummel the boat and wash over it, spouting down through the new holes in the bow, through the gap left from the kerosene chimney, and pouring down like a continuous waterfall through the spaces in the broken window, stuffed with the cushion, sleeping bag and an old raincoat.

Twelve hours passed and still Jarle remained at the helm. He told me to stay inside, to lie down and try to get some sleep. In my mind there was no way I was going to fall asleep – ever again. Certainly not that night. Still, he persisted. 'I'll need you fresh when you take over,' he said.

I did not know when that would be, but hoped it would be no time soon. We were still mired in a life-or-death scenario with conditions that changed by the minute. I wanted our best man at the helm, the man with the most experience. He understood the conditions and knew best how to handle what might arise – and I was not too proud to admit it. I simply did not want to be responsible for our deaths. One well-placed hit on the side of the boat with the broken window would still put us down and under. Waves whipped at us without rhyme or reason, without pattern, without direction. And now we had no light at all. The dark cloak of night had fallen, heralding the onslaught of the burgeoning southern-hemisphere autumn and blotting out the sky.

On the high sea we could see nothing. Jarle was reduced to staring up at the small Norwegian flag attached to the back stay wire. We knew the drill: a direct wave on either side of the boat would send us over once again; a hit on the bow would topple us. However, we could 'surf' a wave that approached from behind, using the two tillers in combination to steer the boat and keep it upright till the crest subsided.

But Jarle had been staring straight up into the phosphorescent night sky for hours, watching that little tattered flag rip in the fierce wind and keeping the wind at our backs. The green glow of the dark water would light up with the white crest of waves right before they crashed into the boat. Jarle, playing on instinct, much like Luke Skywalker turning off his targeting computer in *Star Wars*, could feel the giant waves approaching under the boat, under his heel. His gift and his experience came into play, and he managed throughout the night to avoid a direct hit.

But the intensity of the storm was just too much. Inside, I shuddered with the crash of each ensuing wave. I could hear the magnified low rumble getting nearer and nearer, unable to discern from which direction it was arriving until it struck the boat with such force that it would send us flying through the air, bouncing hard back down on the water just in time to hear the next low rumble approaching.

My body ached all over. The cold had subsided the swelling in my throbbing, aching muscles, leaving the residue of sharp arthritis in its wake; my legs and feet were bruised and cut open. It was then I realised that we had on board the perfect antidote to soothe the pain: the muscle-relaxing Russian ointment. That mad Russian doctor had seen this very moment. I finally understood. I shivered.

My eyes bolted open as if by preternatural force and remained that way. The hollow wet bow amplified and echoed each crashing wave, like being inside a giant bass fiddle or fibreglass tuba. The longer the night went on, the louder the echo became until soon it was constant, difficult to differentiate between crashes, one loud, interminable, symphonic humming.

I did not get a wink of sleep. Instead, I often walked up toward the hatch to lift it, checking on Jarle to make sure he was OK. And then, I began to notice a look in his eye that I had never seen before, a dizziness. He was steering on instinct, but time and pressure and intensity had taken its natural toll. Without a break, he was getting loopy.

It was then, in the dead middle of the night, as we approached the cold spot before dawn, with all due horror still flowing firmly like cold black ink through my veins, that somewhere deep in my soul a muscle must have relaxed and I felt, for a split second, that maybe we would make it through the night after all. Suddenly, the rear of the boat crested upward, lurched, heaved up, threatening to topple, and simultaneously, as Jarle screamed 'Aaaaaaaaaaaaah!' a giant wave hit us square on the backside with the full fury of Neptune, crashing through the rear hatch like thunder, shattering the planks and splintering the wood that held them in place, filling the entire inside of the boat with water up to my chest once again.

I leapt off the bunk into the cold. 'Are you OK?' I yelled out. I waited to see if he was still there. 'Yeah, but I'm wet,' he answered. I was just glad to hear his voice.

Methodically, accepting that my fate had long ago been decided, I picked up the bucket dutifully and began the long, arduous process of emptying out the boat. It took an hour and a half of continuous non-stop bailing before the bottom became visible. I no longer saw purpose in struggling against the tide, swimming upstream. If we were to go down now, so be it. One more wave like that and it would finally be over, and at least I would be relieved of the agony of waiting. So, weary, muscles aching, I slowly bailed out the *Berserk*.

Luckily I did not have to bother removing the hatch – because there was no hatch. Cold wind gusted in through the open hole, through which I could see Jarle's grim determination, for he had the more difficult job: making sure another wave didn't hit us from either of our openings, behind or on the starboard side.

After this, I never felt the same about being in the bunk, captain's orders or not. It somehow felt wrong; I wanted to face Death head-on, wanted to see it coming. I wanted to spit in its face, to die with my boots on, outside. I always wanted to be outside.

Eventually I managed to clear out the boat. I asked Jarle how he had managed to hang on through such force. He explained that he had instinctively felt the wave encroaching at the last minute, and when the boat had reared up he had wrapped both his arms around the upside-down-Y shaped wires of the back stay and held on for dear life. The enormous monster crested and crashed down right over him, smashing through right behind his neck. In the process, some of the wet wave had crept beneath his hood, meandering its way nefariously behind the nape of his neck, creeping like a cold snake until it spiralled itself around his torso, constricting him with cold.

The second monster wave completely smashed the solar panel tied astern, and with it, any hope of recharging our batteries. A direct hit, a bullseye – score another one for Mother Nature – had left the glass covering the little black round receptacles completely shattered like the broken windshield of a car.

As soon as I finished ridding our innards of water, Jarle called me out to the cockpit. 'David, I need you to steer,' he told me. 'No thanks,' I joked. I didn't want the privilege, and he could probably see it in my face, like I had seen a ghost. I had – my own. 'The wave got me wet and I need to change my clothes,' he went on. He claimed to have one last remaining set of dry clothes double-wrapped in a black plastic rubbish bag safely ensconced beneath the hatch over his bunk. He started to shiver. I had no choice. 'I don't want to,' I muttered, half under my breath, the other half obscured by wind.

'Just until I change my clothes,' he said. He definitely needed the break, but the last wave was evidence that the storm still kicked at our ribs like a stubborn mule. I crept out to his side.

'What do I do?' I asked, even though I already knew the answer, like a little kid who asks his father a question simply because the reassurance is more reassuring than asking nothing.

'Use both tillers,' he said. 'Look up at the flag. Keep the wind at our backs. Whatever you do, don't let that side of the boat hit the water.' He gestured toward the starboard side with the broken window and dropped down inside the boat, through the open hatchway.

I was horrified. It was sometime around three in the morning, so dark I had to squint to see my hand clearly. In low-light conditions such as these, my eyes had difficulty focusing but wearing glasses was out of the question; they fogged and became covered with water droplets instantly. I sat on the left side of the boat, grabbing hold of the thick wood tiller inside the cockpit with my left hand and the cold steel tiller rod of the wind-vane rudder with the right. 'Hurry,' I whimpered.

I did not want to be the one responsible for our deaths, and this was the thought running through my brain as I took over control of the tillers. Jarle was the best man for that job. He knew the boat best, knew how to steer, had sailed through storms before, though unlikely anything of this magnitude. The slightest mistake or error in judgement could cost us our lives. I could handle the responsibility for my own death, but I did not want to sink down to the inky blackness and meet my Maker with Jarle's death, and all the weight that carried with it, on my conscience. I wanted him back out there on the helm as soon as possible. I couldn't see a thing.

I looked up into the black night and saw the tattered Norwegian flag flapping wildly, snapping itself to tatters, the ripping shreds obscured by the whistling wind as it passed through the teeth of our wires and rigging, the ropes holding all equipment in place banging so loudly and constantly against the mast that each bang became indistinguishable from the next, resulting in one loud musical roaring whirr of wind, like the grinding of a loud lawnmower.

I felt the movement of the boat quaking beneath my hands. The thick waves made manipulating our course more difficult, like rowing through chocolate syrup. I had no idea what our course even was. The electricity was long gone and the little light that illuminated the compass with it. I didn't care. My job was simple: crane my neck, look toward the sky and the little flag, and keep the tattered rag immobile and straight, pointing directly toward the front of the boat. I could feel the cold wind brushing against the right side of my face like a wire hairbrush, but relished the sensation because at least it gave the wind direction.

The darkness of the dark of darkest night obscured the size of the waves, though when they crested the small white rail of bubbles illuminated itself briefly with slightly luminous green phosphorescence. But by the time the wave revealed itself it was always too late, too near or too distant, a mistimed jump. The boat bounced along the high swells, up and down; looking up, all perspective was lost, no top or bottom, no up or down, no ability to judge distance, just a flap flap flapping flag and a tug of an arm to adjust the wind. Not too difficult. But the waves, they were another story. I could feel them bumping into us, under us, around us, near us, over us, but I never had any idea where they truly were. I would look down from the flag and cast my eyes out over the side of the boat but could see only murky nothingness until the faint outline of bubbles rose with a hiss and a splash, sizzling like a burger on the grill until fading away to the next one. I looked backwards, over my shoulder, and again, only murky obscurity and oblivion gazed back unblinkingly.

Down through the hatch, Jarle's barely visible figure was fishing through the rubbish bags trying to locate his one set of dry clothes. Double-wrapped and in there somewhere, he was opening various bags, poring through them, trying to find the good stuff.

Beneath me the boat bounced and lurched, and as I settled into my seat my eyes adjusted to the dark. I still couldn't see anything; the mountains of dark blue waves merged seamlessly with the charcoal horizon, making their outlines indistinguishable. Suddenly, with great horror, I noticed a tremendous wave approaching from my right flank, from about four o'clock. Oh my God.

I blinked, squeezing my eyes shut, squinting, trying to focus. It headed straight for us, growing larger and larger. It was so big, I could make out its shadow in the dark. It was reaching out for us like the giant gloved hand of Fate. It was going to swamp us.

I had to get out of its way, quickly. Desperately I pushed with all my might against both tillers simultaneously, making the hardest move possible away from the wave.

The boat started to cut slowly away from the monster – but I didn't see the giant cresting under us from the left. I steered right into its path. It's not supposed to be this way!!! Waves aren't supposed to crash from both sides at once! WHAT THE HELL IS GOING ON?!?

I steered right into the path of an even bigger giant, like turning a car wheel away from a bicycle right into the path of an 18-wheeler. The wave lifted the *Berserk* right off her perch on the stormy sea and kept rising and rising, our starboard side pointing up toward the sky; we caught it flush at its peak of power. Then, with great ferocity it turned suddenly and forcefully downward, thrusting the damaged right side of the boat toward ultimate impact with the plane of the sea.

This is it, I thought to myself, aghast with the most ultimate horror of all. Suddenly in a flash it all made sense: the beckoning dreams, the warnings, the voices. *This is how I bite it. This is how it all ends.* I waited for the impact, my soul racked with great sorrow and the sole reverberating thought: I killed us.

The one soft spot on the boat – the broken open window, our wounded right side – aimed straight toward the nebulous black plane of the water, and now we were airborne, riding the curling crest of quite possibly our strongest wave yet, waiting for the bomb to drop. I had achieved something truly remarkable: I had been on the helm for only a few short minutes, yet had failed, and the cost was that I would ride there for all eternity.

I knew in my heart the laws of physics were against us. Years earlier I had a Driver's Ed instructor in high school who used to say: 'You can break Man's laws and get away with it, but you can't break God's laws and get away with it.' We had dared to violate God's most sacred laws of the sea and we were about to pay the ultimate price.

Thankfully, I thought, it will happen quickly; we'll be in the water, it will be cold, it will be dark, and then it will be over. I accepted it. I waited and braced myself. Here it comes, I thought. I held onto the tillers tightly, pulling them toward me with all my might, instinctively, not sure why, clinging to them, clinging them to me. We were in this together, but it didn't matter to them; the boat was completely out of control.

BAM!! The right side of the *Berserk* slammed into the water with mighty fury, right at the worst possible point, with a loud slap. Water burst through our opening with a cannon-boom crash.

'Aaaaaaaaaaaaaaaaaaaaaaah! Fuck!' Inside, Jarle screamed. Was he drowning already?

I held on tightly, waiting for the boat to flip over and begin sinking. Instead, to my surprise, it popped back up again – like a bobber. A pure sense of electric shock resuscitated my hopes. I can't believe it. We lived. I'm alive, alive!! I felt like screaming, like the guy from the first *Frankenstein* movie.

Then I looked over to my right and saw first Jarle's sleeping bag, and then the stern seat cushion that had stuffed the window, float silently away behind us into the night, gone forever.

'Fuck!!' Jarle screamed again. He shouted something in Norwegian. What now? Was water pouring in? Were we going down?

'Are you all right?' I called out to him meekly.

'You just got my last clothes wet!'

Out there on the stern I smiled and took genuine pleasure in the moment. I paused for a bit, took a deep breath, then called back calmly: 'Oh, is that all? I thought we were going to die.'

Hours later. No sleep, no food, and the hallucinatory dream state of water begins to tighten its grasp.

I roll around the starboard bow, a quarter inch of tenuous, strained-to-the-limit fibreglass separating my head from the monster making the disturbing noise. I look over to see if the corkboard has sprung any leaks but can only see the wet veneer of condensation lining the inside of the boat, unsure of whether the water came from within or without, beyond caring.

Then I hear the voices. Slowly they arrive, like witch ghosts on the wind. I strain my ears to hear what they are saying, and then I realise they are all saying the same thing. They are calling out my name: 'Dayyyy-viiiid! Daaaaayyyyyyyy-viiiiiiidddddd!' First one, then the other, different tones, one low, the next high, one after the other, intermingling, one ending, the next beginning right away, one on top of the other. I strain; I can hear my father's voice among them, calling my name again and again. What does he want? Is he dead? Am I dead??

The water brushes up loudly against the side of the boat, sliding like a trombone, banging like a drum, a symphony of musical sounds. Try as I might, I cannot distinguish the wind calling my name from the sounds of the water rushing up against the boat. Indeed, it seems as though the gurgling water itself is rising up, splashing into the air and forming the words before falling away, back into the mix.

Then I realise: these must be the Sirens of the Sea calling out my name. Many sailors must have heard them in the past. The sea was beckoning.

But then a greater epiphany reaches my mind: these voices are the voices of the Dead calling out to me, summoning me, inviting me to join them. I could hear them clearly, calling out my name again and again, different pitches, emanating some place unknown, riding the wind to my ears.

And then it dawns on me: these aren't the voices of the Dead; they are the voices of all those who have died at sea, those who went down in the great unknown, all the sailors and the mariners who tragically lost their lives leaving loved ones on shore never to know, and here they were now, taking shape, calling out to me, calling my name, warning me, luring me, letting me know that I would soon be amongst their number.

And as I sit there, eyes wide open, ear inches away from the rushing water outside the thin fibreglass bow, straining to make sense of the words riding the air, it dawns on me again: these aren't the voices of the Dead who died at sea at all. Suddenly it makes complete sense and I realise what is going on: I am already dead. Only my limited mental capacity had not allowed me to comprehend the fact of it yet; the event of my death had already occurred, but my limited brain had not allowed me to catch up with an understanding of it yet.

I was already dead, inside my open casket, facing up at the bottom of a long rectangle, and these were the voices of the people passing by slowly in solemn procession, shuffling along in raincoats and trenchcoats, looking down at my dead body, whispering and muttering quietly amongst themselves, in great sorrow calling out my name.

And then it dawns me: I'd better go up on deck and get some fresh air.

Jarle is a sailor of historical proportions. The blood that flows through his veins carries the same chromosomes as Shackleton's, Magellan's, Columbus's. He ticks with the same heart. A sailor's soul reveals itself when rearing to fend off the latest inevitable challenge. I believe this is the part of sailing that Jarle relishes most: his makeshift spinnaker boom-mast borne on Fate's mysterious wings.

That night, Jarle crawled through the storm, out over the bouncing, soaking port side and, holding on tenuously with one arm draped over the wire rail, unscrewed the yellow wooden window protector from in front of the port side window, leaving that glass vulnerable to impact. He then crawled out to the starboard side and affixed the wood in front of the gaping hole – leaving us with two moderately vulnerable impact points rather than one strong spot and one weak one. He stuffed the remaining opening in the starboard window frame with our worst old wetgear, jamming it in tightly and securing it in place firmly. Though water still dripped in through the cracks and openings everywhere, the jerry-rigged contraption significantly reduced our intake, and when the storm finally broke in early afternoon, we were for the first time able to realistically assess our situation: the boat was shattered. Water leaked in from everywhere: on the bow deck, where the dinghy banister wood had been ripped out leaving little holes and the heater chimney had melted the plastic; through the cracked wood base of the mast; through the five-foot long broken window. No electricity. The solar panel: shattered and useless. The VHF radio: destroyed. The beloved boom box: destroyed. The dinghy: gone. The inside of the boat: wrecked. All clothing: soaked. All remaining cushions: soaked. All bunks: soaked. All wood: soaked. Everything: soaked. Engine: soaked to begin with. Half our dried goods: soaked. The other half: might as well be.

Jarle went to the bow and dredged out the protective silver metal case in order to take our first position reading in days. He opened the case to find three of the four portable GPS units inside completely smashed and useless. One, however, had survived intact, and he turned it on and waited impatiently for the coordinates to click in to see if it functioned well enough to give us an accurate reading.

Jarle wanted to keep going; I could feel it in his heart. But I also felt certain that the *Berserk* could not withstand another storm. We were living on borrowed time.

Then I remembered what the MI5 soldier had said to me when he had pulled me aside that drunken night on Port Lockroy and spoken to me in confidence. 'You know,' he said, 'Jarle is young, and he's going to make some mistakes. And when he does, it will be your responsibility to make sure that he takes the right path and makes the right decisions. It will be up to you to save his life.' He hinted that at some point my age and life experience could become as valuable as Jarle's seamanship. He gave me more credit than I was due.

Now, here we were, at the moment of truth, and his words rang true in my ears.

'I think we have no choice but to head for the nearest port of call,' I announced matter-of-factly. 'I think we should head for the Falkland Islands.'

'We could still make it to South Georgia and do repairs there,' he answered, his voice fluctuating with the desire of youth to continue, move forth, ever onward.

The reality of the trip ahead of us across the great South Atlantic began to sink in. Two weeks to South Georgia – then at least another four to Capetown, all without electricity, three hours on, three hours off.

'We have no way of getting ashore,' I answered.

'There is an old whaling station at Grytviken,' he replied. 'We can tie up to the dock and get supplies to fix the boat from the British army.'

'There's no guarantee they'll have what we need. And without the dinghy we can't go exploring. We won't be able to go on shore anywhere.' We wanted to see the gigantic emperor penguins. They would have to wait.

Plus, one other thing, Jarle: there's no guarantee the boat will make it. I didn't say it. I didn't have to. I wasn't sure whether the boat could make it to any shore, to the nearest shore, much less withstand two months of arduous storms and seas. She was not ship-shape; she was not ready to face the unknown, even if we both were.

Out on deck Jarle stood and took our position. Luckily, after a protracted wait, the GPS worked; from then on he handled it with kid gloves. I began to pore over a Norwegian book on how to read a sextant, but I had no clue.

We were five and a half days north, still within striking distance of South America. But we had to decide soon, because we would be doing the very thing Jarle had argued constantly against: travelling against the wind, against the prevailing waters of the great Southern Ocean, right into the teeth of the region where Captain Bligh's beleaguered crew had been driven to insane mutiny by the mere madness of the attempt.

'I will decide in the morning,' Jarle announced.

I had pleaded my case. I wanted to head to the nearest shore. Even then, I did not expect the boat to make it. To continue further would be crazy, but worse, it would be stupid. We would be violating our most sacrosanct rule, one of the only ones we had on board. I felt pretty certain of it, but I hoped that Jarle knew it far better than I.

Hell, I wanted to continue, too. I certainly did not want to turn back or head for the Falklands for that matter. But the boat simply would not handle another storm; another storm was imminent; and the only prudent thing to do would be to hit the nearest shore and fix the boat up, if possible, before continuing on. And the nearest shore happened to be the Falklands.

But then, somewhere in the back of my mind, other thoughts began to creep in, almost seeping in like the water through the cracks in the *Berserk*: once the *Berserk* is safely at dock, Jarle is going to fly out, home to Norway to take care of business. And then, you can make your break; you can fly back to South America from the Falklands and head for home.

The nebulous feeling of home began to beckon – only I realised I had no home. I became flush with a profound sense of unsettled inertia, the tendency of an object at rest to remain at rest, or, more relevantly, an object in motion to remain in motion. I had been set in motion and for the foreseeable future there would be no rest.

We had been blown by the storm to the east and were aware that this was the pattern of all storms in the region. The next one would blow us another 60 miles to the east. Our boat was limping; even if we were to head due north for the Falklands, one storm front would send us off course to be lost adrift in the middle of the South Atlantic. We had to compensate; we had to head due north-west in preparation of the next imminent storm.

The next morning, Jarle announced his proclamation: 'We will head for the Falkland Islands.' I felt relieved. Now we only had to make it back there alive. If I had to be honest with myself, I was not sure that we would. We were simply one swipe away from joining the *Titanic*.

But Jarle was confident that making it back would not be an issue. He had made the only choice he could make under the situation, the only choice a true captain in the vein of his hero Shackleton *could* make. Still, he desperately wanted to continue on to South Georgia and Capetown. But simple facts dictated otherwise. Without the proper equipment and with the boat wrecked, it just didn't make sense.

That afternoon I walked slowly into the boat and dug into my backpack for the krill scientist's block of chocolate. I carried it back out to the cockpit. Jarle smiled. He loved two things – ketchup and chocolate. If he could, he would probably put ketchup on his chocolate. This time he would have to do without the ketchup.

I smiled back reluctantly. I was saving this bar for a special moment. The moment was now. I was not certain we would get another opportunity to eat it.

We broke off chunks and savoured each bite until the entire bar disappeared. There was no point in saving any, really. For what? We could be gone at any moment.

We were at least five hundred miles from the Falklands and would need the wind in our favour to make it.

The first night we pulled out the old black flashlight in the hope that we could use it to check our course. It did not function at all and was completely useless. We were haunted – by the ghost of Manuel – and, the thought not lost on us, we cursed his very name over and over again. I had known in my heart from the beginning that we were going to pay for his error in judgement and now the chickens had come home to roost in a big way. Luckily, Jarle had one other flashlight, a small bulb that fastened to his head like a miniature mountaineer's lantern. It too flickered intermittently and lost power at the most inopportune times, but with a little shaking worked more often than not and would help us in our nightly times of need.

Sometime while wading through the soup Jarle looked over and saw that my legs were blue. When the action finally subsided long enough, he stripped off his own hand-knitted wool underwear and tossed them over to me. I smiled gratefully, becoming the first on the boat to wear every pair.

'What are you going to wear?' I asked.

He rifled through the bow and yanked out a black surfer's wetsuit from one of the compartments underneath, then stripped nude and pulled it on over his wet body. It fit tightly, snugly, and it required sincere effort to squeeze into it, but eventually he managed to get it on, and I helped him zip it up like a woman's dress. Getting it off, however, required even more of a redoubling, especially once the inner perspiration evaporated the water, creating a fluid seal.

Soon, Jarle tired of the effort it took to squeeze out of the suit every time he wanted to take a piss – so he took a pair of scissors and cut a hole around his crotch. He spent the rest of our voyage in this manner, with all his manhood hanging out for all the albatrosses to see.

As the nights grew darker, longer and colder, the *Berserk* bounced along on her north-west tack like a runaway train speeding through a black tunnel through a mountain pass in the dark. The rhythmic pounding actually felt like a genuine runaway train bouncing on the tracks beneath us. The phrase 'runaway train', rang through my head constantly, if not drowning out all other thoughts then accompanying them like the musical underscore to a film.

The sheer horror under the bow bag in the pitch black bouncing hard so bones hurt inside the echo of a drum close to the whispering shrieking screaming agonising lapping crashing water, each bounce more horrifying than the last but not nearly as terrifying as the next, the sound and the pain intermingling seamlessly with the rampant thoughts flashing simultaneously through my brain, left little room for comfort in the night. The only difference during the day was the little bit of light.

Jarle and I were forced by circumstance to share the one remaining dry sleeping bag. The aft portion of the boat lay in ruins and his sole remaining bag – even if there was another usable bunk – was soaking and retained no warmth. At first, when things calmed down enough to even think of crawling into the bag for warmth again (sleep was still out of the question), Jarle announced that we would have to share my bag, and I was a bit concerned because I did not understand how we would be able to keep the thing usable if we were to be constantly shuffling in and out of it like a deck of cards. But then, after Jarle actually tied off the tillers and I became resigned to the runaway train concept of the boat plowing through the dark of night like a haunted coach with a mad ghost at the reins, it became more of an issue. There was only one warm spot on the boat and it would have to be shared.

The mummy-type bag's limited zipper ripped completely the first time we both tried to squeeze into it together. I don't know what was worse: squeezing both of our icy bodies beneath the wet rag; spooning with my captain; getting spooned by my captain in his open-crotched wetsuit; the dark of night; the dark under the bag; the caterwauling of the runaway train; the constant up-and-down to check our course; the lack of sleep; our proximity to the point of the bow, which inevitably would hit something first; or simply shifting positions.

I could not help but think of a time when in high school five friends and I piled into a buddy's big old baby-blue Pontiac Bonneville and headed toward Ocean City, on the Atlantic coast. It was early April and the chill of winter still clung to the air, but we wanted a road trip so we climbed in with beer and pot and pills and popped our way to the shore only to find the place completely vacant, a winter ghost town. We were too cheap to get a hotel room, so we decided to sleep in the car, three in front, three in back. The three in front – I slept on the floor in the back – slept sitting up, on each other's shoulders, taking turns singing out intermittently 'A lean, lean, lean, lean,' and then they would all switch their angles and positions in synchronised unison like the Three Stooges, flopping the other direction to face the other way on the other shoulders.

Nobody got any sleep and the next morning, at the crack of dawn, we drove back home again, hungover and foggy with the haze of the previous night's buzz still ringing between our ears. We never even saw the beach. It was a ridiculous bust of a road trip. Now, every time Jarle and I decided to switch positions, I couldn't help but think of it. This time, the beach was in the boat with us.

There was absolutely no purpose in sitting out in the cold of the cockpit throughout the long night but every few minutes one of us would have to climb out of the bag to check on our progress. Inside the bag it was warm, outside freezing; to climb out an unpleasant experience.

'Skull, go check,' Jarle would call out, and more often than not, I would climb out of the bag and amble out to make sure the ropes held and to squint closely to the compass to see our course. Every time Jarle barked the command, I did not want to get up. It was bitter cold, the clothes wet, and dress required. The entire process disrupted any rest whatsoever. Soon, however, simply getting up and checking our course became the path of least resistance – so even if I felt it wasn't my turn, I would head up and check anyway, just to get it over with.

Each night emergency manoeuvres requiring 'all hands on deck' became necessary. One night we were both resting under the bag in the bow when suddenly we heard a loud pop followed by a terrible ripping sound. Instantly the boat began gyrating wildly, the mast swinging back and forth like a pendulum, our course instantly altered.

Jarle bolted upright, tossing the bag off of both of us, and we quickly prepared for the inevitable re-rigging. Grabbing the mini flashlight, shaking it so it would work, Jarle peeked out, trying to avoid the blistering wind. He shone the light over the edge of the sliding hatch and followed it up to the top of the swinging mast to see that the halyard clip holding taut the front sail had snapped off its rope. '*Fey fawwwwnnnnnn!*' he screamed. '*Helveta*!!!!'

I remained quiet and still as a mouse. The seas were rough, the boat bouncing ridiculously. The wind blew cold, colder than usual, rife with the spiteful, dogged chill of night. Someone would have to climb the 30-foot mast as the entire boat swung back and forth like a pendulum and attach a new halyard. Delicate rope work like that could not be done with gloves – and ten seconds of exposure to the wind was enough to begin the numbing process. Jarle's eyes raged with fury, because that someone would be him.

To make matters worse, I had been the one who had raised the sail up earlier. Often when raising a sail the ropes can become caught on the metal stairs, but in this case, I had taken painstaking care to ensure that the sail had been raised properly – in part because I did not want to be blamed for anything going wrong but also because I lazily did not want to have to get up and fix the ropes from banging into the mast and making noise, a constant on the seas and the bane of my existence. I had checked and double-checked again before tying off the rope as tight as I could. I was certain of two things: one, that the brutal conditions and harsh tugging winds had simply twisted the line with a corkscrew of pressure, inevitably snapping it off; and two, that Jarle would blame me.

Between Norwegian curses, he began venting his frustration as I remained silent, holding the flashlight while he prepared. 'I have to go up and do this because I have an idiot for a first mate who cannot even pull up a sail properly without getting it twisted!' He continued shouting in Norwegian as he dragged out the necessary equipment from under the back hatch and got ready to climb the mast, no easy feat under the best of conditions. Here he would have to take the rope up again with him as he climbed, attach the halyard clip to it after it was placed properly, and get back down again, all while the boat flopped back and forth unsteadily in high seas without rhythm, lurching in the dark, with frostbite-inducing winds increasing in frigidity with every step. He would have to remove his gloves to rig the rope.

I bit my lips, enduring the abuse, as he began his ascent. I stood below holding the small mountaineer's flashlight and pointing it up for him as he made his way through the dark up the mast. The boat swung madly back and forth, all the way to the right, all the way to the left. The higher he went, the more it swung. The cold was so intense that I found myself constantly ducking back into the shelter of the hatch just to get out of the biting wind; even though I wanted to show solidarity with his misery, instinct prevailed, convincing me of its futility.

At the pinnacle of the mast, Jarle quickly stripped off his gloves. Instantly his hands began to freeze. He raced against time, clutching the mast with his elbows, his knees, his teeth as he tried rigging the rope through the pulley as quickly as he could in the dim light, which I tried to focus on his spot but which faded the further it got from the source. The longer he froze, the longer it took.

By the time he clambered back down a good fifteen minutes later, his hands were completely frozen, like gnarled branches. He ducked back under the shelter of the hatch and held them out, crooked and white, fingers bent, and his eyes began to reflexively tear as the pain of the thaw set in. He looked up, crying from the searing agony. I knew it well and had felt it many times: first, the hot throbbing heat like putting your hand on a burner but not realising it until it smoulders; then, the needles exploding like fireworks at the fingertips until you stare at them half expecting to see flames shooting out with the blood.

As he stood below recovering, I hovered over the hatch. 'I put up the sail right,' I said, softly and firmly, 'but you would have blamed me no matter what.'

Once the boat was back underway, we crawled back into the bag again, silently but both wide awake, to begin to regain our warmth. Eventually, Jarle spoke.

'I'm sorry, man,' he said sincerely. 'I have a problem with that.' He had a tendency to blame others when things went wrong, he mentioned, and he didn't really mean it.

By now I knew that. His apology, though welcome, was not really necessary. I did not need to hear it to absolve myself; I knew I had rigged the rope right. Though the yelling made the manoeuvre less pleasant than it normally would have been, I got over it right away, let it slide off of me like the constant sea spray slid off the fibreglass hull. We were sailors. That kind of energy happens on the sea. Still, when he apologised, it alleviated some of the pre-dawn chill.

That night, standing up for myself, it could be said that I took my first step toward becoming a true sailor.

That night, if ever there was a question, Jarle truly ascended to the rank of captain.

As soon as the decision to head for the Falklands was made, there no longer was a reason to ration our food. We had enough on board to last six months and now, if we lasted at all, we were heading more or less straight for the nearest port – so all bets were off.

Unfortunately many of our supplies had been trashed. But the Ukrainians had graciously donated as part of our parting gift a carton of Alpen cereal packets with the occasional hard-as-rock dried raisin, that had been marked with an expiration date of 1992 but had probably been festering in the attic of the old British base since some time in the late 1970s. There must have been 200 of them, most of which survived with little or no damage. We simply added cold fresh water and powdered milk into the plastic cup right on top of the stale Alpen and ate packet after packet until we were about to burst.

Half a box of butter sugar biscuits also survived – they had been donated graciously to us by the Australian mountain climbers who befriended us on Port Lockroy. I popped the sweet, buttery, frosted cookies into my mouth one after the other until I reached saturation point and actually felt queasy – but full and sated for the first time in months. All the labels on the canned goods peeled in the water, so we never knew what was inside until we opened them, but whatever it was, we piled it on top of any dry cracker we could find and down the hatch it went.

Even though it was unnecessary, I stayed outside in the cockpit next to the tied tiller throughout most of the grey daylight hours, scouring the horizon for any signs out of the ordinary, for boats, for the great sea monsters that certainly must exist, for the great vortex of a whirlpool. Watching the albatrosses and the other birds circling overhead, I contemplated the great mercury sea, smooth and shiny and silver like a tea tray, watching the way it moved, so alive, pondering the very nature of liquid, how it moves so seamlessly through itself, the microscopic mini atoms finding their way through each other at the same time, holding hands for the briefest of instances until they had passed through the doorway to the other side – much as we were in the process of passing through our own doorway.

The entire time we made our way north through the Drake, we were waiting for the inevitable next storm, well aware of the damage it would do. Our shields were down; they wouldn't hold through another attack. Each change in the direction or velocity of the wind, each moving cloud, each random wave, each bird, any signal out of the ordinary at all – each moment – became imbued with a foreboding, ominous presence.

Our pace through the Drake seemed excruciatingly slow. Our tachometer, built into the fibreglass next to the hatch, had been smashed by one of the waves, rendering it inoperable, so we had no idea of our speed until Jarle fished out a thin, white rope line with what looked like a mini, spinning dirigible on the end and dropped it off the back of the boat. The backup tachometer was neither accurate nor efficient, but trying to keep it from tangling gave me something to do when sitting at the tiller. It more or less registered our movement at a brisk, constant three knots rather than the normal five or six – making the journey seem even longer.

Suspended in the gossamer dark of night, that very same speed seemed so fast that it felt like we were about to leave the rails. Each bounce of the bow upward followed Newtonian physics to the tee and was answered by a tooth-rattling smash down again; the moments in between seemed interminable, and brace for impact though we might, the sea's answer was always a fraction of a second off, on either side of the expected – as if it were laughing, chuckling, roaring at our expense. We might be ready to hit and the boat would stay airborne just a fraction of a second longer until instinctively I loosened my grasp. Then it would hit even harder, hurting more than ever before, bruises piling on top of bruises, louder and more brutal – and then we were up in the air again, only this time, the bow would hit sooner than expected, and another bruise would open up. The resulting instability kept the muscles of the body at a tense state of readiness at all times, making it impossible to relax or truly rest even for a single moment, that is, until complete exhaustion overwhelmed the form and the mind slid off to a hallucinatory dream state hovering somewhere slightly on the other side of consciousness, never far enough away to allow for refreshment, but always in a state of exhausted irritability, as if one had been woken too soon in the middle of a dream that they could not remember but struggled to recover forever while the entire world painfully swirls around them, slinging stinging shrapnel, hurling abuse and indignities their way.

Twice each day Jarle would pull out the lone remaining GPS handset and turn it on to chart our position. He held it up to the sky like a lightning rod, each time uncertain and expectant, waiting for the device to triangulate its satellite signal and respond with coordinates. We would wait and wait while the device worked, like an outdated computer trying to decipher newfangled signals, until eventually, the yellow numbers would emerge on the digital readout. He would mark our course in pencil on his charts of the sea, drawing a line between the coordinates, connecting the dots with our lives at stake.

Slowly we crawled through the Drake, until it became apparent, much to our surprise, that in our attempt to make up ground to the west, we had actually gotten within striking distance of South America. We had caught the most favourable weather imaginable. Jarle pointed out on the chart how against all odds the winds and the tack had actually favoured us in this way. Heading back toward Cape Horn would be much better for us than landing on the Falklands – if we made it. For Jarle, the familiarity of the territory and the knowledge of supplies and repair facilities made it a more desirable destination.

Personally, I was already thinking of getting off the boat. The *Berserk* was a shambles and would take months to repair, a process that did not enthral me, since I would be doing a bulk of the work. If we got stuck on the Falklands, I would have to arrange an expensive flight back to the mainland of South America; by landing on the continent itself, I would be able to arrange transportation back north and head for Buenos Aires, a city I had always wanted to visit. But in order to get there, we would have to take a harder course due west and endure a longer period of time in the dangerous Drake – and as the days went on and we headed further and further west into its teeth, the likelihood of another storm increased – along with my nervousness.

Finally it became apparent that we were going to go for it. We had been on the tack for a solid week and were within spitting distance of the Cape when suddenly and inexplicably the wind just stopped. Just like that, we were left immobilised on the relatively still waters of the Drake, waiting for the change in the wind and the weather.

For three days, we sat there bobbing on the waters south of Cape Horn – barely moving, waiting, waiting – right in the spot where we had been hit by the first storm, where far below the shelf cut out from underneath us and two oceans met. The most dangerous waters in the world. The most dangerous spot on earth. The odds had finally caught up with us. And from experience, we knew well what awaited.

As the hours rolled on, the internal pressure increased, along with the certainty that the next storm was statistically imminent. It had been ten days since the capsizing and we had crossed the stormiest, roughest seas without further incident – so we must be due. This must be how Fate works, I thought: it lures us nearer and nearer to safety until we can smell the shore, and then it unleashes Fury and devastating Wrath, to pummel us with absolute finality.

When this one hit, there would no longer be a question. Game over, like that, a snap of the fingers. Our boat would crack in half like a twig with God's first malevolent breath. The wind would punch us in the face, blow us out to sea, to the east, and we would be left to fight our way through the Drake once again, toward whatever land, futilely like a gerbil in Purgatory running for all eternity on a never-ending wheel.

And so we lingered there for three days, and as we lingered, the certainty of Doom and Fate bloomed. I sat in the cockpit throughout the day, all day, every day, waiting expectantly for the wind, but each slight breeze seemed to die suddenly as soon as we raised a sail.

We inched and drifted our way until we knew it was likely we would sight land within the next 24 hours. Those hours were the worst.

Again, the wind died completely and left us at the mercy and whim of the Cape. The Cape had claimed many a soul; ghosts abounded; and we were hovering over their graveyard. Strain a bit and you could almost hear them cry. For what seemed to be an eternal Hallowe'en, not nice but evil, we watched and we waited, and we waited and we watched, with nothing to do but eat and wait for the wind, constantly scanning the horizon to see what would arrive first: the storm or the shore, Life or Death.

The next morning I tossed off the bag and walked out into the cockpit where Jarle stood, smiling. 'There's something you should see, man,' he said, grinning. 'Look.'

I scanned the horizon off the bow but could see nothing, only the same dull, foggy, briny mist. I squinted, knowing what must be out there but somehow still doubting its veracity. If I did not see it, if it was not visible, it could not be true. Then I honed in and I felt it, and through the horizon focused in on it – vague, indistinguishable, a shape only slightly darker and ever so slightly more solid than the horizon. I smiled. He handed me the old beat-up binoculars and I looked through them for confirmation, as if I could not believe my own eyes.

'Go ahead,' he said as I stared through the lenses on the deck of the bouncing boat, narrowing my field of vision. I pulled them away from my eyes, my great grin frozen.

And I shouted with glee, like never had been shouted before: 'Land ho!'

But in that instant, I felt not one but two distinct impressions deep in the marrow of my soul, where no one but I could see: one, a sense of complete absolute pure elation, for I knew in my heart that we had made it, survived, actually lived, and were going to continue living, with all that entails, for no storm that now struck would fell us here so close to the sheltering shore and the bosom of Mother Land.

And two, an inexplicable profound sense of complete and utter sorrow and loss, because I knew the trip was over, and I would never experience anything like it in my life ever again.

I turned toward Jarle. 'Well, Captain,' I said, 'You and your hero Shackleton have a lot in common – you both got your crews back safely.'

CHAPTER THIRTEEN
CIVILISATION

'This doesn't feel right,' Jarle said to me, tears forming in his dark eyes. 'You belong on the *Berserk*.'

I probably did – but not when there were two months of solid backbreaking work to be done. It was two weeks after we had landed back in Ushuaia, the very place we had met, and my bags were packed. I was getting off the boat, headed for the Amazon.

A few days earlier, while we were making repairs on the dock, we received a visit from none other than Pascal – the French sailor scrubbing his deck the very day we met. He and his Belgian girlfriend had dropped by to survey the damage. He stood on the dock and just stared at me silently with a mischievous glint. He barely spoke English. While his girlfriend handed Jarle a bottle of red wine, he looked me in the eye with his thousand-mile stare.

'Do you remember what I told you?' he asked.

I nodded my head and smiled. It had been the understatement of the century. For the first time, he smiled back – knowingly, proudly. Sailor to sailor. Nothing else needed to be said.

Now Jarle and I hugged on the dock like brothers and I walked away, without looking back, leaving him there alone.

When I found him, he was full of life, of companionship, stocked for a long voyage toward the unknown; when I left him there silhouetted on the dock, he was by himself and the cupboard seemed bare.

But by then I should have known better: A sailor is never truly alone; as long as there is another single boat afloat on any sea, flying any flag, he would never be alone.

And somehow, I knew in my heart that we would see each other again.

I'm not really sure what happened to him right after that. He told me that he had a friend flying down from Norway in a couple of weeks who would help him get the boat ship-shape once again, and then they would head off.

I asked where he was going. He wasn't sure. He talked about heading west to Easter Island, he talked about heading east to Capetown.

Eventually, after he patched up the *Berserk*, with a new dinghy and a new radio and a new boom box, he headed up the eastern coast of Argentina toward Puerto Piramides, where Manuel had worked as a guide on whale-watching tours with his sister.

It was there, anchored outside of Peninsula Valdes, where *Berserk* met her fate. She was anchored in a little harbour off the coast when without warning something hit her bow hard and the water began to pour in. It poured so quickly in the dead of night that he could not bail out fast enough. It was all he could do to grab a few things, hop in the new dinghy and row to shore.

Jarle shined the beam of a new flashlight back into the dark pool and watched his beloved *Berserk* slowly sink to the bottom. In the cool of the night, quietly, almost silently, she disappeared forever.

I am glad I was not there to see it.

Since the trip to Antarctica, whenever I stare out at the misty grey sea and see a white sail unfurl on the cloud-shrouded horizon, I think of hopping on a boat, any boat, and sailing off to nowhere in particular, just setting sail and leaving it all behind, and living for the day.

I stare at the water and I wonder how I'm going to make it through to the next day. And I think about all the people out there who have spent their entire lives working, supporting families, going to their jobs day-in, day-out, week after week, year after year, dreaming of the opportunity to sail the seven seas, dreaming, and I wonder how the hell they do it – and I wonder why I can't. And I think about how out-of-place I am in society, in the 'civilised' world, and I wonder where I belong, and my mind can't help going back to the *Berserk* again and again. And I know: that was a once-in-a-lifetime experience; let it go. And I turn away from the water, rip myself away – it's always ripping myself away – and I turn back to the emptiness of my life, to the paying of bills and shopping for groceries and brushing my teeth, to a best-case-scenario of dinner parties and white wine and raising children and going out of my mind with boredom and a worst-case-scenario of complete emptiness loneliness nothingness, wondering where I went wrong – and all I have to hold onto is the *Berserk*, and the dream that someday somewhere somehow I might fit in like I did on that boat.

And then one day I found myself all alone on a beach on the coast of Oregon, wondering where it was that I had first gone wrong and wondering if there was ever to be the possibility of redemption for my poor pitiful pained soul. And I walked along that windy cold beach, roiling with one white water wave after the next, and I stared into the fog and the mist and I wondered what was out there that I was missing. And I realised: I had no home, nowhere to go. And I had no name; it too had been lost in the shuffle of existence. I had nothing.

And I walked along that beach for miles, wondering what I was going to do, where I would go.

But then, staring out at the water in the wind and the cold sun that day, I thought once again of the *Berserk*, and her first expedition to Antarctica, and, then and there, that day in the Oregon sun, it dawned on me, after all these years, what the experience had actually taught me, and I smiled: the Earth is my home, and the only name I really need to know is God.

www.summersdale.com